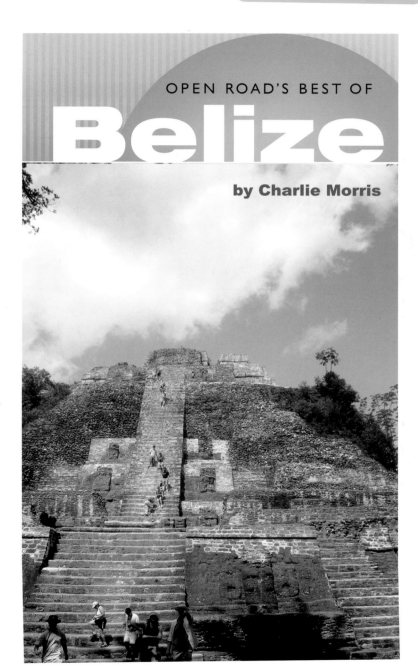

OPEN ROAD'S BEST OF

Belize

by Charlie Morris

Open Road Publishing

Open Road's new travel guides.
Designed to cut to the chase.
You don't need a huge travel encyclopedia – you need a *selective guide* to steer you right. If you're going on vacation for a few weeks or less, get a guide that brings you the *best* of any destination for the amount of time you *really* have for your trip!

Open Road – the guide you need for the trip you want.

The New Open Road *Best Of* Travel Guides.
Right to the point.
Uncluttered.
Easy.

To buy our travel guides and read our travel blog, visit:
www.openroadguides.com

Text Copyright©2013 by Charlie Morris
- All Rights Reserved -
ISBN 13: 978-159360-173-7
ISBN 10: 1-59360-173-5
Library of Congress Control No. 2012947559

About the Author
Charlie Morris is also the author of *Open Road's Best of Costa Rica, Open Road's Best of Honduras,* and *Switzerland Guide.*

Photo credits on page 223

OPEN ROAD TRAVEL GUIDES
Designed for the amount of time you *really* have for your trip!

CONTENTS

5. BELIZE CITY & NORTHERN BELIZE   92

8. PRACTICAL MATTERS   193

Maps

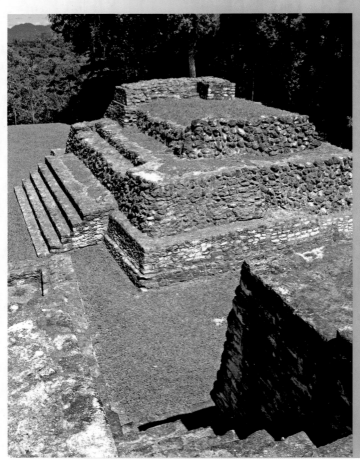

1. INTRODUCTION

Belize is a true tropical paradise, a place where you can explore the wonders of the wilderness while never straying far from the comforts of civilization. All the attractions of Central America are here: palm-shaded Caribbean beaches, azure seas, coral reefs, and vast expanses of uninhabited forest where clear rivers wind lazily past mysterious Mayan ruins, observed only by the monkeys and the birds.

Belize's relative prosperity and English-speaking population make traveling here a breeze. Crime and aggressive hustlers are far less of a problem than in many other tropical destinations. Tourist facilities are well developed: you'll have no problems getting around the country by bus, small plane or rented car, finding excellent accommodations, from modern luxury resorts to charming budget lodgings, and enjoying delightful local or international cuisine.

Belize is one of the world's top ecotourism destinations. The rain forests hold an amazing array of flora and fauna, from playful monkeys to gaudy toucans to elusive wild cats. The seas teem with tropical fish. There's a vast variety of landscapes, from sandy beaches to coastal mangrove swamps to mountains carpeted with lush greenery.

But the greatest asset of this peaceful and serene country is her people, a fascinating mix of Creoles, Mestizos, Garifuna, Mayans and Mennonites. Belizeans are some of the friendliest folks you'll meet anywhere. They've built a strong nation that has avoided the civil wars and poverty that have plagued some of her neighbors, and are doing a good job of preserving their priceless natural treasures.

The activities are endless. With the world's second-longest barrier reef and three coral atolls, Belize has the finest diving in the Western Hemisphere. Fishing is spectacular, from tarpon and snook in the lagoons to bonefish and permit on the grass flats to billfish offshore. The many beautiful rivers offer everything from kayaking to cave tubing. The forested mountain landscapes are full of caves, and are perfect for hiking, birding, horseback riding and mountain biking.

Of course, many travelers also enjoy more sedate pursuits, such as sipping a cool drink while basking on a beautiful beach, and the opportunities for doing that in Belize are second to none.

2. OVERVIEW

Belize has a huge variety of things to see and do for such a small country. You can explore the rain forest-clad mountains and relax on pristine Caribbean beaches, all on the same trip. Ancient Mayan temples tell mysterious stories about the country's previous inhabitants, while today's residents make beautiful music and art. There are fun activities for all interests and all levels of strenuousness. If you want to see the flora and fauna of the rain forest on foot, on horseback or by boat, or if you want to explore the ocean diving, snorkeling, fishing or kayaking, you can find the trip of a lifetime here. Along the way, you'll find attractive and comfortable accommodations, exotic cuisine and charming local crafts.

As a travel destination, Belize is a country in transition. Long an off-the-beaten-path destination for backpackers and birders, the country is quickly becoming a center for mega-tourism. Last year, gargantuan cruise ships disgorged over a million wide-eyed day-trippers to the Tourism Village in Belize City, and Ambergris Caye is evolving into a major upscale resort. As

yet however, there is nothing in Belize to match the crassness of tourist centers such as Nassau or Cancun. Mass tourism is concentrated in a few areas of the country, and there are still vast areas where you can spend days without seeing another tourist.

The Northern Cayes
Off the coast of Belize lies a sprawl of small islands called cayes (pronounced "keys"). The largest and northernmost of these is called **Ambergris Caye**, and it's the country's top tourist destination. Here you'll find lodgings for every taste and budget, from backpacker favorites

to luxury resorts, as well as a huge selection of tour operators offering diving, snorkeling, fishing, and boating trips, and some lively nightlife. **Caye Caulker** is a bit more laid-back, a lazy place where old gringos go to seed and eat cheap lobster. Hard-core divers and fishermen head for a handful of colorful lodges on some of the smaller cayes.

Belize City/ Northern Belize
Most visitors don't linger long in **Belize City**, the country's business capital, but the region has some don't-miss attractions. The **Belize Zoo** and the **Baboon Sanctuary** offer glimpses of the country's animals for the whole family. The Mayan ruins of **Lamanai** and **Altun Ha** are hidden in remote jungles teeming with wildlife. Birders come from all over the world to cruise the lagoons of **Crooked Tree Wildlife Sanctuary**.

Cayo/Western Belize
This is ground zero for ecotourism and adventure travel. Dozens of jungle lodges in all price ranges cater to every interest, including birding, hiking, caving, river tubing and horseback riding. **Mountain Pine Ridge** is a unique ecosystem, and the locale of many caves and waterfalls. This region has the country's highest concentration of Mayan ruins, including Belize's largest, **Caracol**. Just across the border in Guatemala is the largest known Mayan site in the world, **Tikal**.

Southern Belize
Fewer tourists venture to the south, but that's starting to change as people begin to realize how much this region has to offer. Offshore are some of the most pristine dive sites in the country, on the barrier reef and around **Glover's Reef Atoll**. A short way inland, **Cockscomb Basin** and **Mayflower Bocawina** are two of Belize's nicest and easiest to visit nature reserves. The friendly **Garifuna** people have a unique culture and a fascinating musical scene going on in their coastal villages.

Diving
Belize has the most spectacular **coral reefs** in the Western Hemisphere – the world's second-longest barrier reef and three idyllic coral atolls. A rainbow of coral and tropical fish awaits you. A very well developed dive industry

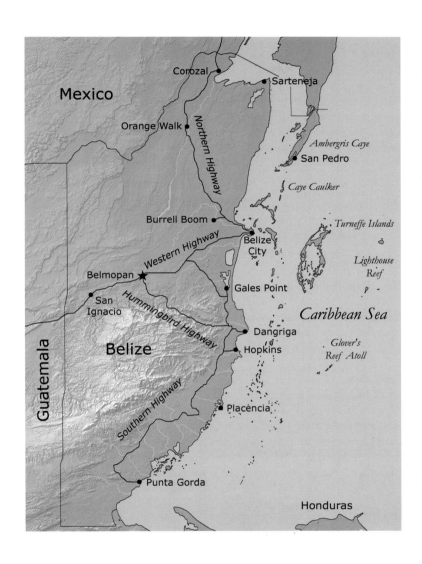

makes it easy to plan the dive vacation of a lifetime. Many reefs are in shallow water just a short way offshore, so the wonders of the undersea world are easily accessible to **snorkelers** too. Even if you've never snorkeled before, you simply must give it a try before you leave Belize.

Fishing

Belize has a huge variety of fishing opportunities. Inside the atolls are vast expanses of sand **flats**, perfect territory for bonefish, permit and tarpon. Silver kings that average 40-80 pounds will trash your tackle with astonishing leaps into the air. The **reefs** hold snapper, grouper and jacks – you might bring home a couple of yellowtail snapper for the grill. **Offshore** anglers battle with blue and white marlin, sailfish, wahoo, dorado, tuna, kingfish and shark. The **rivers and lagoons** are stiff with snook.

Canoeing & Kayaking

Belize's lazy rivers are made for canoeing. You won't find much whitewater, but you will find lovely clear pools surrounded by jungle greenery and melodious birds. A kayak is an excellent way to explore the lagoons and mangrove wetlands of the coast, or the grass flats out on the coral atolls.

Horseback Riding

The best way to explore some of Belize's rugged terrain is on horseback, and riding is a very popular way to enjoy the rain forest. You'll find extensive equestrian centers near Belmopan and Mountain Pine Ridge. You can take a horseback tour or rent horses in most regions of the country.

Spelunking

The **Chiquibul** cave system is one of the largest systems of caverns in the Western Hemisphere. There are caverns and caves suitable for both novice and expert cavers. At a couple of locales, you can go cave tubing. Floating through caves on an inner tube is an unforgettable experience, and one of the most popular activities in Belize. Caves were sacred places to the ancient Mayans, who called the underworld **Xibalba**, and you can visit several caves where skeletons and artifacts of the ancient ones can be seen.

Wildlife

The Belizean government has long seen the value of protecting their wilderness areas, and has created an impressive system of **national parks and nature reserves** throughout the country. Belize has a wide variety of different climates and ecosystems, and the parks have been planned to

Observing the Animals

The greatest thrill in Belize is the chance to see wild animals going about their daily business in the forest. If you spend some time in one or more of the parks and preserves, your chances of seeing some critters are good. However, some animals are much more easily seen than others, and some visitors have unrealistic expectations.

White-nosed coatis (locally known as **quash**) are frequently seen, and they are friendly and fun. Monkeys are everyone's favorites, and they are pretty common (a little too common, say the owners of stolen sunglasses and hats). Belize has two species: **spider monkeys** and **howler monkeys**, whose cries boom through the forest. We'd all love to see a **wild cat**, and Belize has five species: pumas, jaguars, ocelots, margays and jaguarundis. Outside of a zoo or rehabilitation center however, you're unlikely to spot one of these secretive, nocturnal predators.

If you really want to see some of the rarer forest denizens, visit one of the more remote parks, walk quietly, and take your hikes in the early morning or just before dusk. **I highly recommend hiring a local guide**, who can show you animals (and plants) that you would never see on your own.

preserve at least a sample of each one. Visitors can expect to see lovely flowers, butterflies, hummingbirds, colorful parrots and macaws, coatis, monkeys, agoutis, crocodiles and iguanas. The lucky may see anteaters, peccaries, tapirs, ocelots, manatees or whale sharks.

Tropical River Cruises

One of the very best ways to get close to wildlife (without getting out of breath) is to take a **jungle cruise** on one of the many lagoons, canals and rivers. Monkeys and crocodiles are close enough to touch (but don't).

Prime spots are the **New River Lagoon** and **Crooked Tree** in the north, and the **Sittee** and **Monkey** rivers in the south.

Bird Watching

With over 566 (and counting) bird species available for viewing, it's impossible for even the most hard-core birder to visit Belize without adding significantly to their life list. Multicolored **parrots** and **toucans**, along with a wide assortment of Little Brown Birds (LBBs), flit through the forest, and vast flocks of **shore birds** patrol the coasts. If the birding gods smile on you, you may even see a rare **jabiru stork**, a **trogon**, or a **Stygian owl**. Some lodges and tour companies cater specifically to birders.

Mayan Ruins

Belize has thousands of Mayan sites, many as yet unexcavated. However, several impressive ones are very much ready for visitors. In the north are **Lamanai** and **Altun Ha**; in the west **Cahal Pech** and **Caracol**, which has a pyramid that's still the highest structure in Belize; in the south mysterious **Lubaantun**. Just across the border in Guatemala is **Tikal**, the largest known Mayan site in the world.

Garifuna Villages

The **Garifuna** of the southern coast are a unique people, descended from a mix of Africans and Native American Caribs. Many of their picturesque villages, with thatched-roof huts and wooden fishing boats pulled up on the beach, welcome visitors. Waterfront open-air restaurants serve fresh grilled fish. The Garifuna's distinctive, rhythmic **Punta** music is a staple at the country's lively clubs and discos.

Food & Drink

Belizean cuisine is as varied as her people. Fish, lobster and other **seafood** are fresh and delicious. **Mexican** and **Caribbean** cuisine are excellent choices. Ripe **tropical fruits** and locally grown **coffee** are not to be missed. The local beer is tasty and served ice-cold, and a glass of **One Barrel rum** with fresh pineapple juice is the perfect drink to get you in a tropical mood.

Belize Facts

Location:	Central America, with the Caribbean Sea to the east, Mexico to the north, and Guatemala to the west and south
Land Area:	22,806 sq km
Highest Point:	Victoria Peak, 1,160 m
Coastline:	386 km
Biodiversity:	153 mammal species, 566 bird species
Population:	328,000
Languages:	English, Spanish, Garifuna, Mayan. Some Mennonite communities speak German.
Life Expectancy:	69 years
Literacy:	77%
Poverty rate:	43%
Government:	Parliamentary democracy
Independence:	1981 (from UK)
Economy:	Agriculture 10%, Industry 20%, Services 70%

Taking the Kids

Belizeans love kids. Kids love the beach and anything to do with monkeys. On Ambergris Caye and around Cayo, you'll find attractions specially aimed at kids, and most tourist areas of the country have organized tours and activities appropriate for the whole family.

Many lodging places have larger rooms available for family groups. Burgers, chicken, fried potatoes and other kid-friendly food is not hard to find. **Tropical fruits** are a special treat!

3. WILDLIFE OF BELIZE

If you're looking for a place to observe tropical animals and plants in their natural habitat, then Belize is one of the best choices you could make. Like her Central American neighbors, Belize has **an astounding variety of animal and plant life**. Unlike some of her neighbors, Belize has a very low population density, so there are vast wilderness areas where the animals roam free, undisturbed by human contact. And the prosperous Belizeans have so far done an excellent job of preserving their natural treasures. Over 40% of the county has some form of protected status.

Within the borders of this tiny nation are 153 mammal species, 566 bird species, and countless thousands of plant species (and this is just what's been described so far: when it comes to plants and small invertebrates, there are thought to be thousands more that scientists haven't gotten around to classifying yet). Belize has many different habitats, including broadleaf rain forest, tropical pine forest, marshes, mangrove swamps and coral islands. Each has its own unique ecosystem, and its own set of inhabitants.

With **over 40 national parks, refuges and reserves** of various kinds, the critters have plenty of space to roam around, and you are welcome to pay them a visit. Much of the tourist industry is built around showing off the country's natural wonders. Plenty of lodgings and tour operators are at your disposal to help you get a glimpse of those exotic animals and plants. Many of Belize's parks are easy to visit on your own, but for a proper trip,

I recommend going with a local guide or tour company. With a guide, you'll learn much more about the local ecosystem, and probably see animals you would never have seen on your own. At some parks, going with a guide is your only real option: some areas are accessible only by boat, and the most remote have no trails at all, and require hacking a path with a machete.

Mammals

The **white-nosed coati** (*nasua narica*), which locals call a *quash*, is a cute and gregarious creature with a long tail and a prehensile nose that it uses to snuffle among the leaf litter on the forest floor for bugs, small lizards and frogs. You're likely to see at least a few, as they are fairly common, diurnal (active during the day), and not particularly shy. In fact, at some of the more frequented parks, where people have been feeding them, you may be accosted by bands of them begging for goodies. Their antics can be amusing, but you really shouldn't feed them or any other wild animals.

Another common forest dweller is the **gibnut** (elsewhere known as the agouti or paca), a rodent that looks something like a large guinea pig. Gibnuts are often seen in the reserves, poking around on the forest floor, but elsewhere they're scarce, because the locals like to eat them. You may see them on the menu in some traditional Belizean eateries.

The **kinkajou** (*potos flavus*) is called a *night walker* in Belize. These cute little guys live in the trees, and have long prehensile tails like monkeys. Kinkajous aren't rare, but are active mainly at night. The **Belizean gray fox** (*urocyon cinereoargenteus*) is a cool little fox that climbs trees! The very patient may catch a glimpse of some of the rarer mammals, including **anteaters** and the **tayra**, a sleek weasel-like carnivore. Herds of **peccaries** (locally called *warries*), like small wild pigs, root around on the forest floor. You may well see the signs of their depredations. **River otters** are especially fascinating to watch. Small forest mammals also include more mundane species such as **porcupines**, **armadillos**, **skunks** and dozens of species of rodents. There are eight species of **opossum** and over 75 species of **bats**!

The country's largest animal is **Baird's tapir** (*tapirus bairdii*), which locals call a *mountain cow* (see photo on previous page). These pachyderms look something like a rhinoceros without any horns, and can be up to 6 feet long and up to 500 pounds. They are rare, and mostly nocturnal, so you aren't likely to see one in the wild.

Belize has two species of monkeys. The most famous are the **black howler monkeys** (*alouatta pigra*), which Belizeans call *baboons*. These large vegetarians live in troops of 4-8 individuals, and make a loud noise that sounds less like howling than like the barking of a large dog. Even if you don't see them, you're sure to hear them far off in the forest. The **Community Baboon Sanctuary** protects these primates, and releases animals in other protected areas throughout the country. Another good place to see howlers is the **Cockscomb Basin Wildlife Sanctuary**. Belize's other monkey species is the playful **spider monkey** (*ateles geoffroyi*).

The Small Stuff

We all want to see something really cool, such as a large mammal or a particularly exotic bird. But this isn't a TV show, and the critters don't always perform on a schedule. Don't obsess about trophy sightings so much that you miss the less glamorous, but fascinating, beauty all around. Trees, flowers, lush tropical greenery, fruits and spices, butterflies and all kinds of interesting bugs (take a night hike to see some really exotic creepy-crawlies) are easy to see, going about their daily business unnoticed by humans who rush by, searching for the elusive quetzal.

Belize has no less than five wild cats. The kings of the jungle are the magnificent spotted **jaguar** (*panthera onca*) and the **puma** (*puma concolor*), a tawny relative of the North American cougar and Florida panther. Smaller felines are the beautiful little spotted **ocelot** (*leopardus pardalis*) and **margay** (*leopardus wiedii*). The slightly larger **jaguarundi** (*herpailurus yaguarondi*) looks like a strange cross between a bear and a cat.

Belize has one of the healthiest populations of wild cats in Central America, but your chances of seeing one in the wild are almost nil, as they are mostly nocturnal, and very shy of people. At the **Jaguar Reserve** (Cockscomb Basin), you'll probably see at least a paw print or two. **Chan Chich Lodge** in Northern Belize reports cat sightings from time to time. And of course, you can see most of the native cats at the **Belize Zoo**.

Reptiles & Amphibians

To date, 139 species of reptiles and amphibians have been identified in Belize. But they're slippery little critters, and scientists are finding new ones all the time. Snappy saurians may make you think twice about swimming in the rivers. The lagoons are stiff with **crocodiles** and the smaller **caimans**. You'll see a few on almost any river boat ride. There's a huge variety of snakes, including the **boa constrictor**, the bright yellow **eyelash palm pit viper** and the **fer-de-lance** (or *tommygoff*), one of the world's deadliest snakes. Watch your step in the forest, but don't worry – snakebites are rare.

There's a variety of brightly-colored frogs, called **poison-arrow frogs** because the local Mayans used to make poison arrows from them. According to legend, if you lick one you'll get high, but I'd stick to rum if I were you. Notable lizards include enormous green **iguanas** (locally called *wish-willies*), and the **Jesus Christ lizard**, named for its ability to "walk on water" by skipping quickly across the surface.

Birds

The variety of birds is simply amazing (over 566 species). Birders (or *twitchers*, as the British call them) have plenty of opportunities to add species to their *life lists*. The jungles harbor **parrots, toucans, hummingbirds, chachalacas, trogons, woodpeckers, kiskadees, tanagers** and **oropendolas**. At night, you may see one of the many stately species of **owls**. Coastal regions teem with majestic **herons** (including the **rufescent tiger heron**), **egrets, limpkins, ibises, spoonbills, cormorants, ducks** and other shore birds. **Crooked Tree Wildlife Sanctuary**, in the north, is home to flocks of the rare **jabiru stork**.

Birders will find some action almost anywhere in the country. To maximize your sightings, visit both mountain forests and coastal wetlands. The unique ecosystem of **Mountain Pine Ridge** is home to some species that you won't see elsewhere, and some of the remote cayes have birds that are rare or extinct on the mainland. Yes, your chances of seeing something really rare are better in one of the very remote parks of the interior.

However, don't overlook more mundane locations. Mayan archaeological sites can have a surprisingly large number of birds, which may be easier to see at such partially-cleared sites

than they are in the deep forest. A boat ride is almost always one of the best ways to spot birds, whether on a jungle river, a brackish lagoon, or around some of the mangrove islands offshore.

Flora

Plant lovers will likewise be in Heaven. Here are thousands of exotic plant species. The tropical rain forest has many more species of trees than its temperate counterpart. Whereas a typical North American forest is dominated by only a few species of trees, Belizean forests have thousands. Many produce edible fruits or other useful products. The **guanacaste** (also known as tubroos or monkey's ear tree) was sacred to the ancient Maya, and today it's a commercially important tree. The seed pods are used for cattle feed, and the wood is used to make the dugout canoes that locals call *doreys*. Flowering trees such as the **jacaranda** and epiphytes (plants that grow on other plants) such as **orchids** and **bromeliads** add splashes of color amid the green.

Many lodges have hiking trails with interesting plants labeled, and some local guides specialize in medicinal plant tours, pointing out species that the Mayans and other local folks use for food and medicine. The **Belize**

Botanic Gardens (see Chapter 6) are a must-visit for any plant lover. The species are all neatly labeled, and you'll learn a lot about fruit trees and other cultivated plants that you aren't likely to see in the rain forest. Hummingbirds and butterflies are frequent visitors. Dozens of wild and crazy fruits are available, both whole and fresh-squeezed. Whether familiar fruits such as mangos, papayas and pineapples (which are much sweeter and juicier here than the mass-shipped varieties you find at the supermarket in Des Moines) or exotic varieties such as mammee apples, I highly recommend trying them whenever offered.

Marine Life
The magnificent menagerie doesn't end at the water's edge. Belize's many aquatic environments are home to a fascinating array of marine mammals, reptiles, fish and invertebrates. Belize is an important breeding ground for the endangered West Indian **manatee**, and you may see them either in brackish lagoons or offshore on the cayes. Gales Point and Caye Caulker are two favorite manatee-watching areas. Eight types of **dolphin** make their homes in Belizean waters, and several species of whales, including **sperm**, **killer** and **pilot whales**, visit from time to time.

There are seven **sea turtle** species in the world, and four of them nest on Belize's beaches. Female sea turtles return year after year to the beaches where they were born, and lay their eggs in the sand. When the babies hatch, they scamper to the sea en masse. In most of Central America, sea turtles have been hunted almost to extinction, both for their meat and for their eggs, which some fools believe to have aphrodisiac properties. Thanks to Belize's low population density and many protected areas, they are still fairly common here. You're very likely to see some while diving or snorkeling, and if you visit one of the remote cayes at just the right time, you may get to see mama turtle doing her thing on the beach.

Some of the most impressive ocean wildlife is to be seen beneath the surface. Belize is one of the top diving destinations in the world, with the world's second-longest barrier reef (after the Great Barrier Reef in Australia) and three coral atolls. Divers will see a rainbow of **coral** and **tropical fish**, including gobies, blennies, sergeant-majors and angelfish, to say nothing of lobsters, octopi and colorful little shrimp. Coral around the world is dying from increased water temperatures, but Belize still has a lot of live coral.

The largest fish in the sea, the **whale shark**, frequents the area around Glover's Reef Atoll from March-June, and divers can swim with these gentle giants. At Shark Ray Alley, just south of Ambergris Caye, you can snorkel with enormous (but harmless) **nurse sharks** and **Southern stingrays**. More sinister sharks, including **blacktips**, **hammerheads** and **tigers**, are often seen, especially around the atolls.

Anglers haul in a vast variety of species. The grass flats offer some of the world's best fly-fishing for **bonefish, permit** and **tarpon**. Rivers and mangrove lagoons hold several species of **snook**, as well as smaller (only 70 pounds or so) **tarpon**. The coral reefs are thick with **snapper** and **grouper**, and trolling offshore produces **sailfish, marlin, tuna, wahoo, jack**, and **sharks**. See *Best Sports & Recreation* sections for more on fishing.

What is ecotourism, anyway?

Ecotourism is a term that you'll hear kicked around quite a bit on your travels in Belize. Of course, most visitors to the country are here to enjoy the natural wonders, but does that make us all ecotourists? Does spending a couple of hours strolling through the forest with a herd of other gringos make you an ecotourist? Or must you spend a week helping the students with their research at some remote biological station to earn the title?

In fact, ecotourism is a state of mind, **an ideal of sustainable, minimally invasive tourism** that both visitors and those in the tourism industry should strive for (alas, both groups often fall far short of the ideal). Ecotourists leave no litter, don't feed or interfere with the animals, and consume nothing but products that are harvested in a sustainable manner. A true ecolodge recycles and conserves, releases no waste into the environment, strives to use renewable energy, and generally tries to have as little impact on the natural habitat as possible.

Ecotourism is also about preserving a very important species called local workers. One of the central concepts of ecotourism is the idea that local people can make a better living by helping tourists enjoy the rain forest than they could by chopping it down. Good ecotourists hire local guides, patronize local businesses, and buy local products whenever possible.

The **International Ecotourism Society** defines ecotourism as "responsible travel to natural areas that conserves the environment and improves the well-being of local people." Their web site at www.ecotourism.org includes lists of environmentally friendly lodges and tour operators.

You can learn more about tropical forests at www.nature.org. For those of a scientific disposition, **NatureServe** has a searchable database of every species of bird, mammal, and amphibian found in Belize and neighboring countries. *Info:* www.natureserve.org/infonatura.

4. THE NORTHERN CAYES

HIGHLIGHTS

▲ **Hol Chan and Shark Ray Alley** – Safely snorkel with huge nurse sharks and stingrays

▲ **The Blue Hole** – This enormous sinkhole is Belize's most popular advanced dive site

▲ **Fishing on the Flats** – World-class fly fishing for bonefish, tarpon and permit

▲ **Lazing on the Beach** – Doing nothing is a fine art here

Off the coast of Belize lies a sprawling maze of small islands, which the locals call *cayes* (pronounced "keys"). The largest, **Ambergris Caye**, is Belize's most popular tourist destination. A decade or two ago, it was a laid-back, sleepy little island, but it's rapidly growing into one of the Caribbean's major resort destinations. Smaller Caye Caulker remains far quieter.

There are hundreds of smaller cayes, several of them isolated island paradises, home to a single dive lodge. There's little to do on the cayes other than dive, fish and lie around in the sun, but for most of the thousands who visit, that's plenty!

You can get to Ambergris Caye by boat or by plane. Both are quite scenic rides. The plane costs more, but it's quicker, and may be more convenient, especially if you want to give Belize City a miss and head straight for the island. *Info: Both Maya Island Air and Tropic Air offer numerous flights each day to San Pedro's little dirt airstrip from both the Belize City municipal airstrip ($81 round trip) and Philip Goldson International Airport ($135 round trip). www.mayaislandair.com; www.tropicair.com.*

Boat service between downtown San Pedro and Belize City is provided by the (confusingly-named) **Caye Caulker Water Taxi Association**. Open speedboats carry about 30 people and their luggage from Belize City to San Pedro in an hour and a half. *Info: Boats depart from the Water Taxi terminal next to the Swing Bridge in Belize City about six times per day. The price is $27.50 round trip for adults, $15 for kids. www.cayecaulkerwatertaxi.com; Tel. 223-5752 or 226-0992.*

AMBERGRIS CAYE IN A DAY

If you can only spare a day for the islands, then Ambergris is your best bet. There are flights to and from Belize City all day, and there are a few things to do after the diving is done.

Morning
The first destination on our agenda is Belize's beautiful coral reef. If you've never dove or snorkeled before, don't worry – **Hol Chan Marine Reserve** is a perfect place for beginners to

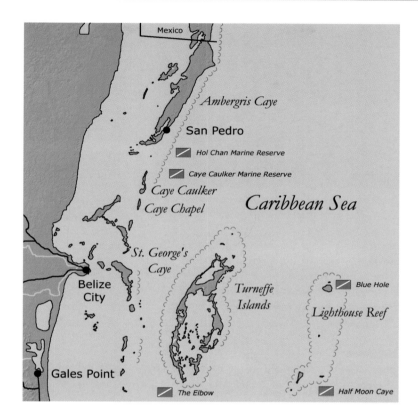

glimpse the glory of the underwater world. It's shallow, it's a short boat ride from Ambergris, and local guides are quite used to taking novices on easy and safe trips. If you can swim, you can snorkel, so let's do it!

For several reasons, early morning is the best time for snorkeling or diving. The seas are usually calmer in the morning, and the hordes of cruise ship day-trippers begin to arrive towards noon. Also, if you get your diving done first thing, you can start drinking cold beer at lunch! So we're going to take the first plane to Ambergris, and head straight for our dive shop. The large and respected outfit at **Ramon's Village** would be a great choice, as it's right by the airstrip. *Info: www.ramons.com; Tel. US 800/MAGIC 15*. **Amigos del Mar** is another large operator that caters to beginners. *Info: www.amigosdive.com; Tel. 226-2706*. Call the day before and line up a trip, so as soon as you arrive, they'll get you fitted out with snorkel, mask and fins, and you can head out to the reef.

The **Hol Chan Marine Reserve** protects a large area of coral reef, as well as mangrove and seagrass habitats. Here you can see a luxuriant ecosystem of colorful coral and fishy life just a few minutes' boat ride from town, including snapper, parrotfish, angelfish, barracuda, moray eels, nurse sharks and lots of lobsters. If you're lucky, you may spot a sea turtle, grouper, tarpon or even a manatee.

At the south end of the reserve, **Shark Ray Alley** is a fine place for novice snorkelers, and an unforgettable wildlife encounter even for seasoned divers. Local fishermen used to throw out their fish waste here, attracting nurse sharks and Southern stingrays. You can swim with these enormous fish in water only a few feet deep. Don't worry, they're not dangerous, but friendly, like big dogs eager for a handout (but be safe – don't touch 'em!).

Afternoon
Our first priority after getting out of the salt water is an ice-cold beer and a hearty lunch at one of the island's many beachfront restaurants. The nearby **Blue Water Grill** at the SunBreeze Hotel is a good choice, or stroll into town and try the inexpensive local favorite **Celi's**, or have a Jamaican-style jerk chicken at the **JamBel Jerk Pit**.

After lunch, take a leisurely stroll around the colorful tourist town of San Pedro. I'm afraid there's no Louvre or Smithsonian here, but there are a few shops that are worth visiting. **Belizean Arts**, located inside Fido's Court-yard, is an excellent art gallery, with a huge collection of oil paintings by local Belizean artists, several of whose works can be seen in local hotels. *Info: www.belizeanarts.com; Tel. 226-3019.*

After we've enjoyed some local art, and maybe bought a t-shirt and a fridge magnet, I'm afraid that's about it for touristy activities. Unlike some other Caribbean resorts, Ambergris doesn't (yet) have any "things 2 do" such as ziplines, wildlife parks or waterslides. But you know what? While I've heard a very few visitors complain that there's nothing to do but "stare at the ocean," thousands more come here and are delighted to do just that! If you came to relax and get away from the world of deadlines and stress, you've come to the perfect place. I know it's a cliché, but it really is true – if you can't relax here, you can't relax!

So, let's do some heavy-duty relaxing. First we'll sit down right here at **Fido's**, a fine place for a cold beverage and a chat with some of the local posse. **Estel's** is a shady spot where we can have another cold one, put our toes in the sand and watch the parade of fun-seekers along the beach.

Evening
The last planes for Belize City leave at 5pm, so if you're heading

Best Beaches

Belize's beaches are beautiful, but frankly, most are not among the world's top swimming beaches. In most areas, the coastline is shallow, so there are no waves to speak of, and the bottom is mostly seagrass and a little muddy, rather than nice granular sand. Another problem is the trash that washes up. Most island lodgings are on the beach, but some are much better for swimming than others. In the *Best Sleeps* section, we let you know which ones have nice sandy strands, and which ones keep them clean.

back this evening, boo-hoo time comes a bit early. If you're spending the night, then a lobster dinner is on the evening's agenda, perhaps at **Elvi's Kitchen** or **Caramba**, two good restaurants in San Pedro. If a candlelight dinner for two is your goal, and price is no object, then take a moonlight boat ride to **Capricorn**, one of the finest restaurants in the country. They only have a few tables, so you'll need to make reservations well in advance (see *Best Sleeps & Eats* later in this chapter).

A WEEKEND ON AMBERGRIS CAYE
A weekend gives you enough time to get a good sample of all the island has to offer: snorkeling, scuba diving, fishing, birding, swimming, eating seafood in funky beach restaurants and sipping umbrella drinks by the pool.

Friday Evening
You can get here by boat from Belize City, or by plane from any of several places in the country. The plane is quicker and cheaper, but either way you come, it will be a scenic trip – speeding through little channels between dozens of tiny mangrove islands or looking down on the islands and shallow grass flats from a low-flying plane.

There's a huge choice of lodging places on Ambergris. When planning your trip, you can pick the perfect spot based not only on your budget, but on the location. Low-budget travelers, or party animals who want to be in the middle of the action, have several good options right in San Pedro town. Those who want to get as far away from civilization as possible will pick one of the upscale resorts to the north of town. Personally, I like to stay south of town, because you get the best of both worlds – it's quiet, with a bit of a secluded atmosphere, but it's easy to walk or bike into town any time you want. For the ultimate in luxury, stay at **Victoria House**. Those of us with more moderate budgets will love **Mata Rocks** (see *Best Sleeps*).

After a short golf cart or boat ride to our hotel, it's time to get into the island lifestyle immediately (the last time we're going to use words like "immediately" all weekend). Take off your shirt and shoes, grab your welcome rum drink from the bar, and stretch out by the pool. As you watch the waves breaking on the coral reef a few hundred feet offshore, you'll feel things like telephones, traffic jams, suburban sprawl and stress begin to fade from your memory. Continue drinking rum until they are completely forgotten. Our only responsibility tonight is to make sure we have a dive trip lined up for tomorrow morning.

Hey! Wake up! The sun's going down, and it's time to think about dinner. The ten-minute walk into town is too complicated to bother with tonight, but that's no problem. Several of the island's finest restaurants are located at resorts just a short walk away. Walking along the beach is a favorite way to go dining on Ambergris.

Saturday Morning

If you see nothing else in Belize, you simply must see her beautiful coral reefs. A living coral reef is the most colorful and fascinating wildlife habitat on the planet, and Belize has some of the finest reefs in the Caribbean,

More Hotels
(by boat)

Sandpiper St.

Blue Tang Inn

Tradewinds Paradise Villas

The Phoenix

Sunbreeze Suites

Caribena St. $

Caramba

Back St.

Pelican St.

Mayan Princess

Ambergris St. $

Middle St.

Elvi's

Park

Buccaneer St.

Front St. $

Black Coral St.

Tarpon St.

Water Taxi Dock
Holiday Hotel

School

Ruby's

Airstrip

Lots More Hotels

Sunbreeze

Ramon's

Downtown
San Pedro

🛏 Hotels
🍽 Restaurants
$ Banks

including the world's second-longest barrier reef. We've all seen reefs on nature TV shows, but nothing comes close to experiencing it yourself. Coral reefs worldwide are threatened, and they may not be around forever, so get wet and see this natural wonder while you're here.

The kicker is that seeing the reef in Belize is easy and fun for people of all ages. While scuba diving (diving while breathing compressed air) requires a certification course, anyone can snorkel. All you need is a mask, snorkel and fins, which you can rent anywhere on the island, and a local guide can show you how to do it in five minutes. If you can swim, you can snorkel, and it's especially easy here on Ambergris. Most dive operators pick you up directly from your hotel, and the reef is just a few minutes' boat ride away.

Early morning is the best time for snorkeling or diving. The seas are usually calmer in the morning, and the hordes of cruise ship day-trippers begin to arrive towards noon. And, there's just something special about a good hearty lunch and a cold beer after a morning out in the sun and salt. We lined up a trip yesterday, so all we need to do this morning is slug down some coffee and stumble to the end of the dock. Within minutes, we'll be underwater.

If you have time for just one dive/snorkel trip, make it to **Hol Chan Marine Reserve**, Ambergris Caye's most popular spot for short reef excursions. Just a few miles south of town is the **Hol Chan Channel**, a steep-walled cut through the reef in 30 feet of water that is particularly rich in sea life and that gives the reserve its name (Hol Chan means "little channel" in Mayan).

Hol Chan's protected status means that you can see a wide range of fishy life just a few minutes' boat ride from town. You'll see schools of yellowtail snapper, parrotfish, angelfish, blue tangs, triggerfish, hogfish, barracuda, moray eels, nurse sharks and lots of lobsters. If you're lucky, you may spot

a blacktip or hammerhead shark, sea turtles, grouper, snapper, tarpon or perhaps even a manatee. There's also a profusion of colorful coral species, including elkhorn coral, brain coral, starlet coral, staghorn coral, sea fans, lettuce coral and other soft corals.

Just south of the channel, and also part of the reserve, **Shark Ray Alley** is one of the top places in the Caribbean to snorkel with large sea creatures. Local fishermen have been discarding fish waste here for years, making the area a frequent haunt of nurse sharks and Southern stingrays. You can swim with these enormous fish in water only a few feet deep – it's a fine place for novice snorkelers, and an unforgettable wildlife encounter even for seasoned divers. The nurse sharks (up to six feet long) and rays (up to four foot wingspan) are not dangerous. On the contrary, they seem friendly, like big dogs eager for a handout (but be safe – don't touch them, and let your guide handle the feeding).

Most of the dive shops on Ambergris run daily snorkeling trips to Hol Chan and Shark Ray Alley. There's a visitors' center in the middle of San Pedro where you can learn more about the ecosystem of Hol Chan. *Info: There's a park entry fee of $12.50 per person, which is included in the price of your trip. The visitors' center is open 9am - 5pm daily. www.holchanbelize.org.*

Saturday Afternoon
The dive boat drops us off back at our hotel worn out and crusty with salt, but happy. First stop is the pool bar for an ice-cold Belikin, and the next is the pool itself for a quick rinse-off. Then I guess we'll have to put on some pants (but not necessarily any shirt or shoes) if we want to have lunch. We'll borrow a couple of bikes from the hotel and ride into town.

San Pedro is a clapboard and concrete Caribbean town that has gradually evolved from a sleepy village into a major tourist resort area. The visitors are a mix of divers and honeymooners, upscale travelers and backpackers, Americans and Europeans. Golf carts and bicycles outnumber cars, but traffic on the sandy (in rainy weather, muddy) streets can be hectic in high season. The town has a Mexican feel: you'll hear more Spanish spoken than English, and excellent Mexican food is to be had.

Speaking of which, it's high time we were sitting down with a menu. Most

San Pedro eateries serve a mix of Mexican dishes, seafood and American favorites. **Elvi's Kitchen** is perhaps the most famous local spot. **Caramba** is also a good choice, and so are the Jamaican-style **JamBel Jerk Pit** and the inexpensive **Celi's**. We'll start with a little *ceviche* (fish or seafood in a lemon marinade, served with chips), then I'll have a large local fish. The kids can have a burrito or a burger.

After lunch, let's walk down **Front Street** and see the cultural sights of the town, such as they are. San Pedro has just three north-south streets, which the locals very sensibly call Front Street, Middle Street and Back Street. There is a half-hearted effort to replace the first two of these functional names with the more colorful Barrier Reef Drive and Pescador Street, but only tourists seem to take much notice. The beach itself serves as a busy pedestrian street – most of the dive shops and bars are located there, so it's the real center of the action (San Pedro's Broadway or Champs-Élysées, if you will).

Belize has a surprising number of fine artists, many of whom paint local subjects in the charming Caribbean Primitive style. **Belizean Arts**, located inside Fido's Courtyard, is an excellent gallery with a huge collection of oil paintings by local Belizean artists, several of whose works can be seen in local hotels. *Info: www.belizeanarts.com.*

And that's about it, folks. There's not much else to do here that doesn't involve getting yourself wet either outside or inside. I say we do both. There's an outfit right here on the beach, **SailSports Belize**, that has all manner of sail-powered craft for rent. How about spending an hour or two making fools of ourselves on a windsurfer or a Hobie Cat? *Info: www.sailsportsbelize.com; Tel. 226-4488.*

Waverunners and other motorized craft are also available. The beach here stays busy with folks doing every water sport known to man, from water-skiing to parasailing to kitesurfing (one of the reasons why the beach in San Pedro isn't especially good for swimming).

Sroll down the beach, stopping in at a few laid-back beach bars such as **Fido's** and sand-floored **Estel's**.

Saturday Evening
Let's dress up (on Ambergris, that means putting on a shirt) and go out for

a really nice gourmet meal tonight. For a delightfully romantic (but expensive) night out, take a moonlight boat ride to one of the gourmet restaurants on the north end of the island. Considered to be one of the best restaurants in Central America, **Capricorn** has been featured in any number of fancy food magazines. A table under the stars is yours for the evening, so take your time savoring Belizean goodies such as lobster tails, stone crab or grouper prepared with Continental flair, and a bottle from the nice wine list. In the same area, and also highly recommended, the **Rendezvous Restaurant & Winery** creates seafood and meat dishes with a fusion of Thai and French influences.

South of town, and easily accessible by foot, bike or golf cart, the **Palmilla Restaurant** at Victoria House is also among the top dining experiences on the island, serving a unique mix of island seafood and Continental cuisine. Their *ceviche* and lobster salad are really special.

See *Best Sleeps & Eats* for more details on these and other restaurants.

After dinner, there's no need to go to bed, as San Pedro has by far the most hopping nightlife scene in Belize. **Fido's**, right in the center of town, is the main hangout, with live music every night. South of town there is **Crazy Canuck's Beach Bar**. If you want to hit the dance floor, make the scene at **Jaguar's**, in the center of town. After midnight, the Red Bull crowd heads to **Big Daddy's**, an after-hours club where the locals get crazy (and I mean very crazy) until dawn. See *Best Nightlife* for more on island nightlife. Amber-gris is a pretty safe place – nothing like Belize City. I don't know if I'd walk back to my hotel all alone, but if you stick with a group and remain reasonably alert, I doubt you'll encounter any problems.

Diving & Flying

You don't want to get the bends at 30,000 feet on the flight back to Newark. This means it is a bad idea to scuba dive on the same day as flying. The cabins of modern airliners are usually pressurized at significantly less than sea level pressure. If your body is still slowly expelling nitrogen absorbed while breathing compressed air on a recent dive, flying with a low atmospheric pressure could trigger problems that would not occur at sea level pressures. This doesn't apply to snorkelers, because they don't breathe compressed air. So: **Scuba divers shouldn't dive within 24 hours before any flight.**

Sunday

No one says you can't snorkel just before flying, so Sunday morning would be a perfect time for a snorkel trip to **Hol Chan** and **Shark Ray Alley** if you didn't go there yesterday (or maybe even if you did). Otherwise, let's take a **boat tour around the island** to see some of the local residents. The sea creatures get most of the press, but Ambergris is also home to **over 260 bird species**, including vireos, flycatchers, kiskadees, woodpeckers and hummingbirds, to say nothing of the many water birds that hang out in the mangroves.

Mangroves

Mangroves are an amazing family of trees that grow on saltwater shorelines, their roots in the tidal water. A mangrove swamp is a unique ecosystem. The underwater forest of their roots makes a perfect habitat for barnacles, oysters, sponges, and sea squirts, which filter their food from the water as the tide goes in and out. Adolescent **fish** (including snook, snapper, shark, sea trout, tarpon and bonefish), shrimp, lobsters and many other creatures find shelter and food among the mangrove roots. **Birds** and **monkeys** live in the trees. Mangrove wetlands have many **ecological benefits**. They prevent coastal erosion, filter out pollutants, and absorb some of the wave energy of storm surges caused by hurricanes.

At the **Caribbean Villas Hotel**, south of San Pedro, aspiring birder Susan Lala has built a three-story "people perch" that offers a panoramic view of the entire island and plenty of interesting bird sightings. It's open to the public daily. Read about her birdy experiences at *www.caribbeanvillashotel.com/birds/cvbirds.html*. Other great places to spot birds are **Little Iguana and Rosario Cayes**, two small protected mangrove islands just off Ambergris, and **San Pedro Lagoon**, in the north part of the island. The island's greatest bird guru is **Elbert Greer**, who writes a weekly column about birds for the San Pedro Sun, and offers guided bird watching tours by boat around the island. He works as a guide at Ramon's Village (see *Best Sleeps*), so you can contact him there, or see *www.scubalessonsbelize.com/birds*.

A WEEKEND ON CAYE CAULKER

Caye Caulker is smaller and mellower than Ambergris. There are no large luxury resorts, nor are there crowds of American spring-breakers (although cruise-shippers do haunt the island during the day). Things are much cheaper here, and it's closer to the hottest dive sites. Personally, I love Caulker – spend more than a weekend if you can.

Friday Evening

You can get here by boat or by plane. Flying is more expensive, but it's quicker, and it has the added advantage that you can get here directly from the airport, without having to set foot in Belize City. However you get here, you'll need to slow down and adjust to island time as soon as you arrive – nothing happens quickly here. When we arrive at our hotel, there may be nobody around. No big deal – we'll go next door and have a cold drink, and somebody will show up before too long.

Caulker has a good selection of very nice places to stay, including **Island Magic** on the beach and the **Iguana Reef Inn**, over on the lagoon side. There are also several nice upscale condo-style lodgings, and plenty of offerings in the rustic-but-colorful category. Low-budget travelers can find clean and pleasant waterfront rooms pretty darn cheap (see *Best Sleeps*).

Have dinner and line up some activities for tomorrow. After chilling out with a welcome drink at our hotel, we'll take a stroll down the main street. If you're a certified diver, stop in at one of the island's dive shops and check out their offerings for tomorrow. Otherwise, hook up with one of several outfits that do snorkeling tours.

At the north end of the village is the **Split**, a little pass that a hurricane carved through the island a few years ago. Here we find the **Lazy Lizard**, a colorful local hangout, and the perfect place to have a drink and watch the sunset.

Getting hungry? I don't know about you, but I've been thinking about lobster tails ever since the ride to the airport this morning. Here on Caye Caulker, my favorite crustacean is abundant and cheap, and we can have it served in a wide variety of ways. At the south end of the village, the **Tropical Paradise Restaurant** serves great lobster specials. The last time I was there, I had a huge portion of lobster in a tasty marinara sauce for about $12. However, the walk all the way from the Split to the Trop is a bit far for a group of lobster-hungry tourists, and we might just get sucked in by one of the streetside barbecue stands that are grilling up lobster, fish and chicken. Some of these are nothing more than a grill, made out of half an oil drum, and a cooler full of drinks. This may be the cheapest way of all to enjoy a grilled lobster tail.

Sated with lobster, cold beer and rum, let's toddle off to our hotel and crash, so we can get an early start on our full day of Caribbean fun tomorrow.

Saturday

A weekend on Caye Caulker is guaranteed to relax even the most stressed-out, high-strung overachiever. The small village has **three dirt north-south streets** (Front, Middle and Back), any of which may be adorned with a soundly-sleeping dog right in the middle. The population is only about 1300 people, mostly Mestizos, whose traditional occupations are fishing, lobstering and boat building. The name of the island is believed to derive

from *hicaco*, the Spanish name for the cocoplum tree. Caulker has been a stop on the hippie trail since the 1960s. Nowadays you'll see more groups of wide-eyed day-trippers from the colossal cruise ships that anchor in the channel just to the south.

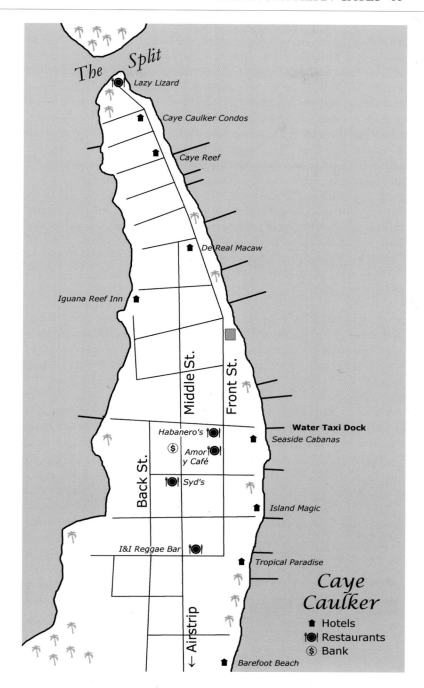

The Split

Lazy Lizard

Caye Caulker Condos

Caye Reef

De Real Macaw

Iguana Reef Inn

Middle St.

Front St.

Habanero's

Amor y Café

Syd's

Back St.

Water Taxi Dock

Seaside Cabanas

Island Magic

I&I Reggae Bar

Tropical Paradise

Airstrip

Barefoot Beach

Caye Caulker

🛏 Hotels
🍽 Restaurants
$ Bank

Today we're going to visit with some of Caye Caulker's marine life. Caulker is surrounded by prime snorkeling reefs, and you simply must get out there and see some of the underwater beauty. Many trips also make a stop off nearby **Swallow Caye** to swim with the manatees. The West Indian **manatee**, or sea cow, is a docile and friendly marine mammal that is found in shallow waters throughout the Caribbean and the Gulf of Mexico. Sadly, Caye Caulker resident Chocolate, who was the prime mover in getting the area around Swallow Caye designated a protected manatee sanctuary, has retired from giving tours, but there are several local operators who run half- and full-day trips for some snorkeling and manatee-watching.

We arrive back at Caulker late in the afternoon, and I for one am mighty thirsty. At the south end of town, there's a little stand that sells all kinds of fresh-squeezed tropical juices in plastic milk jugs. I'm getting a jug of mango and one of papaya to take back to the hotel and slug down at leisure. After a couple of tall glasses and a refreshing dip in the pool, it's time to think about dinner.

Strolling down Middle Street, we pass a couple of good possibilities. **Habanero's** is a very pleasant spot that's popular with visitors, serving spicy Caribbean-Mexican fare such as fajitas and firecracker prawns (made, of course, with habanero peppers). **Syd's** is a local institution, serving excellent (and cheap) Belizean fare on cheesy chrome dinette tables.

After dinner, there are plenty of places to while away the evening. No glitzy discos, but plenty of colorful little bars offering stiff drinks and loose conversation. Several spots have live music from time to time, but we'll

have to ask around to find out where it's happening. We'll definitely visit the **I&I Reggae Bar**, where roots reggae will be cranking, and we might catch a whiff of some herbs that aren't on the menu.

Sunday Morning

The place for breakfast on Caye Caulker is **Amor y Café**, on Front Street (formerly Cindy's). Every morning, there's excellent organic coffee from Guatemala, as well as chai, smoothies, homemade muffins, banana bread, fruit plates and other healthy treats. It's a great spot to hang out and swap stories with other travelers.

After a leisurely breakfast, let's head south of the village to visit a small forest reserve, an outpost of the much larger **Caye Caulker Forest Reserve** that covers the northern end of the island. Here we can take a hike to see native trees such as red, white and black mangroves, three varieties of coconut palm, buttonwood, gumbo-limbo, poisonwood, and the colorful ziracote. There are over a hundred species of birds on Caulker, including some that are rare on the mainland.

Sand Fleas, Anyone?

Many Belizean beaches are thick with irritating **sand fleas**, almost invisible little buggers that swarm around the beach. Many people have their favorite sauces to drive away the little ankle-biters but, to my knowledge, none of these spreads works for everyone. Many swear by **Avon's Skin-So-Soft**, so it's a good idea to bring some as well as the usual high-DEET mosquito repellant.

FOUR DAYS OF SERIOUS DIVING

Belize is one of the best places in this hemisphere for a dive vacation. The country has the **world's second-longest barrier reef**, with thousands of great dive sites, and it's far more pristine and laid-back than mass dive destinations such as Cozumel or the Caymans. On this four-day trip, we'll sample the most spectacular dive sites with a minimum of distractions.

Friday

Where should the hard-core diver stay? I recommend somewhere on the water. In fact, almost anywhere you stay on the coast, you'll have access to superb diving, but each region has its own pros and cons. **Ambergris Caye** has a huge variety of dive operators, plenty of nice sites just offshore, a wide choice of resorts in all price ranges, and a fair number of activities for non-diving companions. Ambergris also has crowds of other divers and the highest prices in the country. **Caye Caulker** is smaller, cheaper and closer to advanced dive sites such as the Blue Hole and Turneffe. Down south in **Dangriga** and **Placencia**, you'll also find nice prices, a laid-back vibe and lots of pristine dive sites nearby (see Chapter 7).

Dive Buddy Selection!

It's a good idea to be sure the people you'll be diving with over a few days have **similar interests and skill levels** as yourself, so you won't spend your valuable vacation time diving in areas that hold little interest for you. If you like drift dives best, floating around quietly looking at big fish and coral, you do not want to spend your time poking in and out of caves. So select your dive buddies with care.

On this trip, our goal is to get in as much diving as possible, without having to worry about details such as transport, meals or non-diving wimps, so we'll choose an all-inclusive dive lodge on one of the small cayes. **St. George's Caye Lodge** is a highly-respected dive lodge that's just a short boat ride from Belize City, but close to lots of great sites. The three lodges on **Turneffe Atoll** are just minutes away from some of the country's most spectacular diving (see *Best Sleeps*).

The folks from our lodge will meet us at the airport, and take us by van and boat out to where the fish are. Over a welcome drink, we'll meet with our divemaster and decide where we want to go tomorrow, then give our equipment a quick checkout and load it onto the boat. After dinner and an evening of swapping dive stories with fellow gung-ho guests, it's off to bed.

Saturday

The **Blue Hole** is Belize's Eiffel Tower, the sight that everyone back home will ask you about. This enormous sinkhole (1,000 feet across and 400 feet deep) is almost perfectly round, and its water is bright blue. It formed as a limestone cave millions of years ago, when this region was dry land. When sea levels rose, the weight of the water caused the roof to collapse, and this unique geological feature was formed.

The main attraction for divers is the cavern formations that open up into the sheer walls, beginning at a depth of about 110 feet. You can swim beneath vast overhangs, among massive stalactites. Sizable sharks patrol the limestone cathedrals, adding to the adventure. However, not everyone loves diving the Blue Hole as much as the tourist hype suggests. It's a very deep dive, which means you only get to spend a few minutes at depth, light levels are low, and there's little in the way of fish to be seen. Around the rim of the crater however, you'll see plenty of coral and its attending fish life.

There are several excellent shallow and medium-depth sites around the atoll that make great second dives. Perhaps the most spectacular is **Half Moon Wall**, where you can see a wide variety of underwater habitats in a small area, at moderate depths (30-70 feet). Here are dozens of spur-and-groove coral formations, overhangs and tunnels, as well as sand flats that are home to a colony of thousands of garden eels. Large sharks, eagle rays and manta rays are frequent visitors.

After the diving, most trips make a stop at **Half Moon Caye Natural Monument**, a tiny and remote island that's home to an amazing variety of wildlife. The most famous residents are the red-footed boobies, which nest here in the thousands. From a viewing platform adjacent to their colony, you can watch them feeding their chicks and flying about in their inimitable booby fashion. Magnificent frigate birds hang about waiting for the chance to snatch a booby egg. Over 120 other bird species visit here on their migrations, and three sea turtle species nest here at certain times of the year.

We'll return to the lodge and have a hearty family-style dinner of fresh seafood, then start getting ready for a night dive. Tonight's the night to do it, because tomorrow night might be pushing a little too close to the 24-hour mark before flying home on Monday. Also, by tomorrow night we are sure to be totally exhausted, in shape for little more than drinking beer and telling dive stories. Diving at night lets you see the reef from another perspective. You'll see fish snoozing away, some of them in cocoons of mucus that they spin for their bed each night (mmm, sounds comfortable). You may also see nocturnal creatures that don't come out during the day. Our divemaster will pick out a great shallow or medium-depth site for our night dive.

Sunday

Rise and shine! Grab a cup of coffee and hurry down to the dock, because today we're going to visit a place that many have called the most spectacular diving area in Belize: **Turneffe Atoll**. The largest of Belize's three coral atolls, Turneffe is a huge ring of coral reefs, dotted with over 200 tiny mangrove islands. The vast mangrove wetlands nurture a veritable Eden of sea life, and the remote location means that the reefs are in pristine shape and the visibility is usually spectacular. Lots of dive boats visit Turneffe, but the sheer number of great dive sites keeps the diving pressure low.

At the south end of the atoll is the **Elbow**, a steep coral wall that drops off into a deep channel swept by strong ocean currents. This is one of the few drift dives in Belize, and perhaps the best place to see really big fish. As we drift with the current along the wall, we'll swim amid vast schools of snapper, grouper, mackerel, jack, permit and tuna, and might even get a glimpse of pelagic creatures such as lemon, blacktip, and hammerhead sharks, manta and spotted eagle rays, green and hawksbill turtles, and bottle-nose and spotted dolphins.

For our second dive, we can choose among some of the finest wall dives in the Caribbean. **Myrtle's Turtles** is an awesome wall that starts at 60 feet and drops off to infinity. Here you'll see schools of jacks, snappers and permits, and a huge resident turtle. **Lefty's Ledge**, another wall dive starting around 50 feet, offers consistent sightings of large pelagics, including jacks, mackerel, eagle rays, and occasional hammerhead, blacktip, and bull sharks. If you'd rather dive a wreck, let's check out the **Sayonara**, an old passenger boat that was intentionally sunk in 1985 at a depth of 50 feet.

Monday Morning

Monday morning – time for one last visit to the beautiful coral reefs. We won't dive this morning, because we'll be flying back home this evening, but we may have just time to squeeze in a snorkel.

The western edge of Turneffe Atoll has lots of shallow reefs, perfect for beginning divers and snorkelers. The most popular is **Rendezvous Cut**, an area of large coral heads in 40-50 feet of water. Other easy dive sites include the **Aquarium**, a shallow (12 foot) spot with a lot of nice coral and a wealth of little reef fish; Hollywood, a sheltered site with depths of 20-45 feet and lush forests of soft corals and sponges; and **Susie's Shallows**, an area of colorful reef with a maximum depth of 15 feet.

Once we're all packed up and ready to go, the resort's boat will take us back to Belize City, where we'll transfer to a van to the airport and (sniff!) home.

A WEEK IN THE CAYES

The **cayes of Belize** have plenty to keep you busy for a week (or a lifetime), at least if you're into water sports. Diving, snorkeling, fishing and sailing present endless possibilities. Above the waterline, birders, manatee-watchers and lobster-eaters will be more than content. And it's amazing how many people are delighted to lie around on the sand and do absolutely nothing!

In a week, you could easily visit several of the cayes, but all offer similar activities, and access to many of the same dive sites, so it makes more sense to choose the island that best fits your idea of a perfect vacation, and spend your week there. That's what most visitors choose to do, so many lodgings specialize in **weeklong all-inclusive packages**. If you want a luxury resort, or you want to be a part of the tourist scene and the nightlife, opt for Ambergris. If you want a mellower scene and lower prices, head for Caulker. If you want a week of hard-core diving or fishing with no distractions, choose one of the lodges on the small islands.

San Pedro
The largest, and nicest, and only town on Ambergris Caye is San Pedro, a clapboard and concrete Caribbean town that is evolving from a sleepy village into a major tourist resort area. The visitors are mostly Americans, a mix of divers and honeymooners, upscale travelers and backpackers, as well as plenty of spring-break types. Cars are outnumbered by golf carts (both gas and electric) all-terrain-vehicles, and bicycles. Taxi vans ferry visitors to and from the various resorts, most of which are located just outside of town. Traffic on the sandy (in rainy weather, muddy) streets can be hectic, especially in high season. The town has a Mexican feel – you'll hear more Spanish spoken than English, and excellent Mexican food is to be had.

There are only three north-south streets in San Pedro. The one nearest the beach is called either Front Street or Barrier Reef Drive, the next one is called either Middle Street or Pescador Street, and the third one back is called Back Street. The alternate names are interchangeable, but for clarity, this book will refer to them as Front, Middle and Back Streets. The beach itself serves as a pedestrian street, and is where most of the dive shops and many of the restaurants are located.

Bikes are to be had (free or paid) at almost every hotel. If you're really lazy, you can rent a golf cart from **Carts Belize** (*www.cartsbelize.com*) or **Cholo's** (*www.ambergriscaye.com/cholos*). Golf cart rentals cost about $70 per day. A driver's license is required to rent or drive a cart.

There are several hotels right in San Pedro, mostly along or just off Front Street. A string of larger resorts spreads out to the south of town. To the north, there are several (mostly higher-end) resorts that are accessible only by boat. Most dive shops and other tour operators will pick you up from your hotel, so staying outside of town needn't be a problem.

Belizean Arts, located inside Fido's Courtyard, is an excellent art gallery with a huge collection of oil paintings by local Belizean artists, several of whose works can be seen in local hotels. *Info: www.belizeanarts. com; Tel. 226-3019.*

If you're on Ambergris for a week, and run out of things to do, don't forget that it's easy to take a day trip to the mainland to visit the **Lamanai ruins**, **Caves Branch**, the **Baboon Sanctuary** or any of various other attractions. Check with any of the island tour operators to see what's offered. *Info: www.ambergriscaye.com.*

Hol Chan Marine Reserve
This protected marine reserve a few miles south of San Pedro is by far the most popular spot for short snorkel and dive trips. The reserve includes sections of mangrove and seagrass habitat that, together with the coral reef, form an interconnected ecosystem where fish and other sea life grow up, feed and breed. The dive action is in the area around the **Hol Chan Channel**, a steep-walled cut through the reef in 30 feet of water that is particularly rich in sea life and that gives the reserve its name (Hol Chan means "little channel" in Mayan).

Ambergris History

When the first Europeans arrived on the island in 1508, they found several thriving Mayan villages. It is believed that the Mayans dug the channel that turned the southern end of a peninsula into an island. There are several **small Mayan ruins** scattered about the island. In the 1600s the island was a haven for **British pirates** who preyed on Spanish shipping in the region, and it was they who named the island for ambergris, an oily substance produced by sperm whales that was very valuable in those days for making perfumes. In the 19th century, **refugees from the Caste War** in the Yucatan came to Ambergris and mingled with the British settlers already there, forming the ancestry of today's mostly bilingual islanders. Traditional economic activities are logging, fishing, chicle, coconuts, lobster, and now tourism.

As elsewhere in the Caribbean, coral reefs near human settlements tend to be devoid of large fish, for the simple reason that the locals caught and cooked them long ago. Hol Chan's protected status means that you can see a wide range of fishy life just a few minutes' boat ride from town. You'll see schools of yellowtail snapper, parrotfish, angelfish, blue tangs, triggerfish, hogfish, barracuda, moray eels, nurse sharks and lots of lobsters. If you're lucky, you may spot a blacktip or hammerhead shark, sea turtles, grouper, snapper, tarpon or perhaps even a manatee. There's also a profusion of colorful coral species, including elkhorn coral, brain coral, starlet coral, staghorn coral, sea fans, lettuce coral and other soft corals.

Just south of the channel, and also part of the reserve, **Shark Ray Alley** is one of the top places in the Caribbean to snorkel with large sea creatures. Local fishermen have been discarding fish waste here for years, which has made the area a frequent haunt of nurse sharks and Southern stingrays. You can swim with these enormous fish in water only a few feet deep – it's a fine place for novice snorkelers, and an unforgettable wildlife encounter even for seasoned divers. The nurse sharks (up to six feet long) and rays (up to four foot wingspan) are not dangerous. On the contrary, they seem friendly, like big dogs eager for a handout (but be safe – don't touch them, and let your guide handle the feeding).

All dive shops on Ambergris and Caulker run daily snorkeling trips to Hol Chan and Shark Ray Alley. There's a park entry fee of $12.50 per person, which is included in the price of your trip. There's a visitors' center in the center of San Pedro where you can learn more about the ecosystem of Hol Chan. *Info: www.holchanbelize.org.*

Ambergris Caye Birding

The marine creatures get most of the press, but Ambergris is also home to over 260 bird species, including vireos, flycatchers, kiskadees, woodpeckers and hummingbirds, to say nothing of the many water birds that hang out in the mangroves.

At the **Caribbean Villas Hotel**, south of San Pedro, aspiring birder Susan Lala has built a three-story "people perch" that offers a panoramic view of the entire island and plenty of interesting bird sightings. It's open to the public daily.

Other great places to spot birds are **Little Iguana and Rosario Cayes**, two small protected mangrove islands just off Ambergris, and **San Pedro Lagoon**, in the north part of the island. Take a boat tour around the island, and you may also spot crocodiles, manatees or dolphins.

The island's greatest bird guru is **Elbert Greer**, who writes a weekly column about birds for the San Pedro Sun, and offers guided bird watching tours by boat around the island. He works as a guide at Ramon's Village (see *Best Sleeps*), so you can contact him there, or see *www.scubalessonsbelize.com/birds*.

Ambergris Caye Diving

The majority of visitors to Ambergris are there for the diving. Even if you've never dove before, when in San Pedro you must at least take a snorkeling trip. The abundance and beauty of the world beneath the sea will amaze you.

Ambergris has a passel of dive operators to choose from. A few of the resorts have their own dive shops, and there are a dozen more on the beach in downtown San Pedro. Many of the hotels have arrangements with certain dive operators, but most dive outfits will pick you up from any hotel dock. All the shops offer equipment rental and PADI instruction, and all offer similar prices, but be sure to inquire as to what's included, as some may nickel-and-dime you on equipment rentals and such. See *Best Sports & Recreation* for information on Ambergris dive operators.

You'll pay around $70-80 for a two-tank local dive. Most of the dive sites are very close to shore, so boat rides are short, and trips leave at a civilized hour, usually 9am or so. Many operators also offer afternoon and night dives. Most of the dive shops also arrange snorkeling and fishing trips.

Belize's most famous dive spot, the **Blue Hole**, is accessible from San Pedro, but it's a rather long boat ride. Most Blue Hole trips leave at 5 or 6 in the morning, and return about 12 hours later. You'll pay about $250 for a three-tank dive trip, including lunch (snorkelers pay around $150).

Ambergris Caye Water Sports

Fishing plays second fiddle to diving on Ambergris. Not because the fishing isn't great (it is!), but because San Pedro isn't known as a fishing resort (hard-core fishermen tend to stay out on Turneffe, or down south). Fishing charters from San Pedro are run by freelance boat captains. You can book a trip either through your hotel, or through any of the dive operators.

There are all kinds of other water sports going on, so many that the beach in San Pedro often resembles a busy train station more than a peaceful vacation spot, as people tear around on all manner of watercraft. **SailSports Belize**, located at the Caribbean Villas Hotel, rents all things with sails, from windsurfers to Hobie Cats to Lasers. *Info: www.sailsportsbelize.com; Tel. 226-4488.*

For kiteboarding, the latest extreme sport, check out **Kitexplorer**. With a board strapped to your feet and a huge kite up in the air, it's a bit like a cross between windsurfing and parasailing. *Info: www.kitexplorer.com; Tel. 635-4967.*

Lighthouse Reef & The Blue Hole

The **Blue Hole** is Belize's Eiffel Tower. Every tourist brochure features a picture of it, every dive shop runs trips to it, and when you get back home, everyone will ask you if you saw it. Completing the Parisian metaphor, the reality falls far short of the hype. Like the Eiffel, the Blue Hole is grand and impressive, but there are far more interesting dive sites in Belize.

Located at the center of **Lighthouse Reef**, a coral atoll about 60 miles southeast of Belize City, the Blue Hole is an enormous round sinkhole, over 1,000 feet across and 400 feet deep. Its almost perfect circular shape and the bright blue color of its water make it a unique sight from the air. It formed as a limestone cave millions of years ago, when this region was dry land. When sea levels rose, the weight of the water caused the roof to collapse, and this unique geological feature was formed.

The main attraction for divers is the **cavern formations** that open up into the sheer walls, beginning at a depth of about 110 feet. You can swim beneath vast overhangs, among massive stalactites. Sizable sharks patrol the limestone cathedrals, adding to the adventure. Because of the depth, the

caverns and the long boat ride to get here, this dive should be made by advanced divers only. However, the coral-lined rim of the crater is a good spot for shallow diving and snorkeling.

There's no question that the Blue Hole is a truly unique place, but many divers find the dive itself disappointing. It's a very deep dive, so you only get to spend a few minutes admiring the sights. As with all deep dives, light levels will be low, and you'll see little in the way of fish and other sea life. At the end of your dive however, as you poke around in the shallows, you'll see plenty.

There are several excellent shallow and medium-depth sites around the atoll that make great second dives. Out here in the open ocean the visibility is usually superb, and you may catch a glimpse of some large pelagic fish. The most spectacular site of all is **Half Moon Wall**, where you can see a wide variety of underwater habitats in a small area, at moderate depths (30-70 feet). Here are dozens of spur-and-groove coral formations, overhangs and tunnels, as well as sand flats that are home to a colony of thousands of garden eels. Large sharks, eagle rays and manta rays are frequent visitors.

After the diving, most trips make a stop at **Half Moon Caye Natural Monument**. This tiny island so far from the mainland is home to an amazing variety of wildlife. The most famous residents are the red-footed boobies, which nest here in the thousands. From a viewing platform adjacent to their colony, you can watch them feeding their chicks and flying about in their inimitable booby fashion. Magnificent frigate birds hang about waiting for the chance to snatch a booby egg. The best time to see the boobies is March-July, when the young are in the nests. Over 120 other bird species visit here on their migrations, and three sea turtle species nest here at certain times of the year. There are also scads of iguanas, geckos and anole lizards, as well as pretty orange flowers called ziricotes.

Lighthouse Reef is within day-trip range of just about everywhere in Belize. Dive boats come here from Ambergris Caye (2.5 hours), Caulker, Belize City and even down south in Dangriga. Live-aboard dive boats also frequent the area. If you want to be right here, stay at one of the small island lodges. There's no lodging right on the atoll, but the lodges on Turneffe are a short boat ride away.

Turneffe Islands
The largest of Belize's three coral atolls is 25 miles east of Belize City. This huge ring of coral reefs is dotted with **over 200 tiny mangrove islands**. There's nothing out here but mangroves, palm trees, birds, fish and the humans who stalk them. Here you'll find what may just be the best diving and fishing in all of Belize. The vast mangrove wetlands nurture a veritable

Eden of sea life, and the fairly remote location means that the reefs are in pristine shape and the visibility is usually spectacular. The sheer number of great dive sites keeps the diving pressure down. Turneffe is no secret – it's visited by several dive boats every day – but with over 160 miles of reefs and walls, there's plenty of room to spread out. There's a huge range of different kinds of diving, and plenty of sites suitable for all skill levels.

The western edge of the atoll has lots of shallow reefs, perfect for beginning divers and snorkelers. The most popular is **Rendezvous Cut**, an area of large coral heads in 40-50 feet of water. Other easy dive sites include the **Aquarium**, a shallow (12 feet) spot with a lot of nice coral and a wealth of little reef fish; **Hollywood**, a sheltered site with depths of 20-45 feet and lush forests of soft corals and sponges; and **Susie's Shallows**, an area of colorful reef with a maximum depth of 15 feet. **Triple Anchors** is a 40-60 foot site where three anchors and some other remnants of an old sailing ship lie encrusted with corals and sponges. **Permit Paradise** is a 60-foot dive where you'll see schools of the eponymous (and delicious) game fish.

There are several wrecks around Turneffe. The most popular, and an excellent choice for a beginning wreck diver, is the **Sayonara**, an old passenger boat that was intentionally sunk in 1985 at a depth of 50 feet.

Intermediate divers enjoy some of the finest wall dives in the Caribbean. **Myrtle's Turtles** is an awesome wall that starts at 60 feet and drops off to infinity. Here you'll see schools of jacks, snappers and permits, and a huge resident turtle. **Lefty's Ledge**, another wall dive starting around 50 feet, offers consistent sightings of large pelagics, including jacks, mackerels, eagle rays, and occasional hammerhead, blacktip and bull sharks. **Gail's Point** is yet another awesome wall frequented by large open-ocean fish and turtles. When diving these walls, you're likely to be enthralled by the huge fish you'll see swimming in the water column. But don't forget to turn your gaze back to the wall from time to time, as the variety of hard and soft corals, sponges, gorgonians, starfish, shrimp and flamboyant little reef fish is amazing.

At the south end of the atoll is the **Elbow**, one of the most impressive dive sites in the country. A steep coral wall drops off into a deep channel where strong ocean currents sweep around the south end of the atoll. This is an excellent drift dive, and perhaps the most likely place in the area to see really big fish. Advanced divers can drift with the current along the wall, swimming with vast schools of snapper, grouper, mackerel, jack, permit and tuna, and perhaps getting a glimpse of pelagic creatures such as lemon, blacktip and hammerhead sharks, manta and spotted eagle rays, green and hawksbill turtles, and bottlenose and spotted dolphin. A few divers have even spotted marlin and sailfish! Because of the strong current and rough seas, the Elbow is for advanced divers only.

The miles of shallow **seagrass flats** inside the atoll are one of the world's finest places for flats fishing. Anglers come from all over the world to try to catch a wily bonefish or a tackle-busting tarpon on a fly. Fishing on the reefs for grouper and snapper, and offshore for billfish, are similarly spectacular.

There are three diving/fishing lodges on the atoll: **Turneffe Island Resort** (*www.turnefferesort.com*), **Blackbird Caye Resort** (*www.blackbirdresort.com*) and **Turneffe Flats** (*www.tflats.com*; see *Best Sports & Recreation*). **The Oceanic Society**, a non-profit conservation group (*www.oceanic-society.org*), operates a research station here that also welcomes visitors on weeklong packages to dive and participate in their studies.

Not all the wonderful wildlife lives below the surface. Turneffe is the most biologically diverse coral atoll in the Western Hemisphere. **Over 60 bird species** have been spotted here, some of them rare or extinct on the mainland. Obviously there's a huge variety of water birds (magnificent frigate birds, kingfishers, double-crested cormorants and several species of herons) and raptors (ospreys, peregrine falcons). You may also see mangrove warblers, golden-fronted woodpeckers, mockingbirds, hummingbirds, vireos, swallows, tanagers and brown boobies.

The vast atoll is home to many rare creatures, including the endangered **American crocodile** and **West Indian manatee**. Several species of dolphins are frequently seen. Turneffe Flats offers wildlife tours of the islands for those who prefer to enjoy the natural world without getting wet.

Caye Caulker

Caulker has a very different vibe than Ambergris. Most visitors find Ambergris to be pretty laid-back (although it is steadily becoming less so), but Caulker makes Ambergris seem like downtown Paris. There's *nothing* going on here but water sports, lying around on the beach and perhaps languidly gazing at a bird from time to time. Even the dogs seem lazier.

With its two nature reserves and lack of large resorts, Caulker has a green feel. You'll see more Rastas and more European visitors on Caulker than on Ambergris. You'll also find slightly lower prices, particularly for the lovely local lobster. When you arrive at your hotel, there may be no one in the office (which may be located in a nearby shop, or someone's house). Go relax on the beach, or have a drink next door – they'll be back soon.

As Belize rapidly evolves from a sleepy backwater to a major tourist destination, the character of the island is changing, for better or for worse. Caye Caulker is a short boat ride away from the main channel where the gargantuan cruise ships anchor, and groups of t-shirt-buying, ice-cream-cone-gobbling day-trippers are now mingling uneasily with the hairy backpackers that have traditionally been Caulker's main visitors.

There are three main north-south streets, called Front, Middle and Back streets. Most of the best accommodations are located on Front Street, right across from the sea. There is nothing on Caulker that could really be called a luxury resort, but there are a couple of very nice midrange lodgings, and lots of lower-budget options (see *Best Sleeps*).

The airstrip on Caye Caulker has direct air service from Goldson International Airport, Belize City Municipal Airstrip, and San Pedro. Contact **Tropic Air** (*www.tropicair.com*) or **Maya Island Air** (*www.mayaislandair.com*) for current schedules.

Boats leave several times per day from the **Water Taxi Terminal** in Belize City, and stop at Caye Caulker on the way to Ambergris. The fare to Caulker is $10 one-way, $17.50 return for adults, and $5/$10 for kids. *Info: www.cayecaulkerwatertaxi.com; Tel. 223-5752 or 226-0992.*

The main activities on Caulker involve watching wildlife. The **Caye Caulker Marine Reserve** includes all of the barrier reef that runs parallel to the shore, as well as the turtle grass lagoon on the west side of the island. There are plenty of excellent dive sites along the barrier reef just a short boat ride offshore. Caye Caulker dive operators also run trips to Hol Chan, as well as the Blue Hole and the Turneffe Islands, both of which are closer from here than they are from Ambergris. See *Best Sports & Recreation* for information on Caulker dive and snorkeling operators.

One of the most popular spots is **Sergeant's Caye**, a tiny island right on the barrier reef south of Caulker. It has a beautiful swimming beach and excellent snorkeling on the coral reef. Novice snorkelers can paddle around in the shallow protected waters on the lagoon side of the island, while more adventurous types can check out the deeper and more spectacular reefs on the ocean side. You'll see a wealth of colorful coral species, including elkhorn coral, brain coral, starlet coral, staghorn coral and sea fans, with swarms of brightly-colored tropical fish such as blue tangs, sergeant majors, parrotfish and angelfish. You may also encounter barracuda, moray eels, nurse sharks and lobsters.

Another favorite place to visit from Caulker is the nearby **Swallow Caye Wildlife Sanctuary**. The West Indian manatee, or sea cow, is a docile and friendly marine mammal that is found in shallow waters throughout the Caribbean and the Gulf of Mexico. Sadly, Caye Caulker resident Chocolate, who was the prime mover in getting the area around Swallow Caye designated a protected manatee sanctuary, has retired from giving tours, but several local operators include a visit to the manatees in their daily snorkeling tours. You can also arrange to simply cruise around the grass flats and mangrove islands around Caulker, observing the manatees, perhaps also some dolphins and certainly vast flocks of seabirds. *Info: www.swallowcayemanatees.org.*

Caye Caulker is also the home of a less cuddly sea creature, the American saltwater crocodile. These endangered reptiles are now protected in Belize, and they are common in the lagoons around the island. It's also exciting to go crocodile hunting at night (in the safety of a boat, of course).

The northern 100 acres of Caye Caulker is also part of the **Caye Caulker Forest and Marine Reserve**, which is managed by a consortium of local tourist and conservation groups. The Forest Reserve has a small visitors' center and picnic area, and is a common stop on boat tours. There's also a two-acre mini-reserve just south of town, where you can take a hike to see native trees such as red, white and black mangroves, three varieties of coconut palm, buttonwood, gumbo-limbo, poisonwood, and the colorful ziracote.

There are over **a hundred species of birds** on Caulker, including some that are rare on the mainland. There's a huge profusion of water birds, from egrets to cormorants, raptors such as hawks and ospreys, and rarities like the black catbird and rufus-necked rail. *Info: Guide Ellen Macrae does birding tours. Tel. 226-0178. For more info on island activities, see: www.gocayecaulker.com; www.cayecaulkerchronicles.com.*

Other Northern Cayes
St George's Caye is one of the closest cayes to Belize City, but it surely feels isolated. There is nothing here but two resorts and a couple dozen private homes (see *Best Sleeps*). A couple of rusty cannon recall the 1798 Battle of St. George's Caye, in which the Spanish were defeated and ceded control of the region to Britain. Water taxis between Belize City and Ambergris Caye will stop here on request.

There are lots and lots of tiny islands (over 200 at last count) strung out along the coast. A few, including **Gallows Point Caye** and **Spanish Lookout Caye**, have a single diving/fishing lodge (see *Best Sleeps*). A few others are visited by tourists on day-trips or overnight camping trips. Others are visited only by birds and drug smugglers.

BEST SLEEPS & EATS
BEST SLEEPS ON AMBERGRIS CAYE
This slender island is Belize's most popular tourist destination, and it is rapidly growing into one of the Caribbean's major resorts. There are well over 75 hotels and guest houses, and more are under construction (although the building goes slowly, as all supplies must be brought by boat from the mainland).

When choosing a place to stay, location is the key. There are plenty of places right in the town of San Pedro, mostly mid-price and budget options. A road south of town leads to many more lodgings, including a few upscale establishments. Most of the real luxury resorts are north of town, accessible by boat only. If you want to be in the middle of the party, stay in town. If you want a more secluded island experience, stay north or south of town. Any place on the island is fine for diving, as most dive operators will pick you up from your hotel's dock.

Both lodging and food are more expensive here than anywhere else in the country. Truly low-budget travelers should head for Caulker or Punta Gorda instead. If you're staying for a while, or are with a large group, consider one of the many places that offer suites with kitchens.

Lodging Prices

Prices quoted are for one double room.

$$$$$ Luxury: $200 +
$$$$ First-class: $125-200
$$$ Midrange: $60-125
$$ Budget: $25-60
$ Backpacker: $25 or less

SAN PEDRO

Being in town gives you easy access to a range of restaurants, night spots and dive shops. San Pedro is a party town, so rooms may be noisy, especially if you need to leave the windows open. The beach in central San Pedro is a narrow pedestrian thoroughfare, and boats and watercraft of all descriptions race around madly, so it's not much good either for lounging around or for swimming. There are a lot of new lodgings under construction, which will make the already large selection even greater, but for now it means that several hotels are located next to noisy construction sites.

The Phoenix $$$$$

This newer luxury resort rose from the ashes of the former Paradise Hotel. The condos are attractive and modern, if a bit stark, with tile floors and bamboo furniture. Everything's sleek and elegant, from the two pools to the Red Ginger restaurant, which serves a fusion of Belizean and world cuisines. *Info: www.thephoenixbelize.com; Tel. 226-2083 or 877/822-5512 US.*

Ramon's Village $$$$

This is one of the best-known lodgings on the island, and the only sandy-compound-thatched-hut-style place right by town (just a short walk south of the airstrip). The 61 cabanas are quaint, the grounds are lush, the beach is nice and the staff are friendly. Some cabanas are by the beach, and some are by the noisy road, so choose carefully. Ramon's has their own dive operation with six boats, rentals and PADI instruction. They also do fishing tours and rent windsurfers, bikes and scooters. The food is only fair, but there are plenty of great eateries nearby. *Info: www.ramons.com; Tel. 800/MAGIC 15 US.*

Tradewinds Paradise Villas $$$$

These modern one-and two-bedroom villas on the north edge of San Pedro have central air, kitchens, daily maid service and free wi-fi. They're a good value for families. The palm-shaded compound includes a pool and has a laid-back feel. *Info: www.belizeparadisevillas.com; Tel. 226-2822 or 800/451-7776 US.*

Blue Tang Inn $$$$

This nice three-story building surrounds a shady courtyard in a peaceful location just north of San Pedro. The 14 newly-renovated suites have kitchens, AC and ceiling fans. Large windows let you enjoy the cool tropical breeze. The third-floor suites have Jacuzzi bathtubs and vaulted ceilings. There's a nice pool with a wooden deck. *Info: www.bluetanginn.com; Tel. 226-2326 or 866/881-1020 US.*

Sunbreeze Beach Hotel $$$$

This is a very nice motel-style place, two stories around a central courtyard. The location, across from the airstrip at the south end of town, is not as

noisy as it sounds, as the airstrip serves prop planes only, and most flights are during the day. The décor features nice tile and paintings by local artists, while the pleasant sandy compound lends a laid-back tropical feel. The 43 comfortable rooms each have two double beds, private bath with large tiled shower (and blasting hot water), phone, TV, wi-fi, AC and ceiling fans. Premier rooms have Jacuzzi baths and refrigerators. The attractive pool and open-air restaurant and bar invite you to linger. Hugh Parkey's Belize Dive Connection is on site, as is a spa and massage studio. *Info: www.sunbreeze.net; Tel. 226-2191 or 800/688-0191 US.*

Sunbreeze Suites $$$$
Run by the same folks as the Sunbreeze Hotel, this resort (formerly Aquamarina Suites) is toward the north end of town. The large air-conditioned rooms have full kitchens and sitting areas. Some rooms overlook the ocean, and some overlook the cemetery next door. There's a small pool, a nice beach and a gift shop. *Info: www.sunbreezesuites.com; Tel. 226-4675 or 800/820-1631 US.*

The Palms $$$$
Just south of the airstrip, these 13 apartments have AC, full kitchens, TV, phones, and private porches. Charming local art graces the walls. There's a nice pool and lush grounds. *Info: www.belizepalms.com; Tel. 226-3322.*

Mayan Princess Hotel $$$
If you're here to dive and party, this would be a good base, right in the center of town in front of the Amigos del Mar dive shop and next to lively Fido's. The rooms have typical tile floors and rattan furniture, kitchenettes and oceanfront balconies. *Info: www.mayanprincesshotel.com; Tel. 226-2778 or 800/850-4101 US.*

San Pedro Holiday Hotel $$$
This small colonial-style place is great for the price. Managers Celi and Kim are longtime pillars of the local tourist industry. The 16 rooms are clean, the AC works fine and the staff are great. Right here are the Bottom Time dive shop and Celi's, one of San Pedro's most popular restaurants. There's a nice little swimming area and some beach loungers for chilling out. *Info: www.sanpedroholiday.com; Tel. 713/893-3825 US.*

Hotel San Pedrano $$
This small central hotel is the nicest of the cheapies, basic but clean. All seven rooms have private bath and AC. They open onto a balcony with a bit of a sea view. *Info: Tel. 226-2054.*

Another decent budget option on Front Street is **Ruby's**, which has rooms with or without private bath and AC. *Info: www.ambergriscaye.com/rubys; Tel. 226-2063.*

The cheapest place to stay is **Pedro's Inn**, a nice little hostel just out of town, with rooms starting at $10. *Info: www.backpackersbelize.com; Tel. 226-3825.*

NORTH OF SAN PEDRO

These resorts are accessible by boat only. Most offer a free boat trip to town only upon arrival and departure, so you may have to pay for every trip into town. The idea is that you'll stay at your resort and chill out for your entire stay (except for a couple of dive trips from their private dock). There are no "things to do" up here, and boat rides back to town are expensive, as are drinks and food. That's Ambergris.

Capricorn Resort $$$$$

Capricorn is renowned as one of the finest restaurants on Ambergris, if not

in all of Central America (see below under *Best Eats*). It also might be your perfect honeymoon getaway, just you, the staff and the sea. It's an intimate lodging, with only three beachfront cabanas. They are charming and comfortable rather than luxurious, with AC, private porches, colorful décor and local art. *Info: www.ambergriscaye.com/capricorn; Tel. 226-2809.*

El Pescador $$$$$

As the name implies, this place caters to anglers, with a special emphasis on flats fishing for bonefish, tarpon and permit. They have what is probably the largest fly fishing shop in Belize. This is no gaudy luxury resort, but the accommodations are first-class. Rooms in the colonial-style main lodge have AC and ceiling fans. All face the ocean and overlook the pool. There are also four three-bedroom villas in beautiful tropical style. You'll find a full range of amenities – three pools, an exercise room, free kayaks and bikes, wireless internet, a tour office and gift shop, and a restaurant serving fresh local fish on an outdoor deck. But the best feature of all is the family that runs the place. "We never say no" is their motto, and a steady stream of delighted guests can tell you that it's true. Divemaster Alonzo guides small groups on dream trips to the local reefs. *Info: www.elpescador.com; Tel. 226-2398 or 800/242-2017 US.*

Tranquility Bay Resort $$$$$
This luxury resort is the northernmost lodging on the island, a remote and relaxing getaway. The eleven beachfront cabanas have AC, comfortable beds and casually elegant furnishings. The restaurant features fresh seafood, and even offers a few vegetarian dishes.

Timeshare Pitch Alert!

Sooner or later on Ambergris Caye, you'll be accosted by a pitchman who offers you a free weeklong stay at one of the island's best-known luxury resorts – a $2,000 US value – what a great deal! The catch? You must sit through a presentation that culminates in a high-pressure sales pitch for timeshare units (timeshares will not be mentioned until you've committed yourself to hearing the spiel). You may be tempted to endure the pitch in order to claim that free week's vacation, only to find that the "prize" is so hedged with conditions as to be practically worthless.

The resort has its own in-house dive operation, and a collection of kayaks, windsurfers and other watercraft. The reef is closer up here than elsewhere on the island, and some folks actually kayak out to the reef for a snorkel. *Info: www.tranquilitybayresort.com; Tel. 220-5880, 888/843-2293 US.*

Captain Morgan's Retreat $$$$$
This is the best-known resort on the island, the one that everyone talks about. It's a fully-equipped and well-run upscale resort with 32 thatched-roof air-conditioned cabanas and all the expected amenities. Most visitors

love it, but it is showing its age a bit, and some hip travelers may be put off by the Disneyesque feel of the place – a trashy American TV show was filmed here, and smarmy salespeople hawk timeshare units. *Info: www.belizevacation.com; Tel. 888/653-9090 US.*

Belizean Shores $$$$$

Everyone loves this beachfront resort. The suites are large and luxurious, with full kitchens and dining areas, as well as private balconies, some with views of the sea. The grounds are green and peaceful, and the large infinity pool with its swim-up bar is a wonderful highlight. The restaurant has a panoramic ocean view and serves a delicious mix of Caribbean and international cuisine. There's a dive center on site, as well as kayaks and even a tennis court. *Info: www.belizeanshores.com; Tel. 226-4478 or 800/ 319-9026 US.*

Las Terrazas $$$$$

This is one of the island's newest resorts, but the construction phase is long over, and everything is very much up and running. It features a very contemporary design, with a hint of Miami Beach. The 37 one- to three-bedroom condos have full kitchens, laundry facilities and balconies or terraces. The Serenity Spa offers massages and exotic treatments such as seaweed wraps and mango baths right on the beach. There's a pool with a bar, a five-star PADI dive facility, a fitness center, a tour desk and free wireless internet. If you tire of lazing about, try one of the free Hobie cats or kayaks. People come from all over the island to dine at the O Restaurant, with its striking modern decor and its fusion of local seafood and trendy world cuisine. *Info: www.lasterrazasresort.com; Tel. 800/447-1553 US.*

Matachica Beach Resort $$$$$

Rustic elegance and personal service are the pride of this well-known resort, one of my favorites on the island. The staff who pick you up at the airport

greet you by name, and call in a drink order on the way, so your favorite libation will be waiting as you step off the boat. The 26 villas have AC and open floor plans with high thatched ceilings, but no TVs or phones. Some have quirky touches such as hand-painted murals and open-air showers. Have a massage or a banana facial at the Jade Spa, or relax in the Jacuzzi (conveniently close to the bar) or the palm-lined infinity pool. The Mambo restaurant is exquisite. *Info: www.matachica.com; Tel. 220-5010 or 223-0002.*

Coco Beach Resort $$$$
This large (62 units) newer resort has a variety of accommodations, all luxuriously appointed, with sumptuous decor. Most units have TVs, wi-fi and private balconies or patios. The hotel rooms have mini-fridges and microwaves, and the one-bedroom casitas and two-bedroom villas have full-size modern kitchens. The two pools are impressive – one extends under one of the buildings, so you can swim in the shade as you sip an umbrella drink from the swim-up bar. Guests can use the restaurant and tennis courts at the sister property Belizean Shores, next door. The service here is top-notch, and the romantic atmosphere makes this a good choice for honeymooners. *Info: www.cocobeachbelize.com; Tel. 226-4840 or 800/499-3002 US.*

SOUTH OF SAN PEDRO
The road south of town is lined with midrange-to-upscale lodgings. Staying in this area gives you the best of both worlds – you're out of the noise and bustle, but it's easy to take a bike or a golf cart into town when you want to. You can also walk along the beach and sample the restaurants and bars of the various resorts.

Victoria House $$$$$
This is the poshest of the resorts south of town, and many call it the nicest on the island. The beautiful beach, luxuriantly landscaped compound and three swimming pools are kept immaculate by an army of groundskeepers. The 42 units offer a range of options, from second-floor State Rooms to thatched Casitas to the four-bedroom Casa Azul with its private pool. All have nice beds with mosquito nets, minibars and efficient AC, but most have no phones or TVs. The Rainforest Suite is especially nice, with charming tropical décor and French doors opening right onto the beach. The Restaurant Palmilla is probably the most expensive on the island. There's also more casual

dining at the poolside restaurant or beach bar. Or, why not have your meal delivered to your own patio? Victoria House has their own Fantasea dive shop, offering daily dive trips from their private pier. A massage after your dive trip is easily arranged. *Info: www.victoria-house.com; Tel. 226-2067 or 800/247-5159 US.*

Villas at Banyan Bay $$$$$

Each of these oceanfront suites has two bedrooms, two baths (one with a Jacuzzi tub), a full kitchen and a nice veranda. This is a good place for

families, with a nice swimming beach and a huge pool including a kids' wading area. The on-site dive shop makes this a good choice for divers, too. Rico's restaurant serves a splendid conch *ceviche*, and the staff is friendly and helpful. *Info: www.banyanbay.com; Tel. 226-3739 or 866/352-1163 US.*

Xanadu Island Resort $$$$

Located just a short way south of town, this elegant tropical resort has 19 suites with full kitchens, dining areas, central air, ceiling fans, and all the goodies. There's a nice pool with a wooden deck, a private dock and plenty of hammocks for lazing about. Repeat guests rave about the service and the peaceful atmosphere. Wedding packages are a specialty. They'll put on a complete tropical wedding for you, taking care of the license, a minister, flowers, a band and all the trimmings. *Info: www.xanaduresort-belize.com; Tel. 226-2814 or 866/351-4752 US.*

Pelican Reef Villas $$$$

These 24 two- and three-bedroom villas have full kitchens, laundry facilities and bathrooms with Jacuzzi tubs. The décor is a blend of antique and modern, with granite countertops and dark wood furniture. The palm-shaded infinity pool invites you to lounge around, but scuba tanks beckon on the dock. Next door, the companion property Athens Gate offers similar amenities in a four-story faux Greek-style building. *Info: www.pelicanreefvillas.com; Tel. 226-2352 or 281/394-3739 US.*

Mata Rocks Resort $$$$

This small and friendly beachfront resort a mile south of town has eleven rooms arranged around a swimming pool, all with ocean views. Downstairs rooms open onto the pool deck; upstairs rooms have private balconies. All have private bath, AC, TV, and a small refrigerator. There are also six Junior Suites, each with full kitchenette. There are no phones in the rooms, but there is wi-fi, as well as a phone in the office available for guests. There are also bicycles that are free for guests' use, but during daylight hours only (too many guests were taking the bikes to bars at night, then forgetting where they were). The daily happy hour at the Squirrel's Nest, the cool and breezy beachside bar, is a good time to compare notes on the day's adventures with your fellow guests. Canadian owners Terry and Liz have been here since 1995. They embrace the casual Belizean lifestyle, and their excellent local staff will cater to your every desire. *Info: www.matarocks.com; Tel. 226-2336 or 888/628-2757 US.*

Exotic Caye Beach Resort $$$$

Just south of town. All rooms have AC, kitchens and sea views. There's a pool, an attractive beach and an on-site dive shop. Crazy Canuck's Beach Bar is one of the local hot spots, with frequent live bands. *Info: www.belizeisfun.com; Tel. 226-2870.*

Corona del Mar Apartment Hotel $$$

This is one of the best values on the island, a first-class hotel at midrange prices that gets consistent rave reviews. A short walk south of San Pedro are twelve rooms and four apartment suites with all mod cons. The AC works great (not always the case in Belize), the beds are comfortable, and there's even an elevator! Some rooms have balconies with splendid ocean views. They serve a nice breakfast on the beach, and keep a pitcher of free rum punch in the lobby all day. The staff are what really keep the guests coming back.

Vacation Lodgings

If you plan to stay in one place for a week or more, renting an apartment is an economical alternative to a hotel room. Actually, the line between the two is blurry, as many hotels have suites with kitchens, and many offer special rates for longer stays. Local real estate agencies have vacation rentals available, from moderately-priced apartments to luxurious seaside villas. Use one of the Belize-based search engines to find a local agent in the region you're interested in.

Miriam, Pamela and Frank are friendly and attentive, and will get your tours and other activities set up in an efficient manner. Don't let Frank hustle you at horseshoes! *Info: www.ambergriscaye.com/coronadelmar; Tel. 226-2055.*

BEST EATS ON AMBERGRIS

Ambergris eateries range from elegant restaurants, perfect for a candlelit dinner for two, to casual sand-floor places and streetside stalls where you can grab a quick burger. Several of the fancy places are located at resorts south or north of town, so you may have to take a boat or bike (and make reservations in advance), but the dining is often worth the effort. The variety of cuisines includes Belizean, Mexican, Italian, Chinese, Thai, Jamaican, and American. Seafood is naturally a specialty, and you'll find lobster prepared in a wonderful variety of ways, as well as snapper, conch and other delights. *Ceviche* (fish or seafood in a lemon marinade, served with chips) is an excellent choice for an appetizer.

Restaurant prices are not necessarily cheap. You can get a good Belizean or Mexican-style dinner at a bargain price, but seafood dishes can get spendy. San Pedro's favorite crustacean is still reasonably priced by US standards – expect to pay around $25 for a lobster dinner in one of the casual restaurants. Atmosphere is cheap – almost all of the restaurants listed below are oceanfront.

Most restaurants offer food only during the usual meal times, serving lunch from around 11am-2pm, then closing in the afternoon and opening again for dinner around 5pm. Most accept credit cards.

Upscale
Capricorn
Snazzy food mags have called this one of the best restaurants in Central America. The menu is a delightful fusion of Belizean and Continental influences. When was the last time you had fresh stone crab claws with French crepes? The specialty of the house is a grouper filet stuffed with onions, peppers and cheese. Home-baked breads and desserts round out the picture. Capricorn is accessible only by sea. A moonlight boat ride and a table under the stars make the perfect romantic evening. *Info: www.ambergriscaye.com/capricorn; Tel. 226-2809.*

Rendezvous Restaurant & Winery

Also located north of San Pedro, this top-rated intimate (only 24 seats) restaurant specializes in Thai and French fusion cuisine. Offerings include classic Thai dishes (*phad Thai*), French specialties (*creme brulée, escargot*), and such unique creations as salmon mousse with basil and mint rolled in an almond crumble. On my last visit, I especially enjoyed the spider crab soup. The Rendezvous produces their own brand of wine (from imported grapes), which even they seem to realize isn't very good. But don't worry – there are other good libations on their wine list. *Info:ambergriscaye.com/ rendezvous; Tel. 226-3426.*

Palmilla Restaurant

The restaurant at the Victoria House Resort is known to locals and tourists as one of the finest on the island, serving a unique mix of island seafood and Continental cuisine. It's no surprise that excellent *ceviche* and lobster salad are on offer, but what say you to orange-scented seafood bouillabaisse, or shrimp salpicon with chipotle? *Info: www.victoria-house.com; Tel. 226-2067.*

Casual

Elvi's Kitchen

San Pedro's most famous eating spot. Elvi has had a restaurant here for over 25 years, and has won all kinds of awards for her Belizean cooking. Despite all the fame, Elvi's remains a casual place with reasonable prices. Seafood

is the specialty, but the chicken wings and desserts have also won renown. On Fridays there's a Grand Mayan Buffet, one of the few places you can sample traditional Mayan cuisine. *Info: www.elviskitchen.com; Tel. 226-2176.*

Caramba!

Also on Middle Street, this place is only a few years old, but it gets rave reviews from locals and visitors. The main offerings are seafood and Mexican dishes, including burritos and fajitas with fish, shrimp or lobster, jerk fish and of course lobster served a variety of ways. There are several vegetarian offerings. There's a decent wine list and an array of cocktails, smoothies and fresh juices. *Info: www.carambabelize.com; Tel. 226-4321.*

JamBel Jerk Pit

One of the island's best known eateries, JamBel started out years ago as an inexpensive jerk joint, and recently moved to more a more upscale location

at the Xaman Ek resort north of town. The cuisine is JAMaican, with a BELizean touch (get it?). The food is not as cheap as it used it be, but it's consistently good. The menu includes the justly famous jerk chicken, great fish, lobster and conch, served with beans and rice and I-tal vegetables. Reggae music cranks for an Irie dining experience! *Info: www.xamanekbelize.com/restaurant.html; Tel. 226-3009.*

Blue Water Grill

The restaurant at the SunBreeze Hotel (across from the airstrip) serves great seafood dishes, splendid sushi, and wood-fired pizza on a pleasant beachfront deck with a great view. Food is served continuously all day. *Info: www.sunbreeze.net; Tel. 226-2191.*

Caliente

Located in the Spindrift Hotel on Front Street, this place serves very good Mexican cuisine, including *enchiladas de mole, tacos al carbón,* and a particularly good *ceviche.* Vegetarians will dig the vegetable *quesadillas.* Next door, **Wahoo's** bar is famous for the Thursday night Chicken Drop (don't ask – just go).

Celi's

On the beach next door to the San Pedro Holiday Hotel, this local favorite is inexpensive and pretty good. They pride themselves on their burgers, and have weekly beach barbecues with live music. Celi's Deli, on the main street side of the Holiday Hotel, has BLT, turkey, chicken and other sandwiches. *Info: www.sanpedroholiday.com/celis.html; Tel. 713/893-3825 US.*

Lily's Treasure Chest

This recently renovated local institution is on the beach next to the water taxi dock. Lobster, shrimp and conch creole are just a few of the seafood specialties on the menu. Breakfast is served all day, and tourist staples such as chicken and burgers are popular with families. Dine on the beachfront deck or inside. *Info: Tel. 226-2059.*

The Grill At Fido's

Also in the middle of town is this long-time tourist favorite, which features a variety of dishes including inexpensive sandwiches. Fido's is also a local drinking hotspot, with live music most nights. *Info: Tel. 226-2056.*

Estel's Dine by the Sea

Estel's, on the beach just north of the Spindrift, has recently been spruced up, but it's still pretty casual. No shirt, no shoes – no problem! The menu, chalked on a blackboard, consists of simple but hearty standards, filling but undistinguished. Estel's is especially popular for breakfast and lunch. No credit cards. *Info: www.ambergriscaye.com/estels; Tel. 226-2019.*

If you're looking for a cheap snack, check out **Ambergris Street**, off Front Street on the beach side. There's a whole row of "fast food" stalls serving everything from burgers to Salvadoran *pupusas* to fruit smoothies to (of course) beans and rice to locals.

There's an amazing selection of cheese, wines and spirits at the shop **Wine De Vine**, toward the south end of town. *Info: www.winedevine.com; Tel. 226-3430.*

BEST SLEEPS ON CAYE CAULKER

Lodging on Caye Caulker used to be highly colorful, rustic and cheap, but in the past few years, several new, more upscale hotels and condos have been built, and a few of the older places have been nicely spruced up. Prices are still a bit lower here than on Ambergris, with fewer sneaky fees, and hotel staff are very laid-back. In fact, there may not be anyone there when you show up – no problem – have a cold one and wait. Some of the smaller places close in the low season.

Iguana Reef Inn $$$$

This upscale inn is on the lagoon side, not the ocean side, but there's a pleasant beach and swimming area, the staff are super-friendly, and

everyone who comes here seems to have a great time. The 13 bright and airy rooms have tile floors, wicker furniture, pastel walls and artwork by local artists. Pleasant breezes keep things cool, but there's also nice cold AC (none of the rickety old window units you'll find at cheaper places). The pool is splendid. *Info: www.iguanareefinn.com; Tel. 226-0213.*

Island Magic $$$

This new resort (it opened in 2010) seems big, modern and snazzy for Caulker, although it's not really that large (11 rooms) or that expensive (the rooms without an ocean view start at $110). All the mod cons are here – TV, AC, ceiling fans, a mini-kitchen with fridge and microwave, free wi-fi. There's a pool with Jacuzzi and bar overlooking the beach and the private pier. *Info: www.islandmagicbelize.com; Tel. 226-0505.*

Seaside Cabanas $$$

This one is also fairly new and modern, a yellow masonry building right by the water taxi dock in the center of town. The 16 rooms are clean and well-appointed (though some are rather small), with private bath, AC, TV, refrigerators and free wi-fi. Most of the rooms have private verandas, and a few have rooftop terraces with hammocks. There's a nice pool and the water is steps away. *Info: www.seasidecabanas.com; Tel. 226-0498.*

Caye Reef $$$

Up near the Split, each of these six condos has two bedrooms, a full kitchen and a private balcony. All mod cons – TV, wi-fi, phones – are here.

Nice beach, nice pool, rooftop Jacuzzi – what more do you need? *Info: www.cayereef.com; Tel. 226-0382.*

OASI $$$

A quiet location and lush grounds, a couple of minutes from the beach and center of town, these apartments have small kitchens, AC, ceiling fans and TVs. Guests rave about the comfortable rooms and especially about owners Luciana and Michael. There are two dogs and a cat. *Info: www.oasi-holidaysbelize.com; Tel. 226-0384.*

Lazy Iguana $$$

Not to be confused with the Iguana Reef (see previous page), this small upscale B&B has four guest rooms, each with AC and ceiling fans. The rooftop palapa has inviting hammocks and a birds-eye view of the island. The location is secluded and quiet, on the other side of the island from the beach, which some folks love and some don't. However, almost everyone loves the breakfast, which features homemade bread. Tours and massages are available. *Info: www.lazyiguana.net; Tel. 226-0350.*

Caye Caulker Condos $$$

Eight nice units near the Split, all with private bath, kitchens, AC, safes and private verandahs. The rooms are pleasantly tropical, with tile floors and mahogany furniture, and the second-floor ones have excellent views. There are complimentary bikes for guests' use, a nice pool, and a rooftop *palapa* with hammocks. Miss Claudette can cook a Belizean dinner for you in your room. *Info: www.cayecaulkercondos.com; Tel. 226-0072 or 600-8485.*

Kokomo Beach Suites $$$

These pleasantly decorated rooms feature porches, TVs, AC, and little kitchens for basic meals. A colorful wooden building with colorful characters lying about in hammocks, it's got plenty of island character. *Info: www.kokomobeachsuites.com; Tel. 226-0777.*

De Real Macaw $$$

This friendly guest house has seven double rooms and a two-bedroom apartment. All have private bath, AC and ceiling fans, and some have porches with sea views. Pets are accepted, and there are lots of cats hanging around. It can be a bit noisy and raucous here – some guests don't like the fact that the hotel is adjacent to the boisterous street market. *Info: www.derealmacaw.biz; Tel. 226-0459.*

There are a number of newer apartments and condo-style accommodations in the middle price range, some of them pretty luxurious. Property manager **Caye Caulker Accommodations** offers a selection of these in all price ranges. *Info: www.cayecaulkeraccommodations.com; Tel. 226-0382.*

Maxhapan Cabanas $$
These three cabanas offer excellent value for the price, with private bath, AC, ceiling fans and TVs. Owner Louise Aguilar is an interesting character, and everyone who stays here seems to love it. *Info: www.gocayecaulker.com/ accommodations/maxhapan-cabanas; Tel. 226-0118.*

Caye Caulker Plaza $$
This new concrete high rise isn't on the water, but the prices are great and the rooms are pleasant enough, with AC, TV, safes, refrigerators and wi-fi. Some have balconies with nice views. *Info: www.cayecaulkerplazahotel.com; Tel. 226-0780.*

Sea Dreams $$
At the north end, this small hotel has a very tropical look, with thatched roofs and a rooftop cupola to catch the breeze. The rooms and suites (with kitchens) are comfortable, with AC and all mod cons. The dock, right on the Split, is a mellow hangout spot. Fishing tours are a specialty. *Info: www.seadreamsbelize.com; Tel. 226-0602.*

Rainbow Hotel $$
This blue Spanish motelish-looking place in the center of the village has recently been renovated, and by all accounts is now quite modern and trim. The rooms have all the mod cons – AC, TV, fridge, microwave, etc. Watch the parade of local wildlife from the balcony in front of the rooms, or walk across the street to the restaurant, which is built out over the water, and soak up the tropical lifestyle. *Info: www.rainbowhotel-cayecaulker.com; Tel. 226-0123.*

Tropical Paradise Hotel $$
At the south end of the village, next to the old island cemetery, this is a classic tropical hideaway, wooden cabanas in a sandy beachfront compound. The rooms are nothing fancy, but they are clean and have all the amenities you'd expect in this price range. The best is #14, which faces directly onto the beach, and has a nice porch, the perfect place to sit and write your masterpiece. Or, if you prefer, to do absolutely nothing. The restaurant serves Belizean specials at good prices (see below). The owners also operate the cheaper and less pleasant Tropics Hotel in town, as well as Star Tours, which offers daily snorkel tours from Tropical Paradise's private dock. *Info: www.startoursbelize.com; Tel. 226-0124 or 226-0374.*

As we move into the lower price ranges, many of Caulker's lodgings may appear a bit too rustic for the typical American tourist, at least from outside. But if you don't expect luxury, you'll find several places offering clean and adequate rooms right on the beach, at nice prices.

Trends Hotel $$
This one has some rooms on the beach and some a few feet away on Front Street. All have private bath and ceiling fans, and some have AC. *Info: www.trendsbze.com; Tel. 226-0094.*

Popeye's Beach Resort $$
Toward the south end of town, Popeye's has a rowdy bar, not much of a beach, and decent air-conditioned rooms for $60-95. *Info: www.popeyesbeachresort.com; Tel. 226-0032.*

Several other cheap sleeps cluster near the water in the middle of the village. Ask around, and you should be able to find a basic but clean room for 30 or 40 bucks.

Yuma's House Belize $
In its former life as **Tina's Backpackers Hostel**, this place had a bad reputation for sanitary and security issues, but the new owners have really cleaned things up (new mattresses and new door locks, among other

improvements), and it's now getting rave reviews from the backpacker set. The beachfront hostel has always been popular for the social scene and the bargain prices (dorm beds for $12.50 per person, rooms for $28.50, all with shared bath and use of the communal kitchen). *Info: www.yumashousebelize.com; Tel. 206-0019.*

LODGING SOUTH OF THE VILLAGE

Walking south past the Tropical Paradise, you'll find a string of beachfront lodgings, each funkier than the last. Tom's Hotel (*Tel. 226-0102*) has austere but clean rooms with shared or private bath. The Anchorage (*www.anchorageresort.com; Tel. 226-0304*) has 18 rooms, all with private bath, AC, TV, refrigerator and balcony, but has seen better days.

Barefoot Beach $$

This small place (three rooms, one suite and three cottages) was renovated and tidied up a few years ago, and now offers a nice value for the price in a peaceful spot south of town. Clean rooms with private bath and AC start at $50. *Info: www.barefootbeachbelize.com; Tel. 226-0205.*

Ignacio's Beach Cabins (*Tel. 226-0175*) are very rustic wooden cabins on stilts, starting around $20 for a cold-water cabin. Shirley's Guest House (*www.shirleysguesthouse.com; Tel. 600-0069*), the southernmost lodging, has a nice sandy compound and decent little rooms starting under $50.

BEST EATS ON CAYE CAULKER

Caye Caulker's restaurants operate on island time. Shirts and shoes are optional, the floor may be sand, and both menus and opening times may be flexible. Prices for food are much better than in San Pedro or Belize City. If part of your ideal Belize vacation involves gorging on lobster, Caye Caulker is the place to do it. You can have your lobster in a wide variety of Caribbean, Asian and Italian sauces, in a soup or a salad, or just steamed or grilled. A good lobster dinner should cost you less than $25 (much less at one of the streetside barbecue stands).

Habanero's

Since opening a few years ago, this has become one of Caulker's most popular restaurants, and with good reason. The menu has a Caribbean-Mexican vibe, and features imaginative creations featuring (of course) seafood and habanero peppers. Fajitas and lobster-stuffed snapper are specialties. Even vegetarians will find something to like here. *Info: Tel. 626-4911.*

Tropical Paradise Restaurant
Located at the hotel of the same name (see above), this is a good sit-down restaurant, open for breakfast, lunch and dinner. Seafood and Belizean specialties are creatively prepared and reasonably priced. The lobster specials can be very special indeed – the last time I was there, I had a huge portion of lobster in a tasty marinara sauce.

Syd's
On a back street toward the south end of town, this is an institution, the place where the locals eat. It's nothing fancy (décor is chrome dinette and plastic), and don't expect fast service, but the food is excellent and cheap, with main dishes starting around five bucks. *Info: Tel. 206-0294.*

All along **Front Street** during the busy season, you'll see small improvised barbecue stands, sometimes consisting of nothing more than a bisected oil drum grill and a cooler full of drinks. This is the cheapest way of all to enjoy a grilled lobster tail, although some travelers may have misgivings about sanitary issues.

Amor y Café
Located on Front Street, this is a good hit for breakfast or lunch. Every morning, there's excellent organic coffee from Guatemala, as well as chai, smoothies, homemade muffins, banana bread, fruit plates and other healthy treats. This is *the* morning hangout spot, a great place to swap stories with experienced travelers and find out what's happening on Caulker and beyond. *Info: Tel. 610-2397.*

Another great local breakfast hang is **Glenda's Restaurant**, on Back Street. The johnnycakes and sweet rolls are justly famous.

The **Lazy Lizard**, at the Split, is a local hangout where you can swim in the clear, fast-moving water.

BEST ISLAND LODGES
If you really want to get away to a secluded Caribbean paradise, one of the smaller cayes could be the island of your dreams. There are a couple dozen little lodges dotted among the vast sprawl of tiny islands south of Caulker. Most exist for the purpose of diving and/or fishing, and most guests come on weeklong packages. If you're a hardcore sportsman, this could be the perfect option. The really hot diving and fishing sites are closer here than

they are from San Pedro, and you can concentrate on the fishies with no distractions.

However, the remote island experience isn't for everyone, and it's probably not for parties that include non-diving spouses or kids. Most of these places are the sole lodging and dining option on their respective cayes, and there are few "things to do." The only access to most of these spots is by the resorts' private boats, so once you're there, you're there for the duration. Supplies also travel by small boat, so the island lodges tend to be more expensive than their mainland counterparts, and occasional embarrassing shortages are a fact of life. Some of the cayes have beautiful beaches, but most are not world-class swimming spots, as the water tends to be shallow, with lots of sea grass and squishy mud rather than nice sand.

St. George's Caye Resort $$$$
The closest of the cayes to Belize City, St. George's Caye has nothing but two lodges and a couple dozen private homes. This homelike dive lodge has

cozy rooms in the main lodge, and six charming cottages built over the water, with thatched roofs. All have private bath and AC. These folks have been running a dive lodge for over thirty years, and it shows in the excellent dive operation, with first-rate facilities and personal service from some of Belize's most experienced divemasters. Diving possibilities include not only lots of nearby sites (the reef is only a half mile out), but also day trips to Turneffe or the Blue Hole (both much closer from here than from Ambergris or Caulker). After the diving, you can poke around in a kayak, windsurfer or jet ski, then join the other guests for a barbecue and a bonfire on the beach. Boats to Ambergris will stop here on request. *Info: www.gooddiving.com; Tel. 800/813-8498 US.*

Hugh Parkey's Belize Adventure Lodge $$$
This basic lodge on Spanish Lookout Caye consists of 12 rustic cabanas

with private bath and ceiling fans, as well as dormitory-style lodging for student groups. There's a complete PADI dive shop (the long-established company also has a dive shop on Ambergris), and various other water and land activities are on offer. *Info: www.belizeadventurelodge.com; Tel. 220-4024 or 223-5086.*

Turneffe Flats $$$

You can't get any closer to the fish than this. The Turneffe Islands are one of the best areas for diving in the country, and flats fishing is also excellent. One of three lodges that comprise the only human habitation on this remote atoll, Turneffe Flats has pretty nice rooms with AC and private bath. Both diving and fishing guests give this place consistently good reviews. *Info: www.tflats.com; Tel. 888/512-8812 US.*

Belcove Island Lodge $$

You don't have to spend a lot to enjoy the island hideaway experience. This basic little lodge on Gallows Point Caye is run by the same folks as the budget Hotel Belcove in Belize City. The six basic but clean rooms have private shower and fans. Meals are prepared on request, or you can use the kitchen to cook your own. Various diving and fishing packages are available. *Info: www.belcove.com; Tel. 227-3054.*

Crying in the Chapel

The luxurious **Caye Chapel Island Resort**, which occupied an entire small island near Belize City, and featured the only world-class golf course in Belize, recently shut down. No one seems to know if or when it will reopen, or even whether the golf course is being maintained.

See Chapter 7 for several more island lodge options in the south of the country.

BEST SHOPPING

Belize produces some very nice handicrafts, from wood carvings to leather to clothing and jewelry. You'll find crafts on sale throughout the country, especially tourist staples such as hammocks and small Mayan-themed carvings. **Jade**, sacred to the ancient Maya, is a favorite material for upscale artworks. You may also be offered coral, but be aware that it is an endangered species, subject to the Convention on International Trade in Endangered Species. Except for fossils, coral is generally illegal to buy or remove from the country.

Belize has many excellent **visual artists**. Most of them take the natural wonders and colorful people of the country as subjects, and many of them paint in the charming Caribbean Primitive style. Oils, watercolors and sculptures are often reasonably priced.

Coffee and **rum** make good cheap gifts for the folks back home. Both are best purchased in a local grocery store. The duty-free shop at the airport is not any cheaper. Prices in tourist shops around the country are usually higher. Consumer goods of all kinds can be expensive in Belize, so stock up on things like razors, spare batteries and other travel items before you go.

Like all tourist towns, **San Pedro** has any number of shops selling t-shirts, fridge magnets, and "handicrafts" that may or may not have anything to do with Belize. There are some very nice carvings, paintings and clothing to be had, but the good stuff may be hard to find among the tourist junk.

Belizean Arts, located inside Fido's Courtyard, is an excellent art gallery that's well worth a visit, even if you don't plan to buy. The highlight is the huge collection of oil paintings by Belizean artists, several of whose works can be seen in local hotels. Other smaller galleries come and go. *Info: www.belizeanarts.com; Tel. 226-3019.*

On Caye Caulker, **Caribbean Colors Café and Art Gallery** has some nice paintings by local artists. *Info: Tel. 668-7205.*

BEST NIGHTLIFE & ENTERTAINMENT

If you want to party, San Pedro is your place. There are no big glitzy discos, but the beach bar scene is very cool. The classic local drink is called a **panty ripper**, and consists of fresh pineapple juice with a generous shot of the country's finest rum (One Barrel). Of course, plenty of ice-cold Belikin beer and the usual selection of fruity tropical drinks flow freely.

Fido's, an open-air thatched compound on Front Street in the center of San Pedro, has live music most nights *Info: fidosbelize.com*. **Crazy Canuck's**, located just south of town at the Exotic Caye Beach Resort, is a good local nightspot, and has a live band every Monday night. *Info: www.belizeisfun.com/crazycanucksmenu.htm.*

The big nightclub in San Pedro is **Jaguar's Temple**, in the center of town, which has DJs spinning dance music every night. *Info: Opens at 9pm. www.jaguarstempleclub.com.*

Wet Willy's, a nice bar at the end of a long dock, has occasional live music, and sees a huge turnout for ladies' night every Wednesday. **Big Daddy's** is an after-hours club where the locals get crazy (and I mean very crazy) until dawn. The **Pier Lounge** is popular with sports fans, as The Game (including Monday Night Football) is shown on a huge plasma TV. The bar at the **Holiday Hotel** is another good place to watch sports on TV.

On Caye Caulker, the place to go to watch the sunset is the **Lazy Lizard**, at the north end of town. Ask around there to find out where everyone's going after happy hour is over. Several spots have live music from time to time. Be sure to check out the **I&I Reggae Bar**, on the side street just inland from the Tropical Paradise Hotel, where rootsy Reggae music cranks at all hours, and you might just smell some herbs that aren't on the menu.

BEST SPORTS & RECREATION

SCUBA DIVING & SNORKELING

Belize is arguably the finest destination for diving and snorkeling in the Western Hemisphere. The world's second-longest barrier reef (after the Great Barrier Reef in Australia) parallels the shore from north to south. Belize also has three of only four coral atolls in the hemisphere (an atoll is a large ring of coral reefs surrounding a shallow lagoon). Belize's relatively

Be Safe

Outside of Belize City, Belize is much safer than other Central American countries, but you do want to be careful when you go out at night. Excessive boozing, drugs and prostitution are all parts of the scene, so there are plenty of ways to get into trouble. I want you to drink, dance and have fun, but keep your eye on your beverage at all times, and be wary of accepting anything to eat, drink or ingest from a stranger. Ladies should not venture out alone, and everyone should think twice about walking back to your hotel after dark. In Belize City, don't even think once – absolutely, positively take a taxi!

Snorkeling Safety

What's the biggest danger to snorkelers? Sting rays, eels, sharks, fire coral? Nope. None of those things will hurt you if you don't touch them, but **the sun can hurt you badly** if you aren't careful. Always wear a t-shirt when snorkeling. You'll be spending most of your time face-down floating on top of the water, with your back exposed to the broiling sun. You may also want to consider some waterproof sunblock for your neck and legs. And remember, the tropical sun can burn you even on cloudy days.

low population density means that most of the reefs are in good shape, and the country has wisely protected many of the most sensitive areas as marine reserves.

Visibility is usually excellent, and you'll see plenty of live coral in all the colors of the rainbow – brain coral, staghorn, elkhorn, and the stinging fire coral – to say nothing of gigantic barrel sponges and waving sea fans. You'll see plenty of fish large and small. Colorful reef fish include gobies, blennies, sergeant-majors, tangs, angelfish and parrotfish, which crunch coral with their strong beaks, digest the animal matter and poop out sand. Larger predators include barracuda (fearsome to look at, but not dangerous), snapper and grouper. If you're lucky, you may see snook, tarpon or sharks. Sea turtles and stingrays are frequent reef visitors.

The reefs are accessible to everyone, not just scuba divers. Snorkeling is very easy to learn, and some of the most beautiful reef structure is quite shallow. There's a fascinating other world just a short boat ride offshore so, even if you've never tried it before, do not pass up the chance to go snorkeling before you leave Belize.

PLANNING YOUR DIVE VACATION

Each of Belize's regions has its own pros and cons for divers. **Ambergris Caye** has the largest variety of dive operators (well over a dozen at last count), and plenty of nice sites just a short boat ride away. There are some excellent resorts where you can stay in luxury and still concentrate on diving, and there are activities for non-diving companions. On the other hand, Ambergris has crowds of other divers and the highest prices in the country. It's a long boat ride north of the Blue Hole and Turneffe. The more pristine reefs are far from the bubble-blowing hordes on Ambergris, for obvious reasons.

Caye Caulker is smaller (with only a few dive operators), more laid-back, cheaper and a little closer to the action. If you really want to get away from it all and dive dive dive, consider one of the dive lodges on the tiny islands. **St. George's Caye Resort** is even closer to the flagship sites, and there are a couple of lodges on the **Turneffe Islands** that are right on top of them.

There are a variety of resorts that cater almost exclusively to divers (the lodging and food side of the dive resorts is cov-

ered in *Best Sleeps & Eats*). Some resorts run their own in-house dive operations, while others have a quasi-independent dive shop on the premises. Any and all hotels in Belize will gladly arrange dive trips for you, or you can book dives directly with a dive shop. In either case, most operators will pick you up and drop you off at your hotel's dock. Most dive shops also arrange snorkeling and fishing trips.

Most shops offer a range of scuba instruction (almost all are PADI shops). A PADI Open Water Certification course will cost you $400-475. Some shops also offer Advanced, Divemaster, Rescue and Nitrox courses. If you aren't a certified diver, but you really want to blow some bubbles, you can take a resort course, which gives you some brief instruction and a supervised ocean dive, for about $175. Another option for earning your certification is a referral course (around $325), which means that you do your classroom and swimming pool instruction at home, and your certification dives in Belize.

All dive operators offer diving gear for rent, but serious divers will want to bring their own gear. Don't plan on buying dive equipment here, as selection is limited and prices are high.

Belize is often featured in the various dive magazines. Check out some of these sites:
• *www.scubaboard.com*
• *www.divernet.com*
• *www.skin-diver.com*
• *www.scubadivingbelize.com*

DIVE SITES

Hot dive sites are found from north to south, on the barrier reef or one of the three coral atolls. Belize's most popular spot for short snorkel and dive trips, visited by every dive shop on Ambergris and Caulker, is **Hol Chan Marine Reserve**, a few miles south of San Pedro. This section of the barrier reef includes the fish and coral-rich Hol Chan Channel and **Shark Ray Alley**, where you can swim with enormous nurse sharks and Southern stingrays in water only a few feet deep – it's a fine place for novice snorkelers, and an unforgettable wildlife encounter even for seasoned divers. *Info: www.holchanbelize.org.*

Lighthouse Reef Atoll is the location of the **Blue Hole**, Belize's Eiffel Tower (when you get back home, everyone will ask you if you saw it). Cavern formations open up into the sheer walls of this enormous round sinkhole, and you can swim through vast limestone cathedrals, accompanied by sleek sharks. It's a unique place, but some divers find it disappointing. It's a deep dive, so you only get to spend a few minutes admiring the sights, and there isn't a whole lot in the way of fish and other sea life. However, the atoll has no shortage of great dive sites. Out here in the open ocean the visibility is superb, and you may catch a glimpse of some large pelagic fish. At **Half Moon Wall**, you can see a wide variety of underwater habitats in a small area, at moderate depths (30-70 feet). Large sharks, eagle rays and manta rays are frequent visitors.

Turneffe Atoll, the largest of Belize's three coral atolls, is 25 miles east of Belize City. This huge ring of reefs is dotted with over 200 tiny mangrove islands. Here you'll find a variety of great sites suitable for all skill levels. The western edge of the atoll has lots of shallow reefs, perfect for beginning divers and snorkelers. Intermediate divers enjoy some of the finest wall dives in the Caribbean, as well as the wreck of the **Sayonara**. One of the most impressive advanced dive sites in the country is the **Elbow**, a wall that drops off into a deep channel where strong ocean currents sweep around the south end of the atoll. This is an excellent drift dive, and perhaps the best place to see really big fish such as lemon, blacktip and hammerhead sharks, manta and spotted eagle rays, green and hawksbill turtles, and bottlenose and spotted dolphin.

AMBERGRIS CAYE
DIVE SHOPS

Ambergris has a passel of dive operators, as well as the country's only decompression chamber. Several of the resorts have their own dive shops, and there are a dozen more on the beach in downtown San Pedro. Many of the hotels have arrangements with certain dive operators, but most dive outfits will pick you up from any hotel dock. All the shops offer equipment rental and PADI instruction, all make trips to Hol Chan, and most go to the Blue Hole, Turneffe and other favorite sites. A two-tank dive will cost you $70-80, a day trip to the Blue Hole around $250. There are only a couple of places on the island to buy dive and snorkel gear: **Island Divers** downtown, and **Captain Shark's** near the airstrip.

Ramon's Village Dive Shop

This upscale resort just south of San Pedro has a dive operation that's one of the largest and best in the country. They have six boats, including a splendid 42-footer for Blue Hole trips, and

Coral Reefs

Coral is a communal organism. The colorful formations you see are colonies of thousands of tiny animals, which filter food from the water. The calcium they secrete builds a coral reef over hundreds of years. The coral attracts tiny fish and crustaceans, which attract larger predators, and so up the scale. A living reef is an incredibly complex ecosystem, which provides habitat for many important fish species. Like rain forests, reefs worldwide are slowly disappearing. Pollution, sedimentation and overfishing chip away at the reefs as a worldwide catastrophe waits in the wings. Rising sea temperatures are killing reefs in many areas and, worse yet, scientists now fear that, as absorbed carbon dioxide changes the chemistry of sea water, corals' very ability to produce calcium could be impaired. Whatever the future holds, Belize's reefs are beautiful now, so get out and enjoy them!

offer a full array of instruction and rentals. *Info: www.ramons.com; Tel. 601/649-1990 or 800/MAGIC 15 US.*

Ecologic Divers

This well-regarded shop, located toward the north end of town, has nice new boats, nice new gear and some very experienced instructors. They offer trips to all the local hotspots, as well as catamaran charters. *Info: www.ecologicdivers.com; Tel. 226-4118.*

Amigos del Mar Dive Shop

This is the biggest dive outfit on the island, with eight or nine boats, including a wonderful 48-footer that they use for long trips to the Hole and Turneffe. On the way back home, they break out the beer and rum and everyone has a ball. Owner Changa is one of the top dive gurus in Belize. This excellent shop is especially good for novice divers. Their divemasters will get your gear set up and handle every detail for you. *Info: www.amigosdive.com; Tel. 226-2706.*

Patojo's Scuba Center

This respected shop is run by Elmer "Patojo" Paz, Changa's brother and a PADI Instructor with 17 years of experience. He and his wife also own the adjacent Tides, a nice midrange hotel with a pool and AC private-bath rooms for around $125 double. Patojo offers a full range of diving, snorkeling and fishing trips, instruction and rentals. *Info: www.ambergriscaye.com/tides; Tel. 226-2283.*

Ambergris Divers

Located on the beach near the Spindrift Hotel, this highly professional shop offers a wide variety of trips from their fleet of six boats, plus the usual menu of instruction and rentals. *Info: w ww.ambergrisdivers.com; Tel. 226-2634.*

Resorts that have in-house dive operations for their guests include **Victoria House** (*www.victoria-house.com*), **Portofino** (*www.portofinodiving.com*), **El Pescador** (*www.elpescador.com*) and the **SunBreeze** Hotel (*www.sunbreeze.net*).

AMBERGRIS CAYE SNORKELING

A snorkel trip will run you about $35 per person including mask, fins, and snorkel. Most snorkeling trips from San Pedro go to the Hol Chan Marine

Reserve, which costs you an additional $12.50 admission fee. You can arrange a snorkeling trip through your hotel or through any of the dive shops on the beach.

Unlike scuba diving, which requires certification, if you can swim, you can learn to snorkel in a few minutes. Much of the underwater beauty off San Pedro is in shallow water, so snorkeling may be just as spectacular as diving. You do need a boat, however – nowhere on Ambergris is the coral reef near enough to shore for you to swim out to it.

CAYE CAULKER DIVE SHOPS
Prices are a tiny bit lower here than on Ambergris. The Blue Hole is closer, so you should be able to do a 3-tank trip for under $200. A PADI certification course runs about $375.

Belize Diving Services
This shop, at the northwest corner of the village by the soccer field, has been in business since 1978. Their 46-foot boat accommodates 20 divers, and their 27-footer takes ten, with a maximum of four-five divers per divemaster. They offer trips to a wide variety of little-visited sites, and a full range of instruction, including over 24 different courses. *Info: www.belizedivingservices.net; Tel. 226-0143.*

Frenchie's Diving Services
This fine shop has been in business since 1981. Their four boats go to all the usual sites, and they offer a full roster of courses. *Info: www.frenchiesdivingbelize.com; Tel. 226-0234.*

Scuba Sensation
This outfit opened in 2004. Divemaster Bert Pacheco takes a maximum of six divers on trips to all the local glory holes. *Info: www.scubasensation.net; Tel. 226-0127 or 667-4700.*

Don't Touch the Coral

Never touch any coral, ever. In fact it's wise not to touch anything out on the reef. Bright orange fire coral can cause a nasty burn, and there are sharp sea urchins and other nasties awaiting unwary fingers. But the pain that fire coral might cause to your little pinky is nothing compared to what you'll do to the coral. Touching coral tends to kill the little organisms. It's even worse with gloves, which is why some dive shops discourage wearing them.

CAYE CAULKER SNORKELING & BOAT EXCURSIONS

Unlike in San Pedro, snorkeling trips are not generally booked through the dive shops, but rather through any of a dozen tour operators. A snorkel trip should cost you about $30 (or $50 for trips to the Hol Chan Reserve). Some of the best-known outfits are **Star Tours** (*www.startoursbelize.com; Tel. 226-0374*), **Carlos Tours** (*Tel. 226-0058*) and **Raggamuffin Tours** (*www.raggamuffintours.com; Tel. 226-0348*), which has a couple of charming old sailboats, and also offers sunset and overnight sailing trips. Any of the larger hotels will be happy to arrange any tour your heart desires.

Many Caulker boat trips make a stop to see the manatees on nearby Swallow Caye. Sadly, much-loved local guide Chocolate has retired, but any of the local operators can take you to visit the gentle sea cows.

CAYES DIVE RESORTS

Hard-core divers should consider staying at one of the dedicated dive lodges on one of the small cayes. You'll be close to the dive sites and among like-minded souls, but lodgings are usually short of luxury, and there are no "things to do" for non-diving companions (see *Best Sleeps* for more information on these lodges).

St. George's Caye Resort

Just a short boat ride from Belize City, St. George's Caye is close to dozens of barely-touched dive sites. The reef is only half a mile out, and Turneffe and the Blue Hole are both much closer from here than from Ambergris or Caulker. The 30 years of experience shows in the excellent dive operation, with first-rate facilities and personal service from some of the country's most experienced divemasters. *Info: www.gooddiving.com; Tel. 800/813-8498 US.*

Turneffe Flats

You can't get any closer to the fish than this. One of three lodges on the atoll, Turneffe Flats has pretty nice rooms with AC and private bath. Both diving and fishing guests give this place consistently good reviews. *Info: www.tflats.com; Tel. 888/512-8812 US.*

Turneffe Island Resort

Decent rooms with AC and private bath, and two or three great dives scheduled every day. *Info: www.turnefferesort.com; Tel. 713/236-7739 US.*

Blackbird Caye Resort
This Turneffe lodge offers oceanfront air-conditioned cabanas with private porches and hammocks, and dives on over 70 dive sites, most no more than 12 minutes from the dock. *Info: www.blackbirdresort.com; Tel. 866/909-7333 US.*

Belcove Island Lodge
This basic and cheap little lodge on Gallows Point Caye is run by the same folks as the budget Hotel Belcove in Belize city. Various diving and fishing packages are available. *Info: www.belcove.com; Tel. 227-3054.*

FISHING

The fishing in Belize is spectacular, but the charter fishing scene is surprisingly low-key, especially compared to the diving action. You won't see marinas full of sleek sport-fishing boats, as you do in Florida, Mexico or Costa Rica. Most fishing charters are run by freelance boat captains, and you can book a trip either through your hotel or through any of the dive operators. Fishing charters may cost up to double what dive trips cost, because they take fewer people and use more gas. Expect to pay in the neighborhood of $250 for a full-day trip to the flats or the reef, $400 or more for a deep-sea trolling trip.

Anglers come from all over the world to enjoy Belize's world-class **flats fishing**. With vast expanses of shallow flats in and around the cayes, Belize is one of the world's top saltwater fly-fishing destinations. You might even have a shot at a Grand Slam: a bonefish, tarpon and permit in a single day.

Cruising for Disaster

The vast majority of visitors to Belize are now **day-trippers from cruise ships**. Well over a million dropped in this year (three times the country's population). Some Belizeans want to reverse the engines, fearing that the remote cayes and jungle lodges are losing their natural, unspoiled flavor under the onslaught of so many mass-market travelers, who are very different from the backpackers, birders and divers that Belize is used to. Locals complain that too little of the passengers' money ends up in the pockets of ordinary Belizeans, and that too much of the ships' trash ends up on Belizean beaches. In 2011, the Placencia Tour Operators Association succeeded in halting the planned development of a second "cruise tourist village" there.

The biggest tarpon cruise through the area in spring and early summer. The Turneffe Islands are perhaps the top spot in Belize for flats fishing. All three of the lodges there cater to anglers as well as divers (see *Diving*, above). The rivers and estuaries harbor snook, tarpon and cubera snapper. On the reefs, grouper, snapper, jacks, barracuda and other reef species are plentiful. On the seaward side of the reef, ocean depths plummet steeply to thousands of feet, and anglers troll for kingfish, dolphin, wahoo, tuna sailfish and marlin. The best months for billfish are April and May.

El Pescador

This first-class lodge on Ambergris Caye caters to flats anglers, and has what is probably the largest fly fishing shop in Belize (see *Best Sleeps*). *Info: www.elpescador.com; Tel. 226-2398 or 800/242-2017 US.*

Turneffe Flats

The Turneffe Islands have vast expanses of flats, as well as easy access to the ocean depths. Of the three lodges on the atoll, this is the most fishing-oriented, but Turneffe Island Resort and Blackbird Caye also offer fishing trips (see *Cayes Dive Resorts*, above). *Info: www.tflats.com; Tel. 888/512-8812 US.*

KAYAKING & CANOEING

Sea kayaking is an especially nice way to explore the offshore atolls. Most beachfront resorts have kayaks available for rent or even free for guests. In the lagoons and flats, a kayak may be the very best way to navigate the winding mangrove waterways and silently sneak up on shy wildlife.

OTHER WATER SPORTS

The beach in San Pedro often resembles a busy train station more than a peaceful vacation spot, as people tear around on all manner of watercraft. **SailSports Belize**, located at the Caribbean Villas Hotel, rents all things with sails, from windsurfers to Hobie Cats to Lasers. *Info: www.sailsportsbelize.com; Tel. 226-4488.*

For kiteboarding, the latest extreme sport, check out **Kitexplorer**. With a board strapped to your feet and a huge kite up in the air, it's a bit like a cross between windsurfing and parasailing. *Info: www.kitexplorer.com; Tel. 635-4967.*

On Caulker, **Raggamuffin Tours** offers sunset and overnight sailing excursions. *Info: www.raggamuffintours.com.*

GOLF

Belize is not a major golf destination. The only world-class course in the country is (or was) the exclusive **Caye Chapel Island Resort**, which occupied an entire small island a short way offshore from Belize City. The resort recently closed, and one seems to know if and when it will reopen, or even whether the golf course is being maintained. There is an 18-hole course near Belmopan (see Chapter 6).

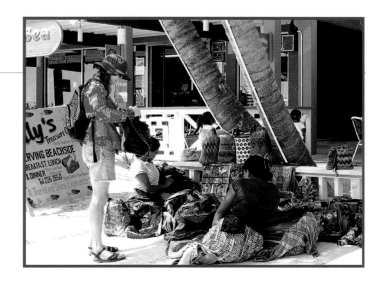

5. BELIZE CITY & NORTHERN BELIZE

HIGHLIGHTS

▲ **Lamanai** – One of the country's most interesting Mayan sites is deep in the jungle, a spectacular spot for birding. The river trip to get there is an adventure in itself.

▲ **The Belize Zoo** – See Belize's forest denizens in large natural-looking enclosures.

▲ **The Baboon Sanctuary** – Everyone loves the black howler monkeys.

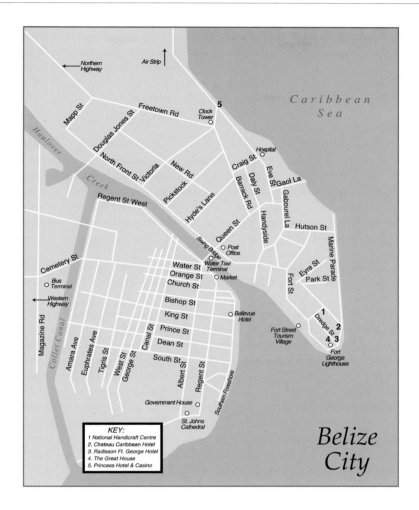

Belize City

Much of Northern Belize is uninhabited jungle and forest, with a few small settlements here and there. Large tracts of the wilderness are protected as nature reserves. Here you'll find two of Belize's most-visited Mayan sites: **Altun Ha** and **Lamanai**.

Belize City, the country's largest, is frankly a place that most tourists don't find very attractive. You'll fly into the International Airport just outside of town, but whether you want to use the city as a hub for visits to the islands and the jungle, or blow right by it, as many visitors do, is entirely up to you.

BELIZE CITY IN A DAY

Belize's largest city is no bustling metropolis, nor is it a quaint seaside village. Rather, it's a somewhat sleepy third-world town, drab and a little mildewy under the oppressive heat and humidity. But I happen to have a soft spot for such places, so let's have a look around!

Morning
We'll start our walking tour in the Fort George neighborhood, the locale of the two best hotels: the popular Radisson and the elegant Great House. Nearby is the **National Handicraft Center**, the best shopping experience in town. Belize has some wonderful artists, and you'll find some of their charming paintings here, as well as carvings in coral, slate and wood, bottled Belizean herbs and sauces, and of course postcards and t-shirts. *Info: 2 South Park Street. Tel. 223-3636.*

The **Museum of Belize**, housed in a former prison, has a splendid collection of Mayan artifacts, and is worth a short visit.

For a look at how the cruise tourists are spending their vacations, let's take a quick look at the **Fort Street Tourism Village**, a walled compound built around the dock where the tender boats from the cruise ships come in. This plastic paradise has several restaurants, bars and shops selling tourist supplies and expensive luxury goods (many of which have nothing to do with Belize). You may scoff at the square megaship passengers, most of them on their first venture out of the States, but I'm happy to see them getting a glimpse of another culture, even if it's a brief, prepackaged glimpse. And, whatever they think of the mass tourism that has recently descended on Belize, locals all concede that the Tourism Village has raised standards of cleanliness and safety in the neighborhood.

Next we'll walk up North Front Street, running the gauntlet of locals aggressively hawking their wood carvings, to the **Swing Bridge**. This bridge across the river serves as a local landmark, dividing the city in two. Crossing over to the south side, we'll pass the **City Market**, a multi-story building full of stalls selling fruits, vegetables and every little thing. Take a look around, but keep your hand your wallet! On the top floor of the market is **Big Daddy's**, where we can have a cheap and filling Belizean lunch with a view of the bay. Or we can cross back over to the north side of town and walk up Queen Street to **Nerie's**, which most folks agree has the best traditional Belizean food in town.

Afternoon

Belize City has its interesting aspects, but Paris it ain't. Our morning walk has already covered most of the tourist highlights, so this afternoon let's head a little way out of town and check out the **Belize Zoo**. We could take a guided tour of the zoo, but it isn't really necessary. Let's just grab one of the taxis that congregate around the Swing Bridge (budget travelers can even take the bus).

Watch Your Step!

Wherever you go in Belize City, or in any city in Belize, watch your step! Covered drains run along the edges of each street, and the covers are very often missing. If you gawk at the sights and don't watch where you put your feet, you risk plunging knee-deep into foul liquid, or worse. All manner of yucky stuff lurks everywhere, just waiting for an unwary tourist's shoe.

Just an hour's ride out of town on the Western Highway, this unique zoo has 125 species of native Belizean animals, all of them rescued as orphans or bred in captivity. They aren't kept in cages, but in large fenced enclosures that duplicate their natural habitats. You'll see jaguars, margays, ocelots, coatis, gibnuts, howler monkeys and tree-climbing foxes, as well as colorful birds such as toucans and scarlet macaws, and scaly reptiles such as crocodiles, iguanas and boa constrictors. The zoo is an absolute must if you're traveling with kids. The mosquitoes here are brutal, so wear long-sleeved clothing and bring your bug spray.

Just past the zoo on the highway heading west is **JB's Watering Hole**, a Belizean institution frequented by a colorful crew of locals, tourists and expats. Let's stop there for a cold beer and a snack before heading back into town. *Info: The Belize Zoo is at mile 29 on the Western Highway. www.belizezoo.org; Tel. 822-8000. Open 8:30am-4:30pm daily. Entry $15 adults; $5 kids.*

Evening

Most parts of town are dodgy to walk around after dark, so our best bet for dinner might be to stick around the relatively safe Fort George area. Fortunately, two of the most atmospheric restaurants in town are right here. The **Harbour View Restaurant**, next to the Tourism Village, has lovely vistas and vaguely Continental cuisine. The **Smoky Mermaid**, at the Great House, has grilled meats, seafood dishes and a special lobster menu with such oddities as lobster quesadillas and lobster burgers. The plant-filled courtyard is a peaceful place for a leisurely dinner.

A WEEKEND IN BELIZE CITY

This wild region has lots of interesting things to see. There's no way we can see it all, but a weekend gives us enough time for a taste of the city, the ruins and the jungle.

Friday

We'll fly into Belize City in the afternoon and take a taxi straight to our hotel. My favorite in town is the elegant **Great House** in the pleasant Fort George neighborhood. It's a comfortable place with character, and for a small extra fee you can use the pool and the other amenities at the **Fort George Radisson** across the street. If you have a lower budget, head for the clean and friendly **Hotel Mopan**, facing the water south of the Swing Bridge.

We need a little time to decompress from the US express lane and get used to the slow dirt road of the tropics, so take off your shirt and shoes, order a panty ripper (rum and pineapple juice) or a cold Belikin beer, and forget about any further activities for the moment.

When the sun starts getting low, we'll start thinking about a big plate of fish. There are several decent restaurant choices in the Fort George area. If the seafood buffet is on tonight, we might eat at the **Radisson Fort George's** third-floor dining room, or we might try their poolside **Stonegrill Restaurant**. Or, we might enjoy the fresh air and charming seascape at the **Harbour View Restaurant**, next to the Tourism Village. If we're in the mood for a peaceful tropical courtyard, we can go to the **Smoky Mermaid**, at the Great House.

Saturday Morning

If you're staying at one of the Fort George hotels, our walking tour starts right outside the door. If you're south of the Swing Bridge, then do this tour in reverse. A couple of blocks from the Radisson is the **National Handicraft Center**, the best shopping experience in town. Everything here is Belizean: charming paintings, coral, slate and wood carvings, baskets, jewelry, bottled Belizean herbs and sauces, Belizean music, postcards and t-shirts. It's a one-stop shopping center for Belizean souvenirs. *Info: 2 South Park Street. Tel. 223-3636.*

Next let's spend an hour or so gazing at the colorful postage stamps and Mayan artifacts at the **Museum of Belize**, which recently opened on the old site of the city's prison.

For a look at how those "other" tourists are spending their vacation, let's pay a quick visit to the **Fort Street Tourism Village**, a McDonaldsesque walled compound where the tender boats from the cruise ships dock. Within this artificial paradise are several restaurants and bars, a bandstand with live music, and lots of shops and stalls selling t-shirts, handicrafts (by no means all local), sunscreen and other tourist supplies. The only really interesting shop is an art gallery that has some nice local paintings on display.

The sophisticated travelers who read this book may be tempted to scoff at the portly cruise ship tourists, with their braided hair and fanny packs. However, the cruise lines provide a safe travel alternative to first-time travelers who might otherwise never encounter even this prepackaged glimpse of another culture. And few would dispute that the Tourism Village has raised standards of cleanliness and safety in the neighborhood.

Next let's have a look at the real Belize City. We'll walk up North Front Street, running the gauntlet of locals aggressively hawking their wood carvings, to local landmark the **Swing Bridge**. This bridge across the river divides the city in two. Crossing over to the south side, we'll pass the **City Market**, a multi-story building full of stalls selling fruits, vegetables and every little thing. On the top floor of the market is **Big Daddy's**, where we can have a cheap and filling Belizean lunch with a view of the bay. Or we can cross back over to the north side of town and walk up Queen Street to **Nerie's**, which most folks agree has the best traditional Belizean food in town.

Saturday Afternoon

Well folks, that's about it for tourist attractions right in the city. After lunch, let's head a little way out of town and check out the **Belize Zoo**. We could take a guided tour of the zoo, but it isn't really necessary. Let's just take a taxi out there (budget travelers can even take the bus). Taxis congregate around the Radisson hotel and the water taxi terminal just north of the Swing Bridge.

The zoo is very convenient from Belize City, just an hour's ride out of town on the Western Highway. It's an absolute must if you're traveling with kids. This unique little zoo has 125 species of native Belizean animals, all of whom were orphaned, injured, rescued from the illegal pet trade, bred in captivity, or donated by other zoos. They aren't kept in cages, but in large fenced enclosures full of trees and plants, as close as possible to their natural habitats. The Belize Zoo isn't just for tourists. Its most important mission is educating Belizeans about their native wildlife, and the importance of protecting it.

You'll see jaguars, margays, ocelots, coatis, gibnuts, howler monkeys, kinkajous, tapirs and the tree-climbing Belizean gray fox, as well as colorful birds such as toucans and scarlet macaws, and scaly reptiles such as crocodiles, iguanas and boa constrictors. Perhaps because of the undisturbed natural state of the vegetation, the mosquitoes here are brutal. Wear long-sleeved clothing and bring your bug spray.

Adjacent to the zoo is the **Tropical Education Centre**, 84 acres of pine savannah. You can take a hike along their nature trail and climb up on several platforms in the forest canopy to see a vast number of resident and migratory birds. There's a small gift shop and snack bar at the zoo.

Just past the zoo on the highway heading west are a couple of restaurants that tend to be mobbed with tour groups. A little farther, at mile 32, is **JB's Watering Hole**, a piece of Belizean history where you can find excellent Belizean food and great conversation with a colorful crew of locals, tourists and expats. *Info: The Belize Zoo is at mile 29 on the Western Highway.*

www.belizezoo.org; Tel. 822-8000. Open 8:30am-4:30pm daily. Entry $15 adults; $5 kids.

Saturday Evening

One of the nicer restaurants in town is **Bird's Isle**, a waterfront restaurant on a little island at the end of Albert Street. The open-air deck is breezy and cool, and the ocean view is guaranteed to keep us in the mellow Belizean frame of mind. It's a ways off the beaten tourist path, so we'll call a taxi to take us back to our hotel.

Take a Taxi

At the risk of being redundant, I have to tell you that it is not safe to wander around Belize City at night (and some areas are dodgy even during the day). After dark, a taxi is the only safe way to travel. Fortunately, taxis are cheap, and they're easy to spot with their green license plates.

Sunday

Even if you're leaving Sunday evening, there's plenty of time for a trip to the **Community Baboon Sanctuary**, an hour's drive west of Belize City, near the village of Burrell Boom. No, these aren't what the rest of the world calls baboons. *Baboon* is the Belizean name for the black howler monkey, a vegetarian monkey that's actually a lot cuter than the fierce and ill-mannered baboons of Africa. This community-based ecotourism project provides protected habitat for over 2,000 howlers.

The endangered black howlers live in troops of 4-12 individuals, and spend most of their time in the trees eating fruits and leaves. Their distinctive call, which sounds more like a big dog barking than like howling, can be heard through the forest for a mile or more. The sanctuary is also home to many other animals, including wild cats and over 200 bird species. We'll take an hour-long tour with a local guide, who can tell us all sorts of fascinating things about the Belizean rain forest. *Info: Entry and tour $7 per person. www.howlermonkeys.org; Tel. 660-3545.*

If we have time, we can visit a couple of other popular attractions nearby: the Mayan ruins of **Altun Ha**, and the

Maruba Resort Jungle Spa, which welcomes visitors for lunch, a swim and a quick spa treatment. Personally, I'm a little wary of both these places because they are sometimes mobbed with day-trippers from the cruise ships (although, as of this writing, few ships are calling in Belize on Sundays). You may want to call Maruba beforehand (see *Best Sleeps*), or check www.cruisecal.com to see if any of the fanny-pack crowd are expected today.

A WEEKEND IN THE JUNGLE

Staying in Belize City and driving around on day trips may be too hectic if you only have a weekend. This trip is more relaxed, a getaway to the jungle. Yyou'll have plenty to do – in fact, the most common complaint heard in Belize is that people wish they could stay longer!

Friday
There are several isolated jungle lodges tucked away in the barely inhabited forests of northern Belize. These resorts are a long ride from civilization, so you don't come for the nightlife or the shopping, but rather to immerse yourself in the natural world for a weekend of hiking, horseback riding, canoeing, birding or relaxing with umbrella drinks.

The **Lamanai Outpost Lodge** offers a chance to enjoy the Mayan ruins, the jungle and the bird-filled **New River Lagoon**. There are several nice trips you can take right from the lodge, with no need to drive anywhere, so it's a perfect place for a short visit (or a long one). The accommodations and service are first-class (see *Best Sleeps*).

Someone from the lodge will meet us at the airport in Belize City and drive us to the little village of Tower Hill, where we'll board a boat for a beautiful ride up the river to the lodge. The whole trip takes about 2.5 hours from the airport. Get your camera out, because we'll be seeing crocodiles, turtles, herons, cormorants and all sorts of water birds as we motor along through the steaming jungle.

The cares and problems of the modern world fade farther away with every mile we travel into the jungle. Traffic jams? Deadlines? What are they? We'll be met at the lodge with a nice cold drink. Take your shoes off. Shirt too. Order another drink, plop down in a hammock and enjoy doing nothing for a while. There'll be plenty of time at dinner to plan our activities for tomorrow.

Chan Chich would be another excellent choice for a weekend jungle getaway. It's also located at a Mayan site on a nice little river in the middle of the jungle. Like Lamanai, it's a first-class lodge that consistently gets great reviews. Birding, hiking, horseback riding and canoeing are on the menu. Travelers with lower budgets may enjoy the **Bird's Eye View Lodge**, on the water adjacent to the Crooked Tree Wildlife Sanctuary with its 250 bird species.

Saturday Morning

One wonderful thing about staying right here at the **Lamanai Ruins** is that we can dodge the cruise ship day-trippers. The t-shirted ones show up at the north end of the ruins, whereas the Outpost is located to the south. We'll get to the site first thing in the morning, and have a couple of hours alone with the howler monkeys and the spirits of the ancient Mayans. By the time the cattle arrive, we'll be thinking about heading back to the lodge for lunch.

For centuries, Lamanai was a wealthy trading center with a population of over 35,000. It had a longer history than most other Mayan cities, and was still inhabited when the Spaniards arrived. The ruins of a Spanish church bear witness to their vain attempts to convert the natives to Catholicism.

The name Lamanai means "Crocodile," obviously a reference to the many crocs in the surrounding waterways, and the many representations of crocodiles at the site. Only about five percent of the 700 structures have been excavated. Some notable ones are the **Mask Temple** with its 13-foot stone carvings of Mayan gods, and the **High Temple**, one of the largest structures in the Mayan world. We can climb to the top for a spectacular view of the forest and lagoon. Finally we'll stop at the museum for a look at some fascinating carvings and other artifacts that have been found at the site.

Saturday Afternoon

Yet another wonderful thing about Lamanai Outpost (there are many) is that there are so many activities right here on-site. Because we don't have to get in a van and ride anywhere, we can get in two nice tours per day, with plenty of time for lying around with umbrella drinks. After lunch, we can hike some of the trails around the lodge. A guide can point out some of the local plants that the ancient Maya used for medicines, some of the resident howler monkeys, or perhaps a few of the over 400 bird species that live in the area. A dozen different herons and egrets, a dozen types of hawks, parrots, hummingbirds, trogons, toucans, motmots…and literally hundreds of **LBBs** (a technical birder term meaning **Little Brown Birds**).

Saturday Evening
After dinner, let's take a cruise around the lagoon on a pontoon boat. With a cooler full of drinks and our own personal bartender on board, we'll watch the sunset and spot even more animals and birds. Later on we can venture out at night with spotlights in search of some of the nocturnal residents. This is our best chance to spot an elusive ocelot or jaguar, to say nothing of owls and nightjars.

Sunday
Every nature lover knows that early morning is the best time to spot animals and birds. Once again, because we're right here on the spot, we can easily be in the woods or on the water in time for the dawn flighting. We can take a hike with one of the resort's resident guides, or paddle around the lagoon in a canoe in search of manatees, otters and crocs.

A WEEK IN NORTHERN BELIZE

In a week you can see the colorful chaos of Belize City, several majestic **Mayan sites**, vast areas of **undisturbed wilderness**, and the pastoral lands of the **Mennonites**.

There's no need to stay in Belize City. Head from the airport directly to one of the jungle lodges in the area. My favorites are **Chan Chich** and **Lamanai Outpost** (see *Best Sleeps*). Both are pretty remote, but both have plenty of activities to keep you busy for a week. Observe birds and animals on jungle hikes, horseback rides and river cruises, take your time visiting the Mayan

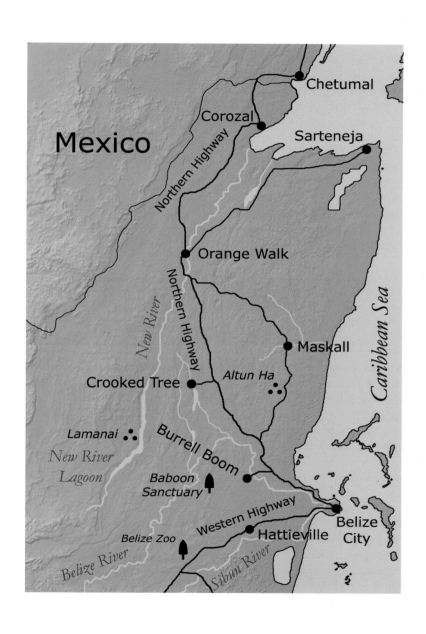

ruins, and spend a couple of days relaxing by the pool. It's no problem to visit the **Belize Zoo** and/or the **Baboon Sanctuary** on the way in or out.

Belize City

Belize City was founded in the 17th century by the **Baymen**, British buccaneers-turned-loggers who used the river to bring lumber from the forests to the coast. The town is said to have been built on wood chips and rum bottles. For much of its history it was a rough-and-tumble boom-and-bust frontier town.

Today Belize City is the country's largest, though that isn't saying much (population is about 70,000). The capital was moved to Belmopan in 1970, but Belize City remains the center of business and finance, and a place where people come from more remote regions to stock up on supplies. One thing it isn't is a major center of tourism, although you can certainly take diving trips and all sorts of other tours from here.

The city is divided in half by **Haulover Creek**, where herds of beef cattle were once "hauled over" by means of a rope. Today it's easier to cross – just walk over the **Swing Bridge**, a swinging drawbridge that opens twice a day to let boats pass.

North of the Swing Bridge is the **Fort George neighborhood**, the nicest (or at least the safest) part of town, the locale of the popular Radisson and the elegant Great House. A couple of blocks from these hotels is the **National Handicraft Center**, the best shopping experience in town. Everything here is Belizean: charming paintings, coral, slate and wood carvings, baskets, jewelry, bottled Belizean herbs and sauces, Belizean music, postcards and t-shirts. It's a one-stop shopping center for Belizean souvenirs. Among the benefits: it's air-conditioned, they take credit cards, and you can buy coral items without worrying about whether they're legal. *Info: 2 South Park Street. Tel. 223-3636.*

The recently opened **Museum of Belize** is housed in a former prison. Exhibits cover the history of the city and the prison, life in colonial times, the country's various ethnic groups, and its colorful postage stamps. The highlight is the large collection of Mayan artifacts. At $5 entry, it's well worth a short visit.

For a fascinating sociological study, and a look at how those "other" tourists are spending their vacation, pay a quick visit to the **Fort Street Tourism Village**, a McDonaldsesque walled compound where the tender boats from the cruise ships dock. Within this artificial island paradise are several restaurants and bars, an internet café, a bandstand with live music, and lots of shops and stalls selling t-shirts, handicrafts (by no means all local), sunscreen and other tourist supplies. The busiest shop of all is the one selling expensive diamond jewelry (no, diamonds have nothing to do with Belize). There's also a nice **art gallery** here, where you can see some of the charming paintings done by some of Belize's many excellent artists.

The Tourism Village has the feel of a gated community. Cruise passengers exit the compound through a couple of exits, each with a posted guard, and must show ID cards from their ships to re-enter. Passengers are funneled into vans that take them on day tours all over the country. Non-passengers may enter after obtaining a visitor's pass from the guard station.

The sophisticated travelers who read this book may be tempted to scoff at the portly cruise-ship tourists, with their braided hair and fanny packs. However, the cruise lines provide a safe travel alternative to first-time travelers who might otherwise never encounter even this prepackaged glimpse of another culture. And few would dispute that the Tourism Village has raised standards of cleanliness and safety in the neighborhood.

Fearing (perhaps correctly) that they would be ripped off six ways from Sunday, were they to wander alone through the streets of Belize City, many cruisers won't bother to leave the safe and sanitary confines of the Fort Street Tourism Village. And that's just fine with the cruise lines, who are skillful at ensuring that most of their passengers' money stays on their ships, or at least in the hands of their chosen local partners. Outside the Wall, taxi drivers, tour operators and touts gather to offer their services to those who venture outside (and sometimes offer lower prices than the cruise line-approved vendors within).

North Front Street, lined with vendors aggressively hawking wood carvings (and other less respectable products) runs from the Fort George area to the Swing Bridge. Stop in at the **Image Factory**, a local art cooperative that has rotating exhibitions of Belizean visual art, as well as a shop selling fine crafts and books. *Info: Open Mon-Fri 9am-5pm; www.imagefactorybelize.com.*

At the next corner is the **Caye Caulker Water Taxi Association**, where you can catch a boat to Ambergris Caye or Caye Caulker. Boats depart every hour or two, starting around 8am (see *Practical Matters*).

Now we're into the real Belize City, where the locals shop. Turn right (north) to head up **Queen Street**, lined with stores and cheap eateries. Turn left and cross the Swing Bridge to get to the **City Market**, a multi-story building full of stalls selling fruits, vegetables and every little thing (it's a great place to see a little local color, but keep an eye out for pickpockets). Heading south from here is **Albert Street**, another shopping street. Here are several record stores where you can buy CDs and tapes of Belizean musicians.

The Belize Zoo

This unique little zoo has 125 species of native Belizean animals. All the animals here were orphaned, injured, rescued from the illegal pet trade, bred in captivity, or donated by other zoos. They aren't kept in cages, but in large fenced enclosures full of trees and plants, as close as possible to their natural habitats. Founded in 1983, the Belize Zoo is not just for tourists. Its most important mission is educating Belizeans about their native wildlife, and the importance of protecting it.

You'll see jaguars, margays, ocelots, coatis, gibnuts, howler monkeys, kinkajous and tapirs, colorful birds such as toucans and scarlet macaws, and scaly reptiles such as crocodiles, iguanas and boa constrictors. My favorite critter is the Belizean gray fox, a cute little fox that actually climbs trees.

The zoo is very convenient from Belize City, just an hour's ride out of town on the Western Highway. It's an absolute must if you're traveling with kids.

Perhaps because of the undisturbed natural state of the vegetation, the mosquitoes here are brutal. Wear long-sleeved clothing and bring your bug spray.

Adjacent to the zoo is the **Tropical Education Centre**, 84 acres of pine savannah. You can take a hike along their nature trail and climb up on several platforms in the forest canopy to see a vast number of resident and migratory birds. They also offer (by advance reservation) half-day guided canoe trips down the Sibun River, and behind-the-scenes tours of the zoo, including a nocturnal tour.

There's a small gift shop and snack bar at the zoo, as well as a few cabins for those who'd like to spend the night. *Info: The Belize Zoo is at mile 29 on the Western Highway. www.belizezoo.org; Tel. 822-8000. Open 8:30am-4:30pm daily. Entry $15 adults; $5 kids.*

Just past the zoo on the highway heading west are a couple of restaurants, beloved of tour groups. A little farther, at mile 32, is **JB's Watering Hole**, a piece of Belizean history where you can find excellent Belizean food and great conversation with a colorful crew of locals, tourists and expats.

The Community Baboon Sanctuary

Baboon is the local name for the **black howler monkey**. The Baboon Sanctuary is a perfect example of the type of community-based ecotourism project that offers the best hope of saving Central America's rain forests and their inhabitants. 200 private landowners have voluntarily agreed to conserve their land to protect the habitat of the endangered monkeys. Since the sanctuary was founded in 1985, the population has grown to over 2,000 monkeys.

There are six species of howler monkey in Central and South America. The endangered black howler lives only in Belize, Mexico and Guatemala, and is one of two monkeys found in Belize (the other is the spider monkey). These vegetarian monkeys live in troops of 4-12 individuals, and spend most of their time in the trees eating fruits and leaves. Their distinctive call, which sounds more like a big dog barking than like howling, can be heard through the forest for a mile or more. The sanctuary is also home to many other animals, including wild cats and over 200 bird species.

There's a small museum and visitors' center at the site, as well as a traditional restaurant. Entrance, including a guided tour, is $7 per person. Various other tours are available, including nighttime walks through the sanctuary and canoe trips on the river. There is some basic lodging available at the site, as well as bed and breakfast options in nearby villages. *Info: An hour's drive west of Belize City, near the village of Burrell Boom. www.howlermonkeys.org; Tel. 660-3545.*

Lamanai Ruins

One of the largest Mayan sites in Belize, the ruins of **Lamanai** include over 700 structures, only about five percent of which have been excavated. Located 35 miles from the town of Orange Walk, it has a spectacular setting, on the banks of the vast New River Lagoon, with trackless jungle for miles around. The name Lamanai means "Crocodile," obviously a reference to the many crocs in the surrounding waterways. You'll see many representations of crocodiles here.

Lamanai was inhabited much longer than most other Maya sites, from 1500 BC until around 1650 AD. In its prime it was a wealthy trading center with a population of over 35,000. Lamanai survived the end of the Maya's Classic Period in the ninth and tenth centuries, when many other Mayan city-states collapsed. When the Spaniards arrived in the sixteenth century, they worked hard to convert the natives to Catholicism, but were never able to completely suppress the Mayan traditions. You can see the ruins of a Spanish church, which the locals burned in 1640.

Highlights of Lamanai include the **Mask Temple**, faced with 13-foot-high stone carvings of Mayan gods; and the **High Temple**, which is one of the largest structures in the Mayan world, over 100 feet high. The view of the forest and lagoon from the top is magnificent. At the **Ball Court**, the

Mayans played a game that involved putting a hard rubber ball through a small hoop. They took the game as seriously as today's Belizeans do their soccer – the losers were sacrificed to the gods! There's a small museum that houses an impressive collection of carvings and other artifacts found at the site, with a basic visitors' center.

Lamanai is also a wildlife reserve, and the area is teeming with birds and other wildlife. You're likely to see some of the resident howler monkeys as you tour the site. Labels identify the various types of trees, many of which were (and are) used by the Maya for food and medicine.

Cruising Buddies

Tour groups from the cruise ships are venturing ever farther into the interior of Belize on day trips. For better or for worse, every place in this chapter is within easy reach of the ice-cream-cone-and-water-bottle posse. You'll encounter the thundering herds not only at the wildlife attractions and the Mayan ruins, but also at jungle lodges such as Maruba. To avoid them, make your visits early in the morning or late in the afternoon. A handy web site is www.cruisecal.com, which has complete schedules for all the major cruise lines. Check it to see when the ships are in Belize, and plan accordingly.

Although it's possible to get to Lamanai by road, it's easier and much more fun to take the 26-mile boat ride up the **New River** from Orange Walk Town. Along the way, you'll see crocodiles, turtles, and maybe even the Jesus Christ lizard, named for its ability to walk on water. Colorful orchids and bromeliads as well as an unbelievable variety of birds round out the show. If you have time, be sure to take a boat ride around the lagoon, where you'll see even more water birds and other wildlife.

Lamanai is remote, so just about the only way to visit is on a guided tour, and that's fine – you'll learn much more about the ruins, and see more wildlife, than you would on your own. The oldest and best-known operator is **Jungle River Tours** (Tel. 302-2293 or 615-1712). If you really want to experience Lamanai, I highly recommend spending the night at the **Lamanai Outpost Lodge** (see *Best Sleeps*). *Info: The park is open daily 8am-5pm.*

Mennonite Country

Mennonites are members of an Anabaptist sect that originated in Europe in the 16th century. They believe in pacifism and a strict separation of church and state. Their resistance to serving in the military and paying taxes tends to set them at odds with worldly governments, so over the years, many have wandered the world looking for a paradise where they can live as they please. Belize's Mennonites began to arrive in 1958, and today they are very successful farmers, producing much of the country's dairy products, as well as sturdy wooden furniture.

Most of the Mennonites live around Orange Walk in Northern Belize, and around Spanish Lookout in the Cayo district. Their country looks rather incongruous, with green pastures and farmhouses that wouldn't look out of place in Pennsylvania.

Traditional Mennonite sects speak a dialect of German, and shun modern technology, getting around in horse-drawn buggies. More progressive types speak English and prefer pickup trucks. You'll see them in town, the men in overalls and cowboy hats, the women in sober long skirts. Some Mennonites are friendly and happy to talk, but others want no contact with our sinful society, so please respect them and don't treat them like a tourist attraction. If you'd like to visit the Mennonite country, try **Hillside Bed & Breakfast** in Blue Creek Village (between Orange Walk and Lamanai), which is run by a local Mennonite family and has basic rooms for $31-60. *Info:* Tel. 323-0155.

Altun Ha

Altun Ha is the best-known Mayan site in Belize – you'll see its **Sun God Temple** every time you hoist a bottle of beer – but it is neither the largest

nor the most interesting. Its easy accessibility from Belize City is its blessing and its curse. Most days of the week it's mobbed with day-trippers from cruise ships. Nearby Lamanai is more interesting, and it has the bonus of the wonderful river trip to get there.

The name Altun Ha means "Rockstone Pond" in the Mayan language, and refers to a rock-lined reservoir that the ancient Mayans built, an impressive feat of engineering for those times. Altun Ha's heyday was during the Mayan Classic era, from around 200 to 900 AD, when the city had a population of about 10,000.

Other Mayan Sites

If you're a true Maya buff, you may want to visit some of the other Mayan sites in the region. **Nohmul**, a large but mostly unexcavated site out in the middle of the sugar cane fields a few miles north of Orange Walk town, has one of the highest pyramids around. **Cuello**, also near Orange Walk on the site of a rum distillery, is one of the oldest Mayan sites, and has a large plaza with three temples. Near Corozal are the sites of **Santa Rita** and **Cerros**. For more information about the ancient Mayans and their works, see Chapter 6.

Crooked Tree Wildlife Sanctuary

About 30 miles northwest of Belize City is an area of intersecting rivers, lagoons and swamps. 3,000 acres of it is a protected sanctuary run by the Belize Audubon Society. This is one of the finest bird-watching areas in Belize, home to vast flocks of water birds and a favorite stopover for migrating birds on their way up north.

Residents include many species of herons, egrets and kingfishers, both of Belize's native duck species, ospreys, hawks, and the star of the show: the **jabiru stork**, the largest flying bird in the Western Hemisphere. These majestic birds, which have a wingspan of up to 12 feet, assemble here in vast numbers during April and May, then again in November. The waterways are also home to scads of crocodiles and turtles, and black howler monkeys hang around in the trees. *Info: www.belizeaudubon.org. Open daily 8am-4:30pm; admission $8.*

The peaceful and charming little village of **Crooked Tree** is on an island surrounded by rivers and lagoons. Until recently, when a causeway was built from the Northern Highway, the village was accessible only by boat. The villagers welcome tourists, especially during the yearly **Cashew Festival**. There are several rustic B&B-style lodgings as well as several forest lodges, of which perhaps the nicest is **Bird's Eye View Lodge** (see *Best Sleeps*).

BEST SLEEPS & EATS

BEST SLEEPS IN BELIZE CITY

Belize City is not that bad a place, but from a tourist's standpoint it can't compare to the jungle or the islands. Plus, the selection of sleeps is poor. The few first-class hotels tend to be second-class, and although there are plenty of lower-priced lodgings, most are in dodgy neighborhoods. Fortunately, frequent air connections mean you need never spend the night in the city. If you do, here are the best options.

Note: as we have for several editions now, we are not recommending you stay at the **Princess Hotel & Casino**. Guests have been complaining of plumbing and AC problems, poor food, clueless staff and sanitary issues. It's a shame, because the hotel has a good view and wonderful facilities.

Radisson Fort George Hotel & Marina $$$$

This historic landmark is the closest thing Belize City has to a first-class American- or European-style hotel, the place for business travelers and tourists who want a safe and clean haven from the city. It's probably the nicest upscale place in town, but that isn't saying much. Everyone enjoys

the facilities – two restaurants, a bar, two pools, a fitness center, a full-service marina, tour and car rental desks, business center and 24-hour security. However, some areas are a bit dingy, and due for renovation. On my last visit, I found the rooms and most of the facilities to be clean enough, but there was a little mildew here, a little chipped paint there – the kind of thing that's hard to avoid in a tropical climate.

The rooms have all the goodies – AC, TV, phones, minibars, coffee makers and nice local paintings on the walls. The best (and most expensive) are the spacious Club Tower rooms, with marble floors and great views of the bay. The St. George's Dining Room is famous for their buffets, but the food here is good, not great. As at many Belize hotels, extra charges add up quickly. Internet access costs $10 per day. The convenient airport shuttle van is $10 per person. The tour desk is handy, but they tack on hefty fees for tours that you could easily book yourself. *Info: 2 Marine Parade. www.radissonbelize.com; Tel. 223-3333 or 888/201-1718 US.*

The Great House $$$$
This is a good place to stay in Belize City, a beautiful old mansion (built in 1927) with colonial-style charm. While it lacks the long list of amenities you'll find at the Radisson (across the street), the

Great House does have most of the modern conveniences, including wireless internet. There are only twelve rooms, each with private bath, AC, ceiling fans, TV, phones, hair dryers, refrigerators, coffee makers and safety deposit boxes. Tile floors and rattan furniture lend a light and airy feel, as sea breezes blow through the wide verandahs. The Smoky Mermaid restaurant is a charming tropical patio with good grilled meats and seafood. *Info: 13 Cork St. www.greathousebelize.com; Tel. 223-3400.*

Villa Boscardi $$$
This may be the best of the mid-price options, a little B&B in a quiet residential area, a block from the water. The six rooms have AC, TV, phone, ceiling fans, hair dryers and desks. *Info: 6043 Manatee Drive, Buttonwood Bay. www.villaboscardi.com; Tel. 223-1691.*

Hotel Mopan $$$
This venerable favorite is a classic old colonial house facing the water a few blocks south of the Swing Bridge. Though the neighborhood is dodgy at night, the hotel is clean and welcoming. The rooms are nothing fancy, but they have nice private bathrooms and TVs. It's worth the extra $10 for the Balcony Rooms, the only ones with really nice views. The owners are pillars of the local scene – stop in at the bar for the latest inside info. *Info: 55 Regent St. www.hotelmopan.com; Tel. 227-7351.*

Belcove Hotel $$
This is an okay hotel in a convenient but seedy location, on the river just around the corner from the Swing Bridge. The plain rooms have private bath and AC. It's run by the same people as the more relaxing Belcove Island Lodge on Gallows Point Caye. *Info: 9 Regent Street West. www.belcove.com; Tel. 227-3054.*

Most low-budget lodgings in Belize City are in neighborhoods that are dangerous after dark. Many have no AC and little ventilation, and some have serious cleanliness and security issues. If you must stay overnight in the city, I highly recommend upping your budget for a night and staying at the Mopan or the Belcove.

The only one of the cheapies that gets pretty good reviews is Smokin Balam, a funky but friendly riverfront hotel and drinking spot where Anna and her family run a tight ship (*59 N Front Street. Tel. 223-3969 or 610-4510*).

BEST SLEEPS OUTSIDE BELIZE CITY
Black Orchid Resort $$$
This fine hotel has 12 spacious rooms with AC and nice tile floors, as well as a pool, restaurant and gift shop. It's situated in a pleasant spot on the river near the village of Burrel Boom, 20 minutes from the airport. You can take a cruise on the river in a canoe, kayak or power boat. They also offer a full range of tours all over the country. If you want a comfortable lodging place not too far from Belize City, in a good spot to serve as a base for exploring the interior, this could be a good choice. *Info: www.blackorchidresort.com; Tel. 225-9158.*

Best Western Belize Biltmore Plaza $$$
This resort-style hotel is located just out of town, on the way to the airport, quite convenient if you're traveling by car. The pool and peaceful garden courtyard are a pleasant oasis, and the list of facilities is first-class: 24-hour security, free parking, laundry service, restaurant, two bars, room service, gift shop, tour desk, business center and small gym. The 75 air-conditioned rooms are well appointed, with phones, TVs, coffee makers, hair dryers and safe deposit boxes. *Info: www.belizebiltmore.com; Tel. 223-2302.*

Belize River Lodge $$$
This fishing lodge is located down a side road and across the river from the airport. The setting is remote and tropical, even though you're near Belize's metropolis. Most guests are here on weeklong fishing packages. *Info: www.belizeriverlodge.com; Tel. 888/275-4843 US.*

BEST EATS IN BELIZE CITY
Belize City is not famous for fine dining. There are several popular restaurants that have beautiful views, nice atmosphere and bountiful

seafood, but most of them suffer from inconsistent quality and service. "Touristy and overpriced" is a description that's often applied to both the hotel restaurants and stand-alone establishments.

The restaurant at the **Fort George Hotel** is pretty good, and their weekly seafood buffet is a feast. Next door at the Great House, the **Smoky Mermaid** has grilled meats, the usual seafood dishes and a special lobster menu. The pleasant plant-filled courtyard is a peaceful place for a cold beer, an umbrella drink or even a bottle from its decent wine list. **Harbour View** lives up to its name and has vaguely Continental cuisine.

Bird's Isle

This place is a little hard to find (unless you simply take a taxi), but it has a beautiful location, on a little island at the end of Albert Street. It's well out of the main tourist area, one of the reasons that it's frequented by locals. The open-air deck is a peaceful and cool place for a meal, and the menu includes all the seafood and Belizean specialties you could wish for. *Info: Tel. 207-2179.*

Sumathi

This Indian restaurant is a favorite of locals. It's also one of the few places with much to tempt the visiting vegetarian. *Info: Tel. 223-1172.*

Riverside Tavern

The cuisine here tends more toward American bar favorites than traditional Belizean, but the food is pretty good and the atmosphere is pleasant. *Info: Tel. 223-5640.*

There are plenty of places for cheap local chow, though many are open only during the day. **Three Amigos** (*2B King St*) offers good Mexican and Belizean dishes. **Nerie's**, on Queen Street, is one of the best bets for Belizean cooking. Another popular local spot is **Big Daddy's**, on the top floor of the City Market.

For light fare, try the **Maya Café** (*160 N Front St*), which serves fresh fruit juices, good coffee and teas. **Super Subs Deli**, inside Brodie's Supermarket on Albert Street, is a good bet for a cheap lunch to go.

BEST SLEEPS IN NORTHERN BELIZE

Hiking, birding and river trips to the Lamanai ruins are the attractions in this region. All these lodges are fairly remote, with no other dining options or "things to do" nearby, so a package that includes meals and possibly some local tours will be your best bet.

Chan Chich Lodge $$$$$

This luxury ecolodge is located on Gallon Jug Estate in the northwestern corner of the country, in the middle of a vast forest area teeming with and

wildlife. The grounds are in the middle of an unexcavated Mayan site, a peaceful and lovely setting for 12 cabanas and a two-bedroom villa. From outside the cabanas look rustic – thatched roofs, louvered walls to let in the breeze, and porches with inviting hammocks. Once inside, however, you'll appreciate the tile floors, big comfortable beds, armchairs, plenty of closet space and huge bathrooms. High ceilings and fans keep things cool. There are several miles of marked hiking trails that are fantastic for spotting wildlife. Over 350 species of birds have been spotted, and wild cat sightings are not rare. Horseback riding, canoeing, and day trips to Lamanai are a few other possible activities. The pool and hot tub are really special, and the food is excellent. Gallon Jug has an airstrip about 15 minutes from the lodge, so you can get here via a 30-minute charter flight from Belize City. *Info: www.chanchich.com; Tel. 223-4419.*

Maruba Resort Jungle Spa $$$$$

Some people find their dream vacation here, others just don't get it – but all agree that Maruba is unique. This all-inclusive resort and spa has mineral baths, two wonderful pools amid tropical greenery, and a full range of massages, multicolored mud baths and other New Age wellness treatments. There's even a Mayan seer on hand for psychic readings. Accommodations are luxurious, especially the suites. Honeymoon packages are a specialty. The location is convenient to many attractions in the region, and a range of tours is on offer. Some people absolutely love the atmosphere, others find it Disneyesque (fittingly, day tour groups from cruise ships often visit). The site is lushly landscaped, not virgin jungle, the exotic "tribal chic" décor – thatched ceilings, wild mosaics on floors and walls – is either really cool or really tacky, and the trance music that plays all over the resort is not for everyone. Don't go near Pancho the monkey! *Info: www.maruba-spa.com; Tel. 225-5555 or 800/MARUBA-7 US.*

Lamanai Outpost Lodge $$$$
Just a few minutes from the Lamanai Mayan site, the unpretentious and laid-back Lamanai Outpost gets a steady stream of rave reviews. There's a huge range of activities – visit the nearby ruins, tour the surrounding waterways by canoe or airboat, go fishing with the local fishermen,

or go out tagging crocodiles with resident biologists. See how many of the 400 local bird species you can check off your list. The waterfront grounds are lovely and peaceful, and the 20 cabanas are attractive and well appointed. Most don't have AC, but you probably won't miss it. The all-inclusive packages are the way to go. *Info: www.lamanai.com; Tel. 220-9444 or 888/733-7864 US.*

Bird's Eye View Lodge $$$
Birders love this place – it's directly on the water, and you can tour the adjacent Crooked Tree Wildlife Sanctuary (with its 250 bird species) by foot, horseback or canoe. You may even spot a wood stork or a kiskadee from your balcony. The lodge itself is not quite luxurious, but the 20 rooms were renovated in 2007, and all have private bath, AC, ceiling fans and nice tight screens. *Info: www.birdseyeviewbelize.com; Tel. 203-2040 or 225-7027.*

BEST SHOPPING
The Fort George neighborhood has several shops selling crafts and other gift items. The best of these is the **National Handicraft Center**, which has much more than just handicrafts, all of it Belizean: charming paintings, coral, slate and wood carvings, baskets, jewelry, bottled herbs and sauces, Belizean music, postcards and t-shirts. It's a one-stop shopping center for Belizean souvenirs. Among the benefits: it's air-conditioned, they take credit cards, and you can buy coral items without worrying about whether they're legal. *Info: 2 South Park Street. Tel. 223-3636.*

The many shops at the **Fort Street Tourism Village** mostly sell overpriced crapola that has nothing to do with Belize, but there is a nice little art gallery there. **North Front Street** is lined with vendors aggressively hawking wood carvings (and other less respectable products). Be sure to stop in at the **Image Factory**, a local art cooperative that has rotating exhibitions of Belizean visual art, as well as a shop selling fine crafts and books. *Info: Open Mon-Fri 9am-5pm; www.imagefactorybelize.com.*

BEST NIGHTLIFE & ENTERTAINMENT

Tourist-oriented nightlife centers around the **Princess Hotel**. Their casino has cheesy live entertainment and a free midnight buffet. The **Calypso Club**, out on a dock over the sea, is a pleasant place for a drink and some seafood. Afterwards, you can step over to the **Vogue Bar**, which has DJs and dance bands on the weekends. In the neighborhood around the Princess are a couple of local nightspots and several places offering late-night eats, but they tend to go in and out of business, so ask the bartender at the Calypso Club where everyone goes these days.

There are a couple of hip local nightspots on **Queen Street** with DJs spinning dance music – again, places come and go. This is a dodgy neighborhood, so use caution and *take a taxi*. Several of the hotels, including the **Fort George** and the **Bellevue**, have live music from time to time. For a mellower scene, you can swap stories with other budget travelers over drinks at **Smokin Balam** on North Front Street, or the bar at the **Hotel Mopan** (see *Best Sleeps*).

BEST SPORTS & RECREATION

BELIZE CITY DIVE SHOPS

Most divers head for the islands, but it's quite feasible to take dive trips from Belize City, and the boat rides to some of the most popular sites aren't much longer.

Hugh Parkey's Belize Dive Connection

This full-service dive operator has a lodge on tiny Spanish Look-Out Caye, 8 miles southeast of Belize City. The lodge has 12 cabanas built over the water with ceiling fans and private baths, as well as a dormitory for student groups. Both the dive operation and the "private island" cater to the cruise ship business. *Info: www.hpbelizeadventures.com; Tel. 220-4024 or 223-5086.*

Sea Sports Belize
This shop on North Front Street has been in business since 1996, and offers dive trips to the usual spots, as well as a range of instruction, gear rental, repairs and sales. They also do snorkeling, fishing and manatee-watching trips. *Info: www.seasportsbelize.com; Tel. 223-5505.*

LIVE-ABOARD DIVE BOATS
For the serious diver, this is the ultimate dream vacation. You'll moor directly at the finest dive sites and dive until you shrivel up like a Greek olive. Two different live-aboards currently operate in Belize, both now owned by the same company. Both of them sail from the dock behind the Radisson Fort George in Belize City, and both do weeklong trips leaving every Saturday. Prices for an all-inclusive trip start around $2,400.

Peter Hughes Diving
The 138-foot Sun Dancer II features nice staterooms with private bath, AC and TV, and most have picture windows. Dive sites include the Blue Hole, Half Moon Caye Wall and the Elbow. *Info: www.peterhughes.com; Tel. 800/932-6237 or 305/669-9391 US.*

Belize Aggressor III
This 110-foot boat carries 18 passengers in nine staterooms, all with AC and TV. Dive sites cluster around Belize's three beautiful atolls. *Info: www.aggressor.com; Tel. 800/348-2628 or 706/993-2531 US.*

FISHING
Action Belize
Captain Van's Action Belize is a tour operator that's been in business since 1979, and specializes in fishing tours. *Info: www.actionbelize.com; Tel. 888/ 383-6319 US.*

Belize River Lodge
This fishing lodge is located near the airport, and runs weeklong fishing packages aboard the Blue Yonder live-aboard yacht. *Info: www.belizeriverlodge.com; Tel. 888/275-4843 US.*

6. WESTERN BELIZE & TIKAL

HIGHLIGHTS

▲ **Tikal** – the ultimate Mayan site just over the border in Guatemala

▲ **Caracol** – this large Mayan site makes a wonderful day trip

▲ **Mountain Pine Ridge** – The largest protected area in Belize, featuring beautiful waterfalls and caves

▲ **Caves Branch** – Tubing through the caves and spelunking

▲ **Cayo Jungle Lodges** – Explore the jungles on foot or horseback, and the rivers by canoe or inner tube

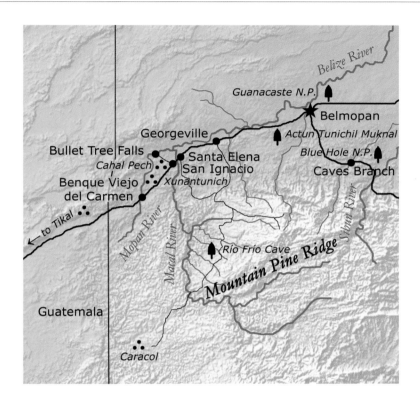

After the cayes, **Western Belize** is the country's most visited region. It's easy to see why, as there's a huge variety of interesting places to see. Here you'll find several major Mayan sites, including **Cahal Pech, Xunantunich, Caracol** and **Tikal** just across the Guatemalan border; vast areas of pristine forest, including distinct broadleaf and pine forest ecosystems; lazy tropical rivers that invite you to paddle or swim; and a spelunker's paradise of caves. Facilities for the visitor are first-rate, with a selection of excellent lodges in budget, midrange and luxury categories.

A DAY IN THE CAYO DISTRICT

Western Belize offers more ways to spend a day than almost anywhere in the world. In **San Ignacio**, an army of tour operators entices you with jungle hikes, river trips, horseback riding, caving…it's tough to choose! We can't do it all, but a trip to **Caracol** will let us check out the **tropical pine** forest, commune with the spirits of the ancient Maya, and cool off in a verdant waterfall pool, all in one day.

Morning

Get up at the crack of dawn and have a Belizean breakfast (beans and fry bread) with some fresh fruit and rich Belizean coffee. Our tour guide will pick us up at our lodge in a nice air-conditioned van, and take us up into the Central American forest (you could also do any of the itineraries in this chapter via **rented car**, though you'd miss the history lessons and local color that you get with a good guide). Caracol is about a two-hour drive from San Ignacio, south over the Mountain Pine Ridge.

Caracol ("Snail") is the largest Mayan site in Belize. Back in the seventh century AD, it was a planned city with a radial street plan and over 140,000 people – twice the size of modern Belize City. The residents were prosperous, and fond of beautiful artworks in jade and obsidian. They were also doughty warriors, and even defeated nearby Tikal in a famous battle.

The site is spectacular, at about 1,500 feet above sea level, with stunning views of the surrounding Maya Mountains. The high point of the city is a complex of structures called Caana. Here is an elaborate tomb, the resting place of the wife of one of the city's most powerful kings, which is still the tallest structure in Belize. The small museum displays artifacts from the site, as well as exhibits on the ancient Mayan world and the history of the excavation of the site. *Info:* www.caracol.org.

Afternoon

After a few hours at Caracol, we'll head back through the **Mountain Pine Ridge Forest Reserve**, the country's largest protected area. The forests of this highland region are mostly pine trees, rather than the broadleaf species that you see elsewhere in Belize. The area is chock-full of wonderful waterfalls and caves. The pine forest ecosystem is home to rare birds such as orange-breasted falcons, not to mention toucans, parrots, humming-birds and animals such as coatis.

On our way back to San Ignacio, we'll take a leisurely ride through the Pine Ridge, stopping off to see a waterfall or two and a cave. There are several very nice jungle lodges in the area, including two of Belize's finest, **Hidden Valley Inn** and **Blancaneaux Lodge** (see *Best Sleeps*). Either of these might be a great place to stop for a nice lunch.

Hidden Valley (or Thousand Foot) Falls, up past the Hidden Valley Inn, is the highest of the many waterfalls in the area, the highest in Central America, in fact. They're worth a quick look. We may also visit **Big Rock Falls** near Blancaneaux Lodge, or **Five Sisters Falls**, by the lodge of the same name. Both of these are beautiful places for a swim, with clear pools amid the verdant jungle.

The most popular stops of all, visited by every day tour group, are the **Río On Pools** and the nearby **Río Frío Cave**. Check out the lovely waterfalls and swim in the warm pools, then explore the large cave. The river running through the cave keeps things cool, and nurtures ferns and mosses.

Evening

No visit to western Belize would be complete without a stop in **San Ignacio** (also known as **Cayo**), the largest town in the region, and a lively little hub of adventure travel and ecotourism. Wide-eyed backpackers roam the streets, courted by tour guides promising days of fun at the ruins, on the rivers or in the caves. **Flayva's Restaurant** (formerly Eva's), on Burns Street in the center of town, is a popular local gathering spot. We'll stop in there for a cold beer and a chat with the posse about what's going on in the region. Alas, I fear it will only get us worked up for the next trip, when we can spend more time here. *Info:* Tel. 804-2267.

A WEEKEND AT TIKAL

Tikal National Park, just across the border in Guatemala, is the world's largest excavated Mayan site. It's possible to visit Tikal on a day trip from San Ignacio, but it really deserves at least an overnight trip. It's a very large and spread-out site, so you're going to do a lot of walking if you want to see even the half of it. Also, it would be a shame not to be there early in the morning, when the site is shrouded in that mysterious jungle mist, and you're more likely to see some of the birds and other wildlife that abound around the site.

Friday Evening
You can fly to the Guatemalan town of Flores from Belize City, or take a bus or rental car from San Ignacio directly to Tikal National Park. There are three inexpensive hotels adjacent to the park. but none of them have much going for them except proximity to the ruins. There are a couple of nicer hotel options around **Lake Petén Itzá**, a bit less than an hour's drive from the ruins (see *Best Sleeps*). My favorite is **La Lancha**, a small, quiet boutique hotel with a pool that's going to feel very good after trudging around the ruins all day.

If we get here early enough, we'll drop by the visitors' center and **line up a guide** for tomorrow morning. It's well worth paying a few bucks to learn about the history of the site, and it's always a good thing to support the local economy. We'll take a guided tour tomorrow morning, then wander about on our own the rest of the day.

Speaking of that pool, it may just be time for a dip and a cold beer, then dinner at our hotel restaurant. There's no big nightlife scene around here, but the hotel bars often harbor some lively conversation among the visitors from all over the world.

Saturday Morning
The name Tikal means "Place of Voices." The voices of the ancient Mayans speak most clearly early in the morning, so we'll be there right at 6am when

the gates open. Early morning mist rises from the jungle, revealing the huge stone heads of long-dead kings. Ceiba roots entwine the stones, flocks of colorful parrots flit about, and deer graze irreverently among the ancient palaces.

By late morning, the hot tropical sun has burned off the mist, and the deer are replaced by herds of irreverent gringos, each clad in ball cap and t-shirt, with an ice cream cone in one hand and a water bottle firmly clutched in the other. It's not possible to evade them altogether, but if you time your visit just right, you can avoid the midday rush.

During the Maya's **Classic Period** (around 300-900 AD), Tikal was one of the largest and most powerful city-states in the Mayan world, a metropolis of over 100,000 residents that traded with cultures as far away as Teotihuacan in Mexico, and made war with neighbors such as Caracol and Naranjo. Rulers such as Dark Sun, Stormy Sky and Jaguar Paw built grand palaces, temples and monuments, and recorded their deeds in Mayan glyphs on **stelae** (stone columns).

The Ancient Maya

During their **Golden Age** (300-900 AD) the Mayans built a highly advanced empire that extended from Mexico through Guatemala and Belize to Honduras. Their calendar and knowledge of astronomy were unequalled until modern times. Their monumental ceremonial sites were the scenes of **elaborate rituals**, including human sacrifice. Although Mayans continue to live in the area today, their advanced civilization collapsed before the Spanish arrived. The exact reasons for their demise are a mystery, but most scientists agree that climate change and droughts did for them. Some believe that poor stewardship of the environment played a role (sound familiar?). With its wealth of Mayan sites, Belize is an excellent place to explore the history of this fascinating people. To learn more, see:

www.mayaruins.com
www.mayan-world.com
www.mayaweb.nl
www.lost-civilizations.net
www.mesoweb.com
www.gomaya.com

Archaeological work at the site began in 1882, but only a fraction of the city of Tikal has yet been excavated. Don't worry though, even that fraction will be enough to keep us stomping about all day: over 3,000 structures, including six large pyramids, 250 stelae, several royal palaces, no less than seven ball courts and hundreds of small residential buildings. The centerpiece is the **Grand Plaza**, where two pyramids, the Temple of the Great Jaguar and the Temple of the Masks, face each other with a large plaza in between, surrounded by dozens of stelae and altars. Around the corner is the complex called the **Lost World**, with a huge pyramid and other structures from several different historical periods.

Visiting Tikal is a good workout, as it is an enormous site. It's no place to visit with small children, or anyone who minds walking. The walk from the entrance to the Grand Plaza is almost a mile. Raised causeways connect other sections of the city. It's another long walk to the **Temple of the Two-headed Serpent**, at 230 feet the tallest Mayan structure in the world. We'll really get a workout as we scramble to the top of the partially excavated pyramid, to be rewarded with a spectacular panorama of the surrounding jungle. The trails that connect the various parts of the site make for a pleasant hike through the jungle. Parrots, toucans, spider and howler monkeys are common, and the partially cleared landscape makes spotting them easier than in the dense jungle.

Saturday Afternoon
When the midday heat becomes oppressive, we can sit down in one of the small *comedores* across from the visitors' center for an authentic Guatemalan meal. After lunch, we'll visit the two small museums at the site. The Morley Museum, named for a colorful character who was one of the early explorers, displays beautiful ceramic and jade artifacts from the site. At the visitors' center, the most interesting of Tikal's stelae are protected.

In this climate, it makes sense to get up early, as we did, and do our walking around before it gets really hot. If you're staying at one of the hotels at the site, you might even indulge in that civilized Spanish/Latin American custom called a *siesta*, and nap for a couple of hours. In the evening, go back into the park for another hour or so, perhaps seeing the **Palace of the Inscriptions**. *Info: Tikal National Park is open daily 6am-6pm. Entry is $20. www.tikalpark.com.*

Saturday Evening
The park normally closes at 6pm, but we have heard that on full-moon nights, you can get a special ticket to go in at night – surely a spiritual and spooky experience! Otherwise, it's another night of drinking beer and swapping travel stories at the hotel bar.

Sunday
If we get going fairly early, we'll have time for a little side trip on the way back to San Ignacio (or, if you haven't had your fill of the Mayans, we could certainly spend another morning at Tikal). The stretch of the Western Highway between San Ignacio and the Guatemalan border is sprouting tourist attractions and lodges at a steady pace. The **Belize Botanic Gardens**, next to Du Plooy's lodge, are worth a visit. You could also do a float down the river here. The Lodge at Chaa Creek, with its butterfly breeding center, is also a nice place for a quick stop.

A WEEKEND IN THE CAYO DISTRICT

The sights in this region are endless – and so are the local tour operators eager to show them to you. On this itinerary, we'll try to see a little of everything – rivers, caves, monkeys and Mayans.

Friday
There are lots of nice places to stay in the region. Most are jungle lodges, and they range from budget-priced rustic cabanas to luxurious all-inclusive resorts. If you want an upscale place in the Mountain Pine Ridge area, you'll love the rooms and the personal service at the **Hidden Valley Inn**. If a place on the river sounds better, try the eco-friendly **Du Plooy's**. If your budget is a little smaller, and you'd like to stay right in town, head for the **San Ignacio Resort Hotel** or **Cahal Pech Village Resort**. One of the best of the really inexpensive lodges is **Midas Tropical Resort**, just outside of town in a pleasant setting on the Macal River (see *Best Sleeps*). Wherever you're staying, I always recommend making a reservation well in advance.

Intercity buses leave Belize City for Cayo about every hour. The local bus takes about four hours, so it may be worth paying a bit more for the more comfortable and faster express bus. Various tour operators operate air-conditioned vans from Belize City to Cayo. Once you get to San Ignacio you can take a van or taxi to your lodge. If you have a rental car, you can drive straight to your lodge, but you should still stop in San Ignacio for a look around.

San Ignacio, also known as **Cayo**, is the largest town in western Belize, and a major center of ecotourism. Cayo serves as a transport hub, a place to stock up on supplies, and headquarters for the area's multitude of tour operators. **Flayva's Restaurant**, on Burns Street in the center of town, is a popular tourist gathering spot, and a likely place to find the latest info on hotels, transportation and tours. *Info: Tel. 804-2267.*

Located on the **Macal River** with the sister town of Santa Elena on the other bank, San Ignacio has a more salubrious feel than Belize City, though some neighborhoods are dodgy after dark. You'll meet a broad mixture of people here – locals in town to do some shopping, travelers en route to and from nearby Guatemala, and of course scads of American and European visitors. There's a good variety of restaurants and bars, and an endless supply of stories to be swapped with hip travelers from all over the world.

San Ignacio is home to a host of tour operators, who can arrange any of an endless list of activities in the nearby wilderness. Canoe trips on the Macal River, birding and hiking trips, horseback riding, mountain biking, caving, visits to the Mayan ruins...the list goes on and on. Contact one of the operators listed in the *Practical Matters* chapter.

Saturday
Caracol ("Snail") is the largest Mayan site in Belize. In its heyday, around

the seventh century AD, it was one of the largest Mayan cities, with a population of over 140,000 people – twice the size of modern Belize City. Unlike other Lowland Maya cities, Caracol was planned on a large scale, with a radial street plan that covered some

65 square miles. Luxurious objects of jade and obsidian have been found throughout the city, indicating that the residents of Caracol were especially prosperous. They were also formidable warriors, defeating the mighty city-state of Tikal in a famous battle in 562 AD.

Caracol was occupied as early as 1200 BC, but most of the major monuments were built during the Mayan Classic Period, between about 500-900 AD. The site was "discovered" in 1937. Excavation began in the 1950s and continues today. The setting is spectacular, at about 1,500 feet above sea level, with stunning views of the surrounding Maya Mountains. Caracol is about 50 miles south of San Ignacio, through the Mountain Pine Ridge area. The road has recently been improved, so it takes about two hours to get there from San Ignacio.

The excavated area of the site is pretty large, with several tombs and temples, and a ball court. The high point of the city, both literally and figuratively, is a complex of structures called **Caana**. Here is a very elaborate tomb, believed to be the resting place of the wife of one of the city's most powerful kings. The magnificent pyramid of Caana remains the highest man-made structure in Belize. You can climb to the top to enjoy an expansive view – nothing but uninhabited forest for miles and miles.

There's a small museum with lots of artifacts from the site, as well as exhibits on the ancient Mayan world and the history of the excavation of the site. You can arrange a tour through any of the local tour operators or lodges. Most visitors opt for an all-day tour: you'll spend the morning at Caracol, then visit a couple of other points of interest on the way back, perhaps the **Río On Pools** for a cooling swim. *Info: www.caracol.org.*

The **Mountain Pine Ridge Forest Reserve** is the country's largest protected area, 300 square miles of wilderness that forms a distinct ecosystem. The Caribbean pine trees contrast with the broadleaf species that dominate the forests in most of Belize. The backbone of the landscape is mostly solid granite, which explains the large number of waterfalls and caves in the area. The wildlife, and especially the birds, are a little different than you'll see elsewhere. Rare orange-breasted falcons, Stygian owls and ocellated turkeys join more commonly seen birdies such as toucans, parrots, hummingbirds and woodpeckers. Baird's tapir, pumas, jaguars and ocelots prowl at night.

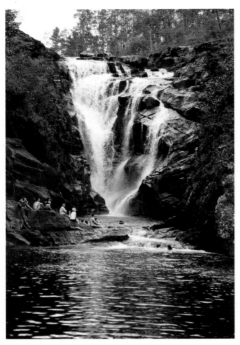

This vast uninhabited area is traversed by a few graded dirt roads that are kept in pretty good repair and should be passable in an ordinary car, except during periods of heavy rain. There are several very nice jungle lodges in the area, including two of Belize's finest, **Hidden Valley Inn** and **Blancaneaux Lodge** (see *Best Sleeps*). Many day tours stop off at one or more of Mountain Pine Ridge's attractions on the way back from a visit to the Caracol archaeological site.

Hidden Valley (or Thousand Foot) Falls, up past the Hidden Valley Inn, is the highest of the many waterfalls in the area, the highest in Central America, in fact. They're worth a quick look. There's an overlook with a picnic area that's easy to reach by road. Near Blancaneaux Lodge, **Big Rock Falls** are shorter, wider and more interesting, and there are nice pools where you can swim. On the grounds of **Five Sisters Lodge**, the falls of the same name are another beautiful place for a swim.

The most popular stops of all, visited by every day tour group, are the **Río On Pools** and the nearby **Río Frío Cave**. Check out the lovely waterfalls and swim in the warm pools, then explore the large cave. The river running through the cave keeps things cool, and nurtures ferns and mosses.

Sunday
This region has all kinds of wonderful eco-adventures. Look for some of the 300 species of birds that hang around the **Belize Botanic Gardens**. Learn about the life cycle of butterflies at the **Green Hills Butterfly Farm**. Ride horses through the jungle from the **Windy Hill Resort** equestrian center. Take a rafting trip on the **Macal River**, or a canoe trip through **Barton Creek Cave** (see *Best Sports & Recreation*).

There are a couple of interesting attractions right around San Ignacio. The **Green Iguana Project** at the San Ignacio Resort Hotel is a must if you are traveling with kids. The resort also has some very easy jungle trails. The small Mayan site of **Cahal Pech** is well worth a visit, and offers a panoramic view.

There are also several worthwhile sights along the Western Highway, so if you're driving back to Belize City, you could easily stop off at **Guanacaste National Park**, **Caves Branch** or the **Belize Zoo**.

A WEEK IN WESTERN BELIZE

A week would give you time to see the best of the **Mayan sites**, hike through the **Mountain Pine Ridge**, visit a cave or two, and do some **rafting** on the river. But that would still only be a taste of all there is to see in this region.

Most of the sights covered in this chapter are in pretty easy day-trip range, whether you stay around **Cayo** or at one of the nearby lodges, so choose the option that fits your personality. If you thrive on the touristy bustle, stay in Cayo. If you'd rather have trackless jungle all around, stay at a remote lodge.

Belmopan
The Belizean government moved the capital to the newly-built city of **Belmopan** in 1970, a few years after Hurricane Hattie wiped out a big chunk of Belize City. Everything about the new city was planned. The name is a combination of "Belize" and "Mopan," one of the rivers in the area. The government buildings were designed to resemble stylized versions of Mayan temples, and they are set in parklike grounds studded with beautiful poinciana trees, and connected by pedestrian walkways.

Despite (or because of) the careful planning, the city has grown very slowly. The US embassy was relocated here from Belize City only in 2006. Many government workers still commute from Belize City. Unless you're interested in the dos and don'ts of city planning, there's nothing in particular for a tourist to see here. However, if you take a bus to any place in Western Belize, you will be stopping here to change buses, whether you want to or not. There is a selection of good restaurants, and a couple of decent places to stay (see *Best Sleeps*). *Info: www.belmopancityonline.com.*

Guanacaste National Park

This tiny (50 acre) park, run by the Belize Audubon Society, is located at the intersection of the Western Highway and the Hummingbird Highway. It makes a very convenient place for a quick walk or a picnic on your way to the Cayo district.

The park is named for a huge **guanacaste tree** overlooking the river near the entrance. The guanacaste (also known as tubroos or monkey's ear tree) can grow to heights of over 130 feet, and is a commercially important tree in Belize. The seed pods are used for cattle feed, and the wood is used to make the dugout canoes that locals call *doreys*. This particular tree escaped being made into a boat because its trunk divided into three at an early age. Today it's a huge spreading old gentleman, covered with epiphytic bromeliads.

Two miles of walking trails feature labels for many other native plants, including mammee apple and mahogany trees, and Belize's national flower, the black orchid. You may also spot a trogon, motmot, kingfisher, magnolia warbler, red-lored parrot or one of over 120 bird species. Deer, kinkajous, pacas, agoutis and enormous iguanas are common. The river is a nice place for a cooling swim. *Info: There's a small visitors' center and gift shop, where you'll pay the entry fee of $2.50. Opening hours are 8am-4:30pm. www.belizeaudubon.org/parks/guanacaste.htm.*

Blue Hole National Park

This park, on the Hummingbird Highway a few miles southeast of Belmopan, covers 575 acres, some of which is primary forest (never logged).

The sinkhole for which the park is named is not to be confused with the more famous Blue Hole offshore (see Chapter 4), but it does resemble it a bit – 25 feet deep and filled with bright sapphire-blue water, it's a capital place for a swim.

The other main attraction here is **Saint Herman's Cave.** This remarkable karst cavern is probably the easiest cave to visit in the country. You can take a peek inside on your own, but to take the grand tour, you'll need a local guide (easily arranged at the visitors' center). You can also take a guided tour of **Crystalline Cave**, where you'll see 2,000-year-old Mayan artifacts and human skeletons calcified in the limestone.

There are five miles of well-marked hiking trails, several picnic areas and a campsite. Over 200 species of birds have been sighted, including trogons, motmots, honeycreepers and cotingas. Other residents include deer, agoutis, tapirs, peccaries and anteaters. A few very fortunate souls have sighted jaguars, ocelots and jaguarundis. *Info: Entry $4. Open daily 8am-4:30pm. www.belizeaudubon.org/parks/bhnp.htm.*

Caves Branch

Western Belize is a spelunker's dream. The limestone landscape is riddled with caves, sinkholes and underground rivers. Caves were sacred spots to the ancient Maya, who called the underworld **Xibalba**, and all sorts of artifacts, skeletons and such have been found in caves in the area, some of them entombed forever in limestone.

The big daddy of caving in Belize is Ian Anderson, a Canadian who began exploring the caves and caverns of the region in the early 1990s, and now presides over an empire of adventure travel that includes a jungle lodge just south of Belmopan and a wide variety of tours in the area (see *Best Sleeps*). Lots of operators run cave tours (and especially cave tubing trips) in this area, but if you're a serious spelunker, **Ian Anderson's Caves Branch Adventure Company** is the place to go. *Info: www.cavesbranch.com.* The nearby **Jaguar Paw Resort** is a worthy competitor. *Info: www.jaguarpaw.com.*

River tubing is an extremely popular activity all over western Belize. Here on the Caves Branch River, you can combine tubing and caving, as the river runs through several underground caverns. It's quite an adventure to float through the darkness, stalagmites sticking up from the river and stalactites hanging from the roof. Underground waterfalls thunder, and openings let n rays of light from the jungle above. Shorter tubing trips are suitable for everyone, but longer trips involve some hiking, both above and below ground. Ian's flagship full-day trip includes over seven miles underground.

Cave tubing is perhaps the single most popular activity on mainland Belize, attracting day-trippers from the many lodges in the area, as well as huge hordes from the cruise ships. During the high tourist season, the masses of tubes jostling down the river seem more like a water ride at Disney World than the wilds of Central America.

Another popular spot is **Crystal Cave**, one of the largest caves in Belize. Here are spectacular crystal stalactites, stalagmites and fanciful formations. Two millennia ago, this was a major ceremonial center for the Maya. Paintings and carvings adorn the walls, and all kinds of artifacts and skeletons have been found here.

The local resorts offer all kinds of activities in addition to caving. Jungle hikes, mountain biking, rappelling, rock climbing and ziplines are on the menu. Horseback riding trips from nearby **Banana Bank** are highly recommended (see *Best Sleeps*). *Info: www.bananabank.com.*

San Ignacio (Cayo)

San Ignacio, also known as **Cayo**, or **El Cayo de San Ignacio**, is the largest town in western Belize (about 14,000 people), and a major center of ecotourism. Although San Ignacio has a good selection of budget lodgings, most visitors to the region don't stay right in town, but rather in one of the jungle lodges in the surrounding countryside. Cayo serves as a transport hub, a place to stock up on supplies, and headquarters for the area's multitude of tour operators. Cheap hotels and tourist restaurants cluster around Burns Street in the center of town, making it a good place to find the latest info on local activities and tours.

Intercity buses leave Belize City for Cayo about every hour. The local bus takes about four hours, so it may be worth paying a bit more for the more comfortable and faster express bus. Various tour operators operate air-conditioned vans from Belize City to Cayo. Ask at your hotel for details.

Located on the Macal River with the sister town of Santa Elena on the other bank, San Ignacio has a more salubrious feel than Belize City, though some neighborhoods are dodgy after dark. You'll meet a broad mixture of people here – locals in town to do some shopping, travelers en route to and from nearby Guatemala, and of course scads of American and European visitors. There's a good variety of restaurants and bars, and an endless supply of stories to be swapped with hip travelers from all over the world.

The **San Ignacio Resort Hotel** operates the **Green Iguana Project**, which is well worth a visit, especially if you are traveling with kids. Green iguanas – very cute when they're small, dinosaurish and scary-looking (but harmless) when they get big – are a vital part of the jungle ecosystem. In many

parts of Central America, they're endangered, mainly because locals like to eat them. The resort runs a captive breeding program, incubating and hatching the eggs and releasing juvenile iguanas into the wild. The exhibit is well-organized and informative, and takes about an hour to see. Also here is a **Medicinal Jungle Trail**, where you can learn about the many native plants that are used as medicine in traditional Mayan and African cultures. This is part of a network of trails that traverse the resort's 14-acre jungle preserve, the home of animals such as gibnuts, agoutis, armadillos, and over 150 species of birds. Some of the trails are very easy, and would be an excellent choice for older (or younger) travelers who may not be up for a strenuous jungle hike.

San Ignacio is home to a host of tour operators who can arrange any of an endless list of activities in the nearby wilderness. Rafting on the **Macal River**, canoe trips through **Barton Creek Cave**, horseback riding and various "extreme sports" are easy to arrange. Contact one of the operators listed in the *Practical Matters* chapter.

Cahal Pech

This Mayan site in the hills above San Ignacio is well worth a visit. Although it's much smaller than Caracol, Xunantunich or Tikal, the site is beautiful, amid bird-infested jungle with an awesome view of the Maya Mountains and the Belize River valley, and it's easily accessible from San Ignacio. Don't let the name, which means "place of ticks," put you off.

Cahal Pech was occupied as early as 1200 BC, making it one of the earliest Maya settlements in Belize. It is believed to have been a major trading center that had contact with other Mayan city-states in Guatemala and the

Olmec to the north. The site consists of 34 structures on a two-acre site, including pyramid temples (the tallest is 77 feet high), palaces, two ball courts, and one of the earliest carved stelae in the region. Cahal Pech was abandoned around 800 AD, during the Maya Collapse.

Caracol

Caracol ("Snail") is the largest Mayan site in Belize. In its heyday, around the seventh century AD, it was one of the largest Mayan cities, with a population of over 140,000 people – twice the size of modern Belize City. Unlike other Lowland Maya cities, Caracol was planned on a large scale, with a radial street plan that covered some 65 square miles. Luxurious objects of jade and obsidian have been found throughout the city, indicating that the residents of Caracol were especially prosperous. They were also doughty warriors, defeating the mighty city-state of Tikal in a famous battle in 562 AD.

Caracol was occupied as early as 1200 BC, but most of the major monuments were built during the Mayan Classic Period, between about 500-900 AD. The site was "discovered" in 1937. Excavation began in the 1950s and continues today. The setting is spectacular, at 1,500 feet above sea level, with stunning views of the surrounding Maya Mountains. Caracol is about a 50-mile ride south of San Ignacio, through the Mountain Pine Ridge area. The road has recently been improved, so it takes around two hours to get there from San Ignacio.

The excavated area of the site is pretty large, with several tombs and temples, and a ball court. The high point of the city, both literally and figuratively, is a complex of structures called **Caana**. Here is a very elaborate tomb, believed to be the resting place of the wife of one of the city's most powerful kings. The magnificent pyramid of Caana remains the highest man-made structure in Belize. You can climb to the top to enjoy a spectacular view – nothing but uninhabited forest for miles and miles.

There's a small museum on-site with lots of artifacts from the site, as well as exhibits on the ancient Mayan world and the history of the excavation. You can arrange a tour through any of the local tour operators or lodges. Most visitors opt for an all-day tour: you'll spend the morning at Caracol, then visit a couple of other points of interest on the way back, perhaps the **Río On Pools** for a cooling swim. *Info: www.caracol.org.*

Xunantunich

This Mayan site is about eight miles west of San Ignacio, on a hill above the Mopan River. The name means "Stone Woman," a reference to a ghost that several people claim to have seen climbing the steps of El Castillo, and then

walking through a stone wall. Getting here includes taking a quaint hand-cranked ferry across the river from the little village of San José Succotz.

Xunantunich was an important ceremonial center, with six plazas and over 25 temples and palaces. Historians believe that the city was an up-and-coming power, but was abandoned after an earthquake destroyed part of the city. The largest structure is the pyramid called El Castillo, which rises 130 feet above the jungle, Belize's second-highest structure after Caana at Caracol. The view from the top is an awesome panorama of Belizean and Guatemalan jungle. A finely-detailed frieze depicting the sun god, attended by the moon and the planets, once encircled the entire pyramid, but only about half of it is still intact (actually, as at many Mayan sites, what you see here is a plaster reproduction – the original has been covered up to protect it from the elements).

Xunantunich was "discovered" by a British medical officer named Thomas Gann in the 1890s. Gann is suspected of removing several art treasures from the site. Anyway, various important artifacts disappeared, and no one knows exactly where they are today.

There's a nice visitors' center with a museum featuring a scale model of the site, three stelae from the site and exhibits on the history of the city. *Info: Open daily 8am-4pm. Entry $10.*

Actun Tunichil Muknal

This cave, called ATM for short, was an important ceremonial center for the Maya. Here they sacrificed young virgins to the rain god Chac. During the Terminal Classic era, the Maya performed these ceremonies ever more often and ever deeper into the cave, as they strove to appease the gods and end the terrible droughts that finally did them in.

The cave was only discovered in 1989 and opened to the public in 1998, and all the artifacts have been left exactly where they were found. You can visit only as part of an organized tour, which you can arrange through your lodge or any of the tour operators in San Ignacio. It's a fairly strenuous trip. To get here, you ride 45 minutes from San Ignacio, and then hike 45 minutes through the **Tapir Mountain Nature Reserve**, crossing three streams on the way. Once you get to the cave, you actually have to swim a short way, and there are several more spots inside where you'll have to wade. And that water is cold! I recommend bringing a large Ziploc bag or two for your camera and a change of clothes. The site can be a bit of a circus during tourist season – there'll be lots of groups visiting and, unlike at large sites like Tikal, you don't have much room to spread out in a cave.

The wonders of ATM are many. There are beautiful stalagmites and stalactites, some of them carved by the Maya so that a light placed in the right spot casts the shadow of a human figure on the wall. There are chambers strewn with ceramic pots and stoneware. There are altars where the Mayan elite performed blood-letting ceremonies, piercing themselves with stingray spines in order to talk to the gods. And of course, there are the macabre skeletal remains of 14 humans, which lie encrusted with calcium that leached from the limestone over the centuries. The most famous of these is the **Crystal Maiden**, the skeleton of a young girl that has become encased in sparkling calcite.

In the immediate area are a couple of other caves, which serious spelunkers or Maya buffs may arrange to visit. **Actun Nak Beh** contains a few human burials and shards of pottery. **Actun Uayazba Kab**, the "Cave of the Handprints" has a very unusually shaped mouth, and extensive carvings, including a large turtle that is believed to have figured in coming-of-age ceremonies, as well as four painted handprints on the walls. In the center of a triangle formed by the three caves is **Cahal Uitz Na**, the "Place of the Mountain House," a ceremonial center consisting of a plaza with six stelae, surrounded by several temples and a ball court.

Cayo Jungle Lodges

Wherever you stay in the Cayo District, you can visit the forests, rivers and caves of the region by taking day trips with any of the hordes of local tour operators (or, if you have a car, by driving around on your own). This can get a little hectic however, and some tour operators will charge you extra if they have to pick you up from a remote lodge. To get the most for your time and money, it makes sense to choose a lodge that offers activities that interest you right on-site.

If you're into birding, you'll love **Du Plooy's**, a very ecologically-oriented lodge right on the Macal River, with the **Belize Botanic Gardens** next door. Expert bird guides on staff can show you some of the 300 species that hang out in the area.

If horseback riding interests you, check out **Windy Hill Resort**, which has an equestrian center and a central location that's convenient for day trips. **Black Rock Lodge** is another eco-friendly establishment directly on the Macal River, surrounded by rain forest, mountains and waterfalls. See *Best Sleeps* for details on these and other area lodges.

Mountain Pine Ridge

The **Mountain Pine Ridge Forest Reserve** is the country's largest protected area, 300 square miles of wilderness that forms a distinct ecosystem. The Caribbean pine trees contrast with the broadleaf species that dominate the forests in most of Belize. The backbone of the landscape is mostly solid granite, which explains the large number of waterfalls and caves in the area. Looking at the pine trees, red clay soil and granite outcroppings, you might almost think you're in Georgia.

The wildlife, and especially the birds, are a little different here than you'll see elsewhere. Rare orange-breasted falcons, Stygian owls and ocellated turkeys join more commonly-seen birdies such as toucans, parrots, hummingbirds and woodpeckers. Baird's tapir, pumas, jaguars and ocelots prowl at night.

This vast uninhabited area is traversed by a few graded dirt roads that are kept in pretty good repair, and should be passable in an ordinary car, except during periods of heavy rain. There are several very nice jungle lodges in the area, including two of Belize's finest, **Hidden Valley Inn** and **Blancaneaux Lodge** (see *Best Sleeps*). Many day tours stop off at one or more of Mountain Pine Ridge's attractions on the way back from a visit to the Caracol archaeological site.

Hidden Valley (or Thousand Foot) Falls, up past the Hidden Valley Inn, is the highest of the many waterfalls in the area, the highest in Central America, in fact. They're worth a quick look. There's an overlook with a

Bark Beetle Infestation

Nasty little bugs called bark beetles went crazy in 2001, and infested some 20% of all the pine trees in Belize. Mountain Pine Ridge was especially hard-hit, with 80% of the trees killed. The forest service has been pretty successful at combating the little buggers, and the pines are now almost fully recovered. A "silver lining" is that the country is now a little bit more open than it was before, making it easier to see the huge variety of birds, who are just as abundant as ever.

picnic area that's easy to reach by road. Near Blancaneaux Lodge, **Big Rock Falls** are shorter, wider and more interesting, and there are nice pools where you can swim. On the grounds of **Five Sisters Lodge**, the falls of the same name are another beautiful place for a swim.

The most popular stops of all, visited by every day tour group, are the **Río On Pools** and the nearby **Río Frío Cave**. Visit the lovely waterfalls and swim in the warm pools, then explore the large cave. The river running through the cave keeps things cool, and nurtures ferns and mosses.

Tikal Ruins, Guatemala

One of Belize's most popular tourist destinations isn't in Belize at all, but rather just across the border in Guatemala. **Tikal** is the world's largest excavated Mayan site. Today it's a UNESCO World Heritage Site, and Guatemala's most popular national park. For details on the site itself, see pages 123-127, *A Weekend at Tikal*.

Many visitors take a guided tour from Belize, but **you can get to Tikal by car or public transport**, and hire a guide at the site. Some buses from Belize City go to Melchor de Mencos on the Guatemalan side, where you can catch a bus for Flores or for Tikal. Both Maya Island Air and Tropic Air offer two flights per day from Goldson International to Flores, which is about a 45-minute ride from Tikal. Border formalities are no major hassle. Visa requirements are similar to those for Belize. You will have to pay a departure tax of $18(!), even if you're just going for the day. If you're driving, expect your car's papers to be closely scrutinized. Guatemala has a higher crime rate than does Belize, and tourists have been robbed on some of the isolated trails at Tikal. Recently-deployed **Tourist Police** have made things much better, but I do recommend that you be more cautious on this side of the border.

BEST SLEEPS & EATS

BELMOPAN

Most travelers visit Belmopan only to change buses – and you will too, if you take a bus to any place in the west or south of the country. There's no real reason to spend the night in the town, but there are a couple of special lodges in the immediate area.

Twin Palms $$$

This small, modern inn, which opened in 2011, is the best lodging in Belmopan. There's a nice pool and attractive grounds, and the rooms have comfortable beds, AC, TV, wi-fi and small refrigerators. There's no restaurant, but a bountiful breakfast is served. *Info: www.belmopancityonline.com/belize-bed-and-breakfast.aspx; Tel. 822-2831 or 610-2831.*

LODGES NEAR BELMOPAN

Banana Bank Lodge & Jungle Equestrian Adventure $$$$
If you love horses, this is the place for you. Banana Bank is an upscale jungle lodge located on the Belize River. The equestrian center is probably the largest in Belize, with about 100 head of quarter horses. There are miles of beautiful riding trails through the jungle. Other ways to spend your time include tubing and kayaking on the river, lazing around the pool, and visiting resident painter Carolyn Carr's studio and gallery. There are several different lodging options, with or without AC, at reasonable prices. *Info: www.bananabank.com; Tel. 832-2020.*

Ian Anderson's Caves Branch Adventure Co. & Jungle Lodge $$$$
If you love caving, this is the place for you. Oops! You say dad loves caves and mom loves horses? Not a problem. Ian's place is not far from Banana Bank – many visitors stay at one and take day trips to the other. This part of Belize has enough adventurous activities to keep you busy for months. There are dozens of interesting caves in the area, and Ian and his merry band of spelunkers know them

better than anyone. However, even they haven't charted them all – you can visit in the off-season and help them scope out new ones. Cave tubing is especially popular – float down the river on an inner tube, rushing in and out of caves! *Info: www.cavesbranch.com; Tel. 610-3451 or 866/357-2698 US.*

Pook's Hill $$$$

At the end of a five-mile dirt road, south of the town of Teakettle, this jungle lodge feels isolated, but is easy to reach. Its proximity to the ATM cave means that you can visit that popular attraction and avoid the worst of the crowds. The site is right on the Roaring River, a splendid place for swimming and kayaking, and right in the middle of the mountain rain forest, adjacent to the Tapir Mountain Nature Reserve. The variety of birds is amazing, and guides are always on hand to answer your ornithological questions. The classic thatched cabanas have nice beds and ceiling fans, and are fully screened, the better to enjoy the sights and sounds of the forest. A couple are raised on stilts, the better to peer into the canopy and observe the doings of the birds and monkeys. *Info: www.pookshilllodge.com; Tel. 832-2017.*

Sleeping Giant Rainforest Lodge $$$$

South of Belmopan, this jungle lodge is on the Sibun River, overlooked by the mountain from which it takes its name, and surrounded by beautiful

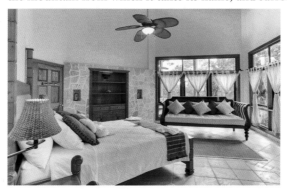

grounds and bird-infested forest. It's near Blue Hole National Park, as well as Caves Branch – many guests take advantage of the huge menu of tours available there. The nine rooms have AC and modern décor, and each has room for either four or six guests. The attentive staff earns rave reviews. *Info: www.sleepinggiantbelize.com; Tel. 822-3850 or 888/332-4268 US.*

BEST SLEEPS IN SAN IGNACIO

Hotel prices in San Ignacio vary according to the season, how full they are and, perhaps, how the owner likes your looks. Especially in the cheaper establishments, it may be worth bargaining for a discount.

San Ignacio Resort Hotel $$$$

This is the best of the hotels right in town. The 24 rooms have recently been renovated, and are well appointed, with private bath, AC, TV and phone. There's a pool, tennis court, hiking trails, tour desk, gift shop, business center, and laundry service. The Green Iguana Project is well worth a visit (especially with kids) even if you aren't staying here. The bar is something of a hangout for colorful US expats. *Info: 18 Buena Vista Street. www.sanignaciobelize.com; Tel. 824-2125 or 855/488-2624 US.*

Mahogany Hall $$$$

In the nearby village of Bullet Tree Falls, this riverside resort has nice air-conditioned rooms with porches and French doors, as well as TV and wi-fi. There's a pool and a restaurant, and tours to the surrounding wonders are easily arranged. *Info: www.mahoganyhallbelize.com; Tel. 844-4047 or 664-7747.*

Midas Tropical Resort $$

This inexpensive lodge features rustic cabanas with private bath just outside of town in a pleasant setting on the Macal River. With seven acres of forest around, it feels secluded, yet it's only a five-minute walk from town. The restaurant serves tasty Belizean food at good prices. *Info: www.midasbelize.com; Tel. 824-3172.*

Burns Avenue in the center of San Ignacio has several economy hotels. Two of the best are the Casa Blanca Guest House (*www.casablancaguesthouse.com; Tel. 824-2080*) and the Western Guest House (*www.westernguesthouse.com; Tel. 824-2572*). The super-cheap **Hi-Et Guest House** (*Tel. 824-2828*) is beloved by backpackers.

Other budget options are listed at www.sanignaciotown.com. You can get a double room with private bath and AC for under $40, or one with shared bath and fan for $15. Be sure to specify a room with a window!

BEST EATS IN SAN IGNACIO

Flayva's

For many years, this place, right in the center of the action on Burns Street, was known as Eva's, and was world-famous, less for its food than for being a clearinghouse for tours and activities in the region. I haven't visited since the recent change of ownership, but by most accounts the food is actually better, and it's still a good place to get the latest local info. Breakfast, lunch and dinner are served, and the menu includes steaks, chicken, curry, Mexican food and vegetarian dishes. *Info: Tel. 804-2267.*

Locals dig **Ko Ox Han Nah**, which offers Asian cuisine, including vegan dishes; and Erva's (*Tel. 824-2821*), which dishes up Mexican and Belizean fare. Hode's (pronounced ho-dee's) Place (*Tel. 804-2522*) serves fine local dishes. It's a great place to bring the kids, as there's a playground and a game room. At night, the place to be is the **Cahal Pech** disco.

JUNGLE LODGES AROUND SAN IGNACIO

Most of these lodges are pretty secluded, but not that far from the Western Highway and San Ignacio. Most visitors come on all-inclusive packages – they'll pick you up from town, feed you each night, and arrange tours and activities for you during the day. This is a good way to go, because there's no other way to get around the area on your own, unless you rent a car. Some lodges have plenty of hiking, birding and other opportunities right on the grounds, and all will gladly arrange excursions to the Mayan ruins, waterfalls, caves, nature reserves and other area attractions.

The Lodge at Chaa Creek $$$$$

This is one of the most venerable ecolodges in Belize, open since 1981, and the recipient of many prestigious awards. Set in a 365-acre private reserve

on the Macal River, the lodge offers plenty of opportunities for rain forest hiking, horseback riding, mountain biking and canoeing. The 23 thatched cottages are each uniquely decorated and lavishly appointed. Some have private Jacuzzis. *Info: www.chaacreek.com; Tel. 824-2037 or 877/709-8708 US.*

Blancaneaux Lodge $$$$$

One of two luxury lodges in Belize owned by Francis Ford Coppola,

Blancaneaux is located on 50 acres of grounds on the Privassion River. The thatched cabanas, some riverfront, are well appointed and very attractive, with all kinds of quirky antiques and local art. There's a fully-equipped spa for massages and mango baths, a stable full of riding horses, and an organic garden and chicken farm to provide fresh produce for the excellent gourmet restaurant. This is an international luxury lodge, not a quaint local establishment, and sometimes it feels as if you're in Europe, not Belize (love it or hate it – personally I think it's a great mix). As you'd expect at an establishment of this caliber, the rooms, food and wine are expensive, but the service is top-notch and very personal. *Info: www.blancaneaux.com; Tel. 824-3878 or 800/746-3743 US.*

Hidden Valley Inn $$$$$

This beautiful lodge sits on a 7,200-acre private estate in the Mountain Pine Ridge preserve, home to 300 species of birds and animals and 76 species of orchids. The 12 rooms are bright, airy and private, set in six adobe-style cottages. Luxuries include the expected (large bathrooms, fireplaces, large comfortable beds, wi-fi) as well as the unexpected but handy (a shoe cleaning kit, a bottle of Skin-So-Soft bug-repellent oil). The lovely waterfall pool and hot tub is perfect for soaking tired feet after a day of hiking. The dining is excellent, with fresh-baked bread, a good wine list and delicious coffee grown and roasted right on the premises. The locally-recruited staff caters to your every whim. There's also a resident naturalist and bird expert who leads tours. 90 miles of hiking trails lead you to idyllic waterfalls and clear pools deep in the jungle. You can hike all day without seeing another human, but luxury is only as far away as you want it to be. *Info: Cooma Cairn Road. www.hiddenvalleyinn.com; Tel. 822-3320 or 866/443-3364 US.*

Windy Hill Resort $$$$$

This resort perches on a hilltop with cooling breezes and nice views, in a central location that's convenient for day trips around the region. The attentive staff and tasty food draw rave reviews. The wood-lined cottages have private bath and ceiling fans, and they are spacious and comfortable. Some have AC. There's a restaurant and bar, a fitness center, an elegant infinity pool and a gift shop. Several hiking trails begin on the grounds, and there are horses and birding guides on staff. *Info: www.windyhillresort.com; Tel. 824-2017.*

Du Plooy's $$$$

Everyone loves this friendly ecolodge. The location couldn't be better, on the Macal River, with the Belize Botanic Gardens next door. It's one of the top birding destinations in the country, with 300 species hanging around and expert bird guides on staff. The rooms are spacious and comfortable, with all mod cons, the personnel are extremely friendly, and the food is great. Unlike at some lodges, you'll have three meal options each night, including a vegetarian one. Du Plooy's gets a big thumbs-up for their environmental awareness. There are no plastic straws or paper napkins, and no beef on the menu (did you know that cattle emit more greenhouse gases than all the cars and trucks in the world?). The doubles are pricey, but there are several rooms for larger groups that are actually quite a good deal. *Info: Ten miles west of San Ignacio. www.duplooys.com; Tel. 824-3101 or 512/707-1863 US.*

Mariposa Jungle Lodge $$$$

This intimate lodge has six 400-square-foot cabanas, each with lovely furnishings and mod cons like wi-fi and hair dryers (but no phones or TVs). No AC either, but you won't miss it, as cool hilltop breezes cool the fully-screened rooms. Hammocks are the perfect place to listen to the birds. The pool is atmospheric and the food is delightful. Mariposa strives to be a true eco-resort, recycling and using biodegradable products whenever practical. *Info: www.mariposajunglelodge.com; Tel. 670-2113 or 304/224-2136 US.*

Mystic River Resort $$$$

This jungle resort gets consistently great reviews. The suites are huge and beautifully furnished. All have verandas overlooking the river. The restaurant and bar have similarly splendid views, and there's a nice little pool. Naturally, the birding is great, and horseback tours are a specialty. *Info: www.mysticriverbelize.com; Tel. 834-4100.*

Macaw Bank $$$

This small eco-friendly lodge is run by an expat American couple. The five cabanas are not luxurious, but are clean and comfortable, with everything you'll need. Ron and Al take great care of their guests, cook great food and follow sustainable practices. River tubing is a short walk away, and the most popular Mayan sites are nearby. *Info: www.macawbankjunglelodge.com; Tel. 665-7241.*

Gaia Riverlodge $$$

Formerly Five Sisters Lodge, this hotel overlooks the beautiful Five Sisters waterfall. There are 16 cute thatched cabanas with private baths, balconies and hammocks. There are plenty of birds and wildlife right on the grounds, and the location is great for exploring the sights of the area. *Info: www.gaiariverlodge.com; Tel. 834-4005 or 800/447-2931 US.*

Maya Mountain Lodge $$

Right in the jungle on lovely grounds, adjacent to a private reserve, are eight basic thatched cabanas, with inviting hammocks hanging from the eaves. This place is nothing fancy, but it's comfortable and friendly, and the forest is just as beautiful here as it is at the Blancaneaux. The rooms all have private bath and AC, but some are nicer than others, so choose carefully. The pool is very cool, surrounded by greenery. *Info: www.mayamountain.com; Tel. 824-2164.*

Moonracer Farm $$

Staying at this place is more like visiting friends than like going to a hotel. There are only two rooms, each with two queen beds and private bath, and everyone seems to love the owners, expats Tom and Marge. This is no luxury resort, but it's clean and comfortable. It's off the grid, so electricity is available only for necessities, such as wi-fi. Lighting is by lantern, and cooling is by the breezes that blow up here on Mountain Pine Ridge. *Info: www.moonracerfarm.com.*

BEST SLEEPS NEAR TIKAL

There are several very nice hotel options around Lake Petén Itzá and the town of Flores, but the ride to the ruins may take up to an hour.

La Lancha $$$$

Francis Ford Coppola's joint is handy enough for easy visits to the park. It is a 10-room boutique hotel with local furniture and colorful fabrics

everywhere. Big hammocks and comfortable spots to hang out are plentiful. There is a pool and the lake is a short walk away. "Gourmet" Guatemalan dishes are served in the restaurant. *Info: www.coppolaresorts.com/ lalancha; Tel. (502) 7928- 8331 or 800/746-3743 US.*

Camino Real Tikal $$$

This is the nicest mid-price place in the immediate area, an international chain-style lakefront resort with 72 first-class rooms featuring AC and other mod cons. Many of the rooms have balconies and a view of Lake Petén Itzá. There are two restaurants and a bar, and kayaks for exploring the lake. The food is fine, which is a good thing, as there is nowhere else to eat nearby. It's about a 45-minute ride to the ruins. *Info: www.caminorealtikal.com.gt; Tel. (502) 2410-5299.*

There are three places to stay right at the Tikal ruins site, but all are mediocre at best. There's nothing particularly wrong with the rooms, which are okay for the price, but the staff are jaded from years of tour-bus tourists whom they know won't ever be coming back. The food is as poor as the service. There are a couple of local-style *comedores* across the street that are cheaper and a little better. The three hotels are:

The Tikal Inn $$

This is the best of the three so-so hotels located adjacent to the ruins. It has a nice pool, and believe me, you will appreciate it after trudging around the ruins in the jungle humidity. *Info: www.tikalinn.com; Tel. (502) 7926- 1917.*

The Jaguar Inn $$
Next door to the Tikal Inn, the Jaguar has similar rooms at about the same price (75 bucks for a double room). *Info: www.jaguartikal.com; Tel. (502) 7926-0002.*

The Jungle Lodge $$
The third member of the Tikal rogues' gallery also has a pool, and is comparable to the other two. *Info: www.junglelodgetikal.com; Tel. (502) 2477-0570.*

BEST SHOPPING

On your way to or from San Ignacio, don't fail to stop at **Caesar's Place**, at Mile 60 on the Western Highway. This is about the best craft shop in the country, with all kinds of carvings, artworks, clothing and gift items from Belize and neighboring countries, as well as a good selection of CDs and tapes by Belizean musicians. There's also a small guest house, a restaurant and an internet café.

BEST SPORTS & RECREATION

SPELUNKING

The porous limestone that lies under much of Western Belize is home to the **Chiquibul** cave system, one of the most extensive in the hemisphere. There are endless opportunities for both beginning and expert cavers. Every tour operator in the west offers cave trips, but the big daddy spelunker is **Ian Anderson**, a Canadian who began exploring the caves and caverns of Belize in the early 1990s, and now presides over an empire of adventure travel that includes a jungle lodge and a wide variety of tours in the area (see *Best Sleeps*). *Info: www.cavesbranch.com.*

BIRDING

Belize is a birder's paradise. The variety of birds is simply amazing (over 566 species). As this small country has more bird species than some continents, birders (or *twitchers*, as the English call them) have plenty of opportunities to add species to their *life lists*.

The jungles of Western Belize harbor parrots, toucans, hummingbirds, chachalacas, trogons, woodpeckers, kiskadees, tanagers and oropendolas. At night, you may see one of the many stately species of owls. The unique ecosystem of **Mountain Pine Ridge** is home to some species that you won't see elsewhere. Many jungle lodges in the region, including the **Hidden Valley Inn**, have resident bird experts.

Yes, your chances of seeing something really rare are better in one of the remote parks. However, don't overlook more mundane locations – you might make a surprising number of sightings right on the grounds of your lodge. Mayan archaeological sites can have a wonderful variety of birds, which may be easier to see at such partially cleared sites than they are in the deep forest.

A few companies specialize in birding tours. Check out **Paradise Expeditions** (*www.birdinginbelize.com; Tel. 824-2772*), **Victor Emmanuel Nature Tours** (*www.ventbird.com; Tel. 800/328-VENT*) and **Exotic Birding** (*www.exoticbirding.com*).

HIKING

Walking and hiking possibilities in this region are endless. Many lodges

maintain their own trails, and most are open to non-guests as well. You can take plenty of nice day hikes right from San Ignacio – if that's all you have time for, then don't fail to do so. But to get the full experience, spend at least one night in the rain forest. The best time to see birds and other wildlife is always early in the morning, and there's simply something magical about waking up to the sounds of water dripping, birds singing and maybe a troop of howler monkeys baying in the distance. There are nice jungle lodges for all budgets (see *Best Sleeps*), so there's no need to rough it to be in position for the best hiking and birding.

HORSEBACK RIDING
Several lodges have equestrian centers on-site, including **Mountain Equestrian Trails** (*www.metbelize.com*), **Windy Hill Resort** (*www.windyhillresort.com*) near Mountain Pine Ridge, and **Banana Bank Lodge** (*www.bananabank.com*) near Belmopan. Horseback tours are available almost everywhere – ask any local tour operator.

CANOEING & KAYAKING
There's no white water around here. River trips tend to be relaxing affairs, unless you're there on a day when the cruise ships are in. **DuPlooy Travel** (*www.belize-vacation.com*) and **River Rat Tours** (*www.riverratbelize.com*) are just two of several operators in San Ignacio that offer canoeing and tubing on the Macal, Mopan and Belize rivers.

Ian Anderson's Adventures in Belize (*www.adventuresinbelize.com; Tel. 822-2800 or 866/822-2278 US*) offers river and sea kayaking trips among their huge menu of tours, as do many of the tour operators listed in the *Practical Matters* chapter.

WILDLIFE ATTRACTIONS
Tourist attractions are sprouting along the Western Highway like foliage in the rain forest, fertilized by a steady stream of day-trippers from the ships. If you are travelling with kids, and their interest in Little Brown Birds and Mayan ruins begins to wane, you'll have no trouble finding activities to keep them entertained, from swimming holes to ziplines to theme park-style water rides (oops, I mean cave tubing).

You can atone for such guilty pleasures by visiting one of several more educational attractions, which adults and kids will enjoy, and where you'll know that you're helping the country's wildlife by supporting the local people who study and preserve it.

Belize Botanic Gardens is a non-profit organization that runs the country's only formal botanic garden, in the beautiful Macal River Valley. Walk around the parklike grounds or take a hike in the jungle. You'll see a huge variety of lovely orchids, learn about the many plants that the local Maya have been using for centuries, and climb the tower to enjoy an expansive vista. You can even swim and tube in the river. If you come around dawn or dusk, you'll see a lot of wonderful birds as well. *Info: Open daily, 7am-5pm. Entry is $5 and a guided tour is $7.50. www.belizebotanic.org.*

Green Hills Butterfly Farm is a research facility featuring a huge screened-in flight area where flocks of flamboyant butterflies flit about freely. Kids and adults learn about the life cycle of these beautiful creatures. The hummingbirds that gather at the feeders are also fascinating to watch, as are the other birds that hang about the lush grounds. *Info: Open daily, 8am-4pm. Entry and guided tour $10 adults, $5 kids. www.green-hills.net; Tel. 834-4017.*

Located at the San Ignacio Resort Hotel right in town, **Green Iguana Project** is well worth a visit. The resort runs a captive breeding program, incubating and hatching the eggs and releasing juvenile iguanas into the wild. The exhibit is well-organized and informative, and takes about an hour to see. Also here is a network of easy hiking trails (see *Best Sleeps*).

GOLF
The only public golf course in mainland Belize (and the only one in the country since Caye Chapel closed down), **Roaring River Golf and Accommodations** is an 18-hole, par-64 course with unique natural beauty. The

river and the jungle surround you, as hundreds of species of birds serenade you. Just watch out for crocs in the water hazards, and ball-stealing monkeys. There are also a few air-conditioned hotel rooms and a restaurant. *Info: www.belizegolfcourses.com; Tel. 820-2031 or 664-5441.*

7. SOUTHERN BELIZE

HIGHLIGHTS
▲ **Cockscomb Basin Wildlife Sanctuary** – The Jaguar Reserve is one of the finest wildlife reserves in Belize, and it's easy to visit.

▲ **Mayflower Bocawina National Park** – This smaller park has most of the same attractions as Cockscomb, but fewer tourists.

▲ **Placencia** – This laid-back beach village has nice beaches and a full range of accommodations from budget to luxury.

▲ **Coral Reefs** – The famous barrier reef and a huge coral atoll are just a short boat ride offshore.

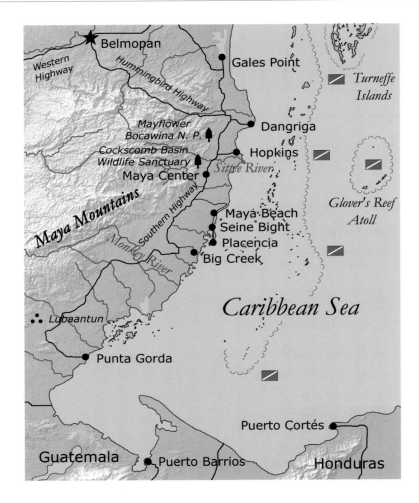

The southern **Stann Creek** and **Toledo** districts are far less known to outsiders than are the Cayes and the Cayo district. This is starting to change, as **Placencia** is evolving into one of the country's top beach resorts, but much of the region is still off the beaten path.

Down south you'll find **some of Belize's best beaches**, isolated islands offering delightful diving and fantastic fishing, jungle reserves teeming with birds and wildlife, and more mysterious Mayan ruins.

COCKSCOMB BASIN IN A DAY

If you have only a day, your best bet is to head for **Cockscomb Basin Wildlife Sanctuary**, also known as the Jaguar Reserve. This is one of the largest and nicest wildlife reserves in Belize, and it's easy to visit, even on a short trip. The 128,000-acre park is the world's only official jaguar sanctuary, and 60-80 of Belize's largest pussycats roam the mountains and river valleys.

Morning
The gateway to the park is **Maya Center**, home to a couple dozen local families who were relocated here when Cockscomb was declared a wildlife sanctuary. The villagers support themselves by providing guided tours, lodging and other services to park visitors. Although many tour operators can take you to the Reserve, the local guides from Maya Center are the best. These guys know the forest better than you and I know the way to our local post office, and if we call ahead, they're happy to pick us up from our lodge in Hopkins (or wherever) and take us straight to jaguar country. *Info: www.mayacenter.com; Tel. 533-7045.*

Cockscomb features an excellent network of **well-maintained trails** of various levels of difficulty. We'll hike along the river through some of the lushest rain forest in Belize, admiring the orchids and bromeliads, and checking off a few of the over 300 species of birds. All five of Belize's cat species live here, as does the rare Baird's tapir. Even here in **the heart of jaguar country**, we're not likely to see one of these shy nocturnal predators. We may very well see their tracks, however, and we're almost certain to hear one of the troops of black howler monkeys that live in the area. After a couple of hours of hiking, we'll stop at one of the lovely waterfall pools and cool down with a swim.

Afternoon
On our way back, we'll make a short stop at the **Maya Center Women's Group Gift Shop**, where you'll find nice wood and stone carvings, woven apparel and jewelry, most with the obligatory jaguar and/or ancient Mayan imagery. This is what the local women do while the men are leading tours in the jungle, and it provides another way for the locals to make some money and preserve their beautiful forest.

If we still have some time, we might pay a brief visit to Dangriga, the largest town in Southern Belize and the country's center of **Garifuna** culture. This colorful and funky town is the home of the **Punta Rock** style of music, and some of Belize's best folk musicians. The sound of drums pulsates through the city night and day.

The **Gulisi Garifuna Museum** has exhibits on the history and customs of this fascinating people, including dancing, drum-making and traditional medicine. *Info: Open Mon-Fri 10am-5pm, Sat 8am-noon. Entry $5. www.ngcbelize.org; Tel. 669-0639.*

There are several local artists and craftsmen who welcome visits to their studios. **Austin Rodriquez** makes traditional Garifuna drums, and **Benjamin Nicholas** paints charming paintings depicting events in Garifuna history.

A WEEKEND IN THE HOPKINS AREA

The sleepy Garifuna fishing village of **Hopkins** is conveniently located for trips to the forests of **Cockscomb** and **Mayflower**, as well as for the excellent reefs just offshore. A weekend isn't enough time for more than a sample of the region's attractions, but with careful planning we can get in visits to the rain forest and the mangroves, with some time left over for enjoying one of the finest beaches in Belize.

Friday Evening
This pleasant little town has a long sandy beach, and a wide selection of waterfront lodgings in all price ranges. **Hamanasi** and **Jaguar Reef** are both excellent luxury lodges. Travelers with moderate budgets will be delighted with the friendly **Hopkins Inn**. Even if you have a backpacker budget, you can stay right on the beach, at **Tipple Tree Beya** or **The Funky Dodo** (see *Best Sleeps*).

Despite the increasing number of tourists, Hopkins remains a fairly low-key village where the locals slowly go about their age-old business of fishing, drumming and carving dugout canoes. After we've lined up a tour for tomorrow morning, let's stroll around and soak up some of the thick Garifuna culture. We can have dinner at **King Kassava**, the main hangout in town, featuring cheap meals, stout drinks and colorful characters. We'll also pay a visit to **Lebeha**, a center for the local music scene. By day, it's a school where local youngsters take lessons in traditional Garifuna drumming. By night, it's a bar with a kicking drum jam where local musicians slap the skins until the wee hours. We'll head back to our hotel fairly early though, because we plan to be up at dawn to visit the rain forest.

Saturday

Cockscomb Basin Wildlife Sanctuary, also known as the Jaguar Reserve, is one of the largest and nicest wildlife reserves in Belize. It was established in 1990 to protect one of Central America's largest remaining populations of jaguars. The reserve includes some of the lushest rain forest in Belize, thick with orchids and bromeliads, and over 300 species of birds. It's home to all five of Belize's cat species – jaguar, puma, margay, ocelot and jaguarundi – as well as the rare

Baird's tapir (see photo), gibnuts, kinkajous, armadillos, boa constrictors and deadly fer-de-lance vipers. Even here in the heart of jaguar country, your chances of seeing one of these shy nocturnal predators are fairly slim. You may very well see their tracks, however, and you are likely to see (and will certainly hear) black howler monkeys.

Various local tour operators offer guided tours to the reserve, but the best deal is to hire a local guide directly from **Maya Center**, a village near the entrance to the sanctuary. Before the establishment of the park, the area was home to a few dozen Mayan families, who were relocated to Maya Center and trained to support themselves by guiding visitors to the rain forest (instead of cutting it down to grow crops). This is a classic ecotourism success story that we want to support with a few of our dollars. If we contact the Maya Center guides ahead of time, they'll pick us up from Hopkins. *Info: www.mayacenter.com; Tel. 533-7045.*

Cockscomb features an excellent network of well-maintained trails of various levels of difficulty. We'll spend a few hours hiking along the river, or perhaps up to Ben's Bluff, an overlook with a panoramic view of the undisturbed forest. Later on we'll cool down with a swim near one of the many lovely waterfalls.

Cockscomb Basin is the most popular park in the area, largely because it's so easily accessible, but it's far from the only one. In fact, over half the interior of this district is protected as some sort of park or reserve. If you'd like to get off the beaten tourist trail a little, visit **Mayflower Bocawina National Park** with its three small Mayan sites and the 100-foot-high **Antelope Falls**.

Sunday
Just south of Hopkins is the estuary of the **Sittee River**, a beautiful area of mangroves, marshes and lagoons that offers a nice contrast to mountainous Cockscomb. A river cruise with local guide **Horace Andrews** is one of the very best ways to see wildlife (and also a good way to rest our feet after all that hiking yesterday). We'll see turtles, crocodiles and iguanas, and some of the 200 species of birds that hang out around the river, from water birds such as tiger herons and snowy egrets to jungle birds such as oropendolas, chachalacas, trogons and parrots. If you prefer fish, Horace can put us on to them too. Anglers bag snook up to 26 pounds and tarpon from 10-70 pounds in the nearby Anderson and Boom Creek lagoons. *Info: www.belizebyhorace.com; Tel. 670-8358.*

A WEEKEND IN THE PLACENCIA AREA

The pleasant peninsula of **Placencia** might just be the perfect spot for a "surf and turf" vacation. We'll spend a day out in the Caribbean on a tiny caye, and a day cruising up a jungle river, getting glimpses of the two most biologically diverse habitats on Earth in a single weekend.

Friday Evening
Placencia is easy to get to. Both Maya Island Air and Tropic Air offer several daily flights from Belize City (see Chapter 8). We can fly to Belize City from the States, change planes, and be at Placencia's little airstrip in the afternoon. Our hotel will send a van to pick us up, and we'll be on island time in no time.

There's a huge selection of lodging in all price ranges, both on the peninsula and in the surrounding area. We plan a day of diving tomorrow, so we may choose one of the resorts that run their own dive operations: the **Robert's Grove** or the super-luxurious **Blancaneaux's Turtle Inn**. Those with more moderate budgets will like the **Sea Spray** or **One World**. See *Best Sleeps* for more information on these.

Wherever we stay, the first order of business on arrival is to remove shirt, shoes and wristwatch, grab an ice-cold beverage, and mosey on over to the beach or the pool.

Once we're properly refreshed from our travels, we'll take a stroll down Placencia's sidewalk, famous as the narrowest main street in the world, line up a dive trip for tomorrow morning, and see about a lobster dinner. Placencia is slowly but surely evolving into a major resort, but it still has a low-key, island-time vibe, more like Caye Caulker than like Ambergris Caye. It's one of the oldest communities in Belize. The ancient Mayans came here for fish and salt. British buccaneers founded the village in the 1600s, and it changed hands between the Spanish and the English a time or two. Today's residents are a broad mix of Creoles, Garifuna, Mestizos and plenty of Anglo expats.

Let's stop in at one (or both) of the two main local hangouts: the **Pickled Parrot** and the **Tipsy Tuna**. Either is a good place to have a cold beer (or the more adventurous may try a glass of "parrot piss") and a chat with some of the locals, expats and tourists propping up the bar at happy hour. When we get hungry, we can grab an inexpensive burger or plate of shrimp here, or we can head back to our hotel for a sit-down dinner. In either case, we'll hit the hay early tonight, so we can hit the reefs early tomorrow. *Info: www.placencia.com.*

Saturday

In the morning, we'll slug down a cup of fresh Belizean coffee, and stumble down to the end of the dock to meet our boat for a trip to the reefs. The barrier reef is quite close to shore in this area, and there's an endless selection of sites for diving and snorkeling. If you leave yourself in the hands of your divemaster, you're almost certain to be delighted with the sites he selects. Today however, we're going to visit some of the most pristine dive sites in the country, off the most remote of

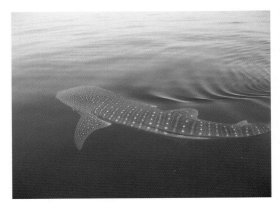

Belize's three coral atolls, **Glover's Reef Atoll**. An atoll is a ring of coral reefs surrounding a shallow lagoon. An atoll is formed when coral reefs grow around the shoreline of an island, then the island itself erodes away as the reefs continue to grow.

Glover's Reef, a protected Marine Reserve and a UNESCO World Heritage Site, offers a vast variety of dive sites for all skill levels, from snorkelers to expert divers. **Emerald Forest Reef** is an excellent site for snorkelers and novice divers, with depths of 15-70 feet, no current, and an amazing abundance of coral providing food and shelter to crabs, sea urchins, starfish and sponges, who are eaten in their turn by large jacks, snapper and grouper. Speaking of which, **Grouper Flats**, a large area of reefs ranging from 30-80 feet, is home to several species of our favorite fish: Nassau, tiger, black, spotted and marble groupers. If you're an advanced diver, we might visit **Shark Point**, a remote site frequented by nurse, blacktip, hammerhead and tiger sharks. Enormous (but harmless) **whale sharks** can be seen around Glover's from March-June. Getting to see the largest fish in the sea is the dive experience of a lifetime.

After the diving, let's pay a visit to one of the tiny coral islands that dot the ring of the atoll. We'll see huge flocks of seabirds, some of them seldom seen on the mainland, as well as wish-willies (iguanas), and possibly a saltwater crocodile or two. Sea turtles nest on the beaches from June-August. By the way, another animal that thrives here is the irritating sand flea, so bring a variety of bug repellents! On the way back to Placencia, we may see huge pods of spotted, bottlenose and spinner dolphins.

Glover's Atoll is also an excellent place for **fishing**. The lagoon inside the atoll has miles of shallow grass flats that are perfect territory for fly-fishing for bonefish, permit and tarpon, as well as over 700 patch reefs thick with yellowtail snapper. Offshore trolling produces billfish, wahoo and shark. Inquire at any of the dive shops about half- and full-day fishing charters.

Sunday
The **Monkey River**, one of Belize's major rivers with its headwaters high in the Maya Mountains, meets the Caribbean Sea about a half hour's boat ride south of the Placencia peninsula. A boat trip up the river is an excellent way to spend a day. A jungle river cruise is my favorite way to observe wildlife. You sit in (relative) comfort, instead of trudging through the mud, and your chances of seeing birds and animals are better than on a hike, because the river provides an opening in the thick forest.

South of the river is the large protected area of **Payne's Creek National Park**. Most of the park is impenetrable jungle, and there are no facilities for visitors, although there are a few hiking trails right around Monkey River Town. There are many troops of black howler monkeys in the area, as well as deer, armadillos, tapirs, ocelots and jaguars. The river is slap-full of crocodiles and manatees (to say nothing of tarpon and snook). Huge colonies of tiger heron and ibis live and breed in the area, and hawksbill sea turtles nest on the beaches.

At the mouth of the river is **Monkey River Town**, a very funky little village of about 200 people. There's no proper road to the village, so almost all access is by boat. Back in the bad old days of the banana industry, Monkey River was a sizable town, but as the banana industry declined, so did the town, and today the few villagers make their living from fishing and guiding ecotourists on trips to the river and the jungle. There are several local families with boats who run day trips, and you can contact them through any of the lodges in the area.

A few of the villagers offer rooms and meals, but the only thing that approximates a hotel is Clive's Place, also known as the **Sunset Inn**. Clive Garbutt is the best-known of the local guides. He and his family run wildlife and fishing trips. The inn has eight rooms with private bath, hot water and 24-hour electricity (a real luxury around here) as well as a restaurant and bar. *Info: www.monkeyriverbelize.com; Tel. 709-2028 or 720-2025.*

A WEEK IN SOUTHERN BELIZE

If you can spare a week for your Belize trip, the south is the best place to spend it. Here you can easily enjoy both the offshore world of the cayes and the jungles of the interior without any rushing around.

Gales Point
A short way south of Belize City, this tiny fishing village sits on a narrow strip of land between the ocean and the Southern Lagoon, a mangrove-lined estuary that's home to the largest community of West Indian manatees in the Caribbean (see the section on Caye Caulker in Chapter 4 for more about these gentle marine mammals). Much of the lagoon is a protected area, the **Gales Point Wildlife Sanctuary**. Inquire at the **Manatee Lodge** (see *Best Sleeps*) for a local guide to take you on a manatee-watching boat tour.

There's also excellent fishing for tarpon and snook in the lagoon and adjoining waterways. Between May and October, hawksbill and loggerhead sea turtles lay their eggs on the beaches around here.

Dangriga
Dangriga, formerly called Stann Creek, is the largest town in Southern Belize (population around 10,000) and the country's center of **Garifuna** culture. Locals claim that **Punta Rock**, the music that rules the Caribbean coast of Central America, originated here. Some of Belize's best folk musicians make their home here, and the sound of drums pulsates through the city night and day. The region is also famous for Garifuna cuisine, which features cassava bread, grilled fish and *hudut*, a savory dish made of mashed plantains.

As you ride into town, you are greeted by a large sign that reads *Mabuiga!* (Garifuna for Welcome!) and the **Drums of Our Fathers Monument**, a bronze sculpture of traditional Garifuna drums. Dangriga centers on a bridge over the North Stann Creek River. The south bank bustles with boats taking travelers to the various nearby cayes. On the north bank is the wild and wooly street market where fruit, vegetables and fresh fish are on sale.

Dangriga is the gateway to several forest reserves, including **Mayflower Bocawina National Park** and the **Cockscomb Basin Wildlife Sanctuary**, as well as the offshore wonders of **Glover's Atoll** and the barrier reef.

Dangriga isn't for everyone. It's more of a regional commercial center than a tourist resort. It's a typical Central American town of decaying wooden shacks on stilts, and the poverty you'll see here may be a little shocking. Though the town is on the water, the beaches right in town are grungy.

There are a couple of very minor tourist attractions in town, and most day tours of the region stop in at one or more of them for a little culture and a chat with some of the locals. The **Gulisi Garifuna Museum** is named for a Garifuna heroine named Gulisi, who came to Belize from Roatan with her 13 children and founded the settlement of Punta Negra. It's worth a short visit on the way out of town. *Info: Open Mon-Fri 10am-5pm, Sat 8am-noon. Entry $5. www.ngcbelize.org; Tel. 669-0639.*

There are several local artists and craftsmen who welcome visits to their studios. **Mr. Austin Rodriquez** and his daughters make traditional Garifuna drums, curing deer and cow hides with lime and salt and stretching them over carved wood bodies.

The Garifuna

The ancestors of the **Garifuna** (or Garinagu) were indigenous Caribs on the Caribbean island of St Vincent, and blacks from West Africa who arrived on the island in the 1600s. During the Napoleonic wars, the Garinagu allied themselves with French settlers, and as punishment, the British deported them to the island of Roatan, off Honduras. Soon the Garinagu began to migrate to the mainland, and today they live all along the Caribbean coast from southern Belize to northern Nicaragua. They have their own Garifuna language (most also speak Spanish or English) and several styles of folk music. Visitors also love Garifuna cuisine, served at thatched beach restaurants: cassava, conch soup and grilled fish. To learn more, see *www.garinet.com* or *www.ngcbelize.org.*

Benjamin Nicholas's charming paintings are in the Caribbean Primitive tradition, and depict events in Garifuna history. Dangriga's most famous son, **Pen Cayetano**, considered the founder of Punta Rock, is also an accomplished painter. His gallery is usually open only in November.

Another popular stop is Marie Sharp's famous hot sauce factory. *Info: www.mariesharps-bz.com.*

The biggest party of the year takes place around November 19, **Garifuna Settlement Day**. The anniversary of the Garinagu's 1832 arrival in Belize is a national holiday, and here in Dangriga it's the occasion for a whole week of revelry, including parades, all-night drumming, dancing and drinking, and a reenactment of the arrival of the first Garinagu in a "dorey" (dugout canoe).

There's a handful of very funky nightclubs and bars that sometimes have live music. You have a better chance here than anywhere else of seeing a good Punta Rock band inducing dancers to shake their hips at unbelievable speeds. You'll have to ask around to find out where the latest happening spot is, however.

The bus ride takes about three hours from Belize City, changing in Belmopan. By car, you should make it in less than two hours on the scenic Hummingbird Highway. Maya Island Air and Tropic Air both offer hourly flights from Belize City. *Info: There's some good info on the city's web site at www.dangrigalive.com and the regional site www.stanncreek.com.*

Hopkins & Sittee River

The sleepy Garifuna fishing village of **Hopkins** is conveniently located for trips to the forests of Cockscomb and Mayflower, as well as for the excellent reefs just offshore. The long and sandy beach is a fine one, and you'll find a nice selection of beachfront accommodations and plenty of beachy activity. A couple of places in town rent windsurfers, kayaks and other watercraft, and two dive resorts just south of town run daily trips to the barrier reef and Glover's Atoll (see *Best Sports & Recreation*).

Despite the fair number of tourists milling about, Hopkins has less bustle than San Pedro or Cayo. The hairy backpackers and tanned jet-setters tend to rush from the rain forest to the reefs, while the locals slowly go about their age-old business of fishing, drumming and carving their dugout canoes. The Garifuna culture is thick here. Be sure to pay a visit to **Lebeha**, a drum school offering lessons by day, a bar with a happening drum jam by night. *Info: The town runs a decent little web site at www.hopkinsbelize.com.*

Just south of Hopkins is the estuary of the **Sittee River**. One of Belize's largest rivers, the Sittee has its source high in the jungles, and ends up here in a vast area of mangroves, marshes and lagoons. Whether you like birds or fish, you'll find them here. Local guide **Horace Andrews** can put you on to either or both. Anglers bag snook up to 26 pounds and tarpon from 10-70 pounds in the nearby Anderson and Boom Creek lagoons.

River cruises are one of the very best ways to see wildlife. You're sure to see turtles, crocodiles and iguanas, and you may see any of the 200 species of birds that hang out around the river. Tiger herons snowy egret kingfishers flycatcher oropendola seedeater kiskadee chachalaca honeycreeper tanager trogon parrots hawks kite, falcons etc etc…It's also easy to rent canoes or kayaks and poke about on your own. *Info: www.belizebyhorace.com; Tel. 670-8358.*

Cockscomb Basin Wildlife Sanctuary

Also known as the **Jaguar Reserve**, this is one of the largest and nicest wildlife reserves in Belize. It's quite easy to visit, whether you're coming for a short hike or a multi-day backcountry trek. The 128,000-acre reserve was established in 1990, largely thanks to the efforts of naturalist Alan Rabinowitz, who came here to study the jaguar, Belize's largest cat (as told in his fascinating book, *Jaguar*). Today the park is run by the Belize Audubon Society, and 60-80 jaguars are believed to roam the jungle-clad mountains in peace. *Info: www.belizeaudubon.org.*

The reserve includes some of the lushest rain forest in Belize, and is home to all five of Belize's cat species, as well as the rare Baird's tapir, howler monkeys, boa constrictors and deadly *tommygoffs*.

It's amazing that a park this accessible is such a great place to see wildlife. On my last visit, we saw a kinkajou, a paca, a tayra and a beautiful margay, as well as jaguar footprints and scat! Comments in the visitors' book detailed recent sightings of pumas, jaguars and jaguarundis. I highly recommend a night hike (guided, of course).

The park features a network of wide, well-maintained trails. You can hike along the river for an hour or two, swim in one of the many lovely waterfalls, or float down the river on an inner tube. One of the most popular medium-difficulty hikes takes you to Ben's Bluff, an overlook with a panoramic view of the undisturbed forest. Serious adventurers can tackle the four-to-five day expedition to **Victoria Peak**, the highest point in Belize at 3,828 feet. Before the establishment of the park, the area was home to a few dozen Maya families, who now live at a place called **Maya Center** near the entrance to the sanctuary. Here you'll find a museum of Mayan culture, a craft shop, some basic lodging and several local guides who offer tours of the reserve.

The villagers used to make their living by clear-cutting the rain forest to grow corn, but now they are doing well providing services to tourists. This is a classic ecotourism success story, but it will only work if the locals do make some money, so be sure to hire a local guide, and stop in at Maya Center and drop a few dollars!

Maya Center is about 20 miles south of Dangriga on the Southern Highway. Here you pay the park entrance fee of $5, then take a dirt road another six miles to the sanctuary entrance. Buses to Punta Gorda will stop here on request.

Tutzil Nah Cottages, run by the Chun family, offers rudimentary rooms with private bath and 24-hour electricity (luxury!) for under $30 double. The ladies cook basic meals on request. Staying here is an unbeatable cultural experience, like staying at the home of a Mayan family. Contact them ahead of time, and they'll pick you up from your lodge. Maya Center has a couple of other families that offer cottages. There are also some very basic cabins and a campground, right at the sanctuary entrance.

Any of the local Maya Center guides will give you a great tour, but if they're available, go with one of the Chun brothers, who lived here before the sanctuary was founded, and know the jungle better than you and I know the way to our local post office. Julian Chun was one of Alan Rabinowitz's main assistants during his work here, as detailed in the book *Jaguar*. A walk with him is the wildlife experience of a lifetime. Tours cost about $50 per person. *Info: www.mayacenter.com; Tel. 533-7045.*

The **Maya Center Mayan Museum** features a traditional Mayan house, but the real attraction is the locals themselves, who will share stories about their culture, play a little of their music, and demonstrate how they process such local goodies as sugar cane, chocolate and coffee. The Saqui family also offers guided tours and basic lodging. *Info: Entry $10. www.cockscombmayatours.com.*

Mayflower Bocawina National Park

Just south of Dangriga, Mayflower is a newer (2001) and smaller (7,000 acres) park than Cockscomb Basin. Mayflower sees fewer tourists, but it has equally beautiful rain forest and a couple of nice waterfalls, it's also teeming with wildlife, and it has a well-maintained network of hiking trails. 238 species of birds have been observed here, including several rare varieties of motmots, trogons, macaws, parrots and toucans. Black howler monkeys are often seen, and you might also spot a coati (a *quash*), a tree-climbing Belizean gray fox, a paca, agouti, kinkajou, peccary, giant anteater or the paw print of a jaguar.

There are three **Mayan sites** in the park, all of them small sites belonging to the Post-Classic Period. The Mayflower Site is right ácross from the visitors' center. A short hike away are the Maintzunun ("Hummingbird") and T'au Witz sites. All are only partially excavated, and not terribly interesting.

The most popular hiking trail is a nice easy walk to the Bocawina and Three Sisters waterfalls, beautiful falls with large pools at the bottom that are perfect for a cooling swim. A more strenuous hike (2-3 hours) leads to **Antelope Falls**, a 100-foot-high cascade that also has nice pools for swimming, as well as an awesome view of the jungle and the Caribbean Sea below.

There are several camping places in the park for those who want to make a multi-day trek. You can hire licensed tour guides in the nearby village of Silk Grass, but the best way to experience this park is to stay a couple of nights at the eco-friendly **Mama Noots Eco Resort**, which is located within the park boundaries. They have basic but comfortable cabins at a moderate price (see *Best Sleeps*). *Info: The visitors' center is about four miles up a well-maintained dirt road that takes off at mile six of the Southern Highway. Entry $5.*

Glover's Reef Marine Reserve

Glover's Reef Atoll, named for pirate John Glover, is the most remote of Belize's three coral atolls (about 35 miles southeast of Dangriga), and it has some of the most pristine dive sites in the country.

An atoll is a ring of coral reefs surrounding a shallow lagoon. An atoll is formed when coral reefs grow around the shoreline of an island, then the island itself erodes away as the reefs continue to grow. There are only four atolls in the Western Hemisphere, and three of them are in Belize. This unique ecosystem is a protected Marine Reserve and a UNESCO World Heritage Site.

The eastern side of the atoll is dotted with tiny coral islands, a few of which have small dive lodges. The nicest (and priciest) is **Isla Marisol Resort**, which has bungalows with private bath, hot water and AC. Also right on the atoll are **Glover's Atoll Resort**, which has camping, dorm beds and thatched cabins, and **Slickrock Adventures**, which has some basic cabanas on Long Caye. These two places are pretty rustic but are perfect for those who want to be right in the middle of the best diving and fishing, and don't require luxury. In case you do, try nearby **Thatch Caye**, or one of the upscale resorts near Dangriga (see *Best Sleeps*).

Glover's offers a vast variety of dive sites for all skill levels, from snorkelers to advanced divers. The outside of the ring has some excellent walls, and within the lagoon are over 700 patch reefs.

Emerald Forest Reef, on the northeast end of the atoll, is an excellent site for snorkelers and novice divers, with depths of 15-70 feet and no current. The site is named for its amazing abundance of coral. Every variety of coral known to live in this area has been seen here, including boulder, finger,

brain, pencil and 10-foot-high stands of elkhorn. Hiding in this underwater rain forest are all kinds of crabs, sea urchins, starfish and sponges. Farther up the food chain, jacks, snapper and grouper prowl.

Long Caye Wall is a great site for both beginners and

advanced divers, and it's possible to dive from shore. Depths range from less than 20 feet to infinity. A shallow reef leads to a sloping region of sand inhabited by a forest of garden eels. Beyond is the wall, dropping straight down thousands of feet to the ocean bottom. All kinds of coral, including black coral, cover the wall, while off in the water column you may see pelagic creatures such as sharks, sea turtles, eagle and manta rays.

Grouper Flats is a name to get any diver's heart pumping. This large area of reefs ranges in depth from 30-80 feet, and is home to several species of our favorite fish: Nassau, tiger, black, spotted and marble groupers.

Shark Point might just kick your blood pressure up yet another notch. It's a remote site requiring a bit of a long boat ride, with typically rough seas and depths down to 90 feet, so it's recommended for advanced divers only. Nurse, blacktip, hammerhead and tiger sharks consistently hang around this large area of reef.

The area is also famous for **whale sharks**. These enormous (but harmless) fish can be seen around here from March-June around full moon nights. Snapper spawn here in vast numbers around that time, and the whale sharks come to feed on the eggs. The sight of thousands of snappers spawning in a huge ball, while giant whale sharks swim overhead slurping up the eggs, could be the dive experience of a lifetime.

There are a few other things to do out here other than dive. There's **excellent fishing** in the lagoon – snapper on the patch reefs, bonefish and permit on the flats. The lagoon is also a splendid place for cruising around in a kayak. Spotted, bottlenose and spinner dolphins hang around in huge schools. Sea turtles nest on the beaches from June-August. On land, you'll see huge flocks of seabirds, as well as wish-willies (iguanas), and possibly a saltwater crocodile or two. By the way, another animal that thrives here is the irritating sand flea, so bring a variety of bug repellents!

Southwater Caye

This little island sits right on top of the barrier reef, about 14 miles off of Hopkins. Splendid wall diving is right offshore, protected by the new Southwater Caye Marine Park. There are three basic dive lodges on the island: **Pelican Beach Resort** (*www.pelicanbeachbelize.com*), the **Blue Marlin Lodge** (*www.bluemarlinlodge.com*) and **International Zoological Expeditions** (*www.ize2belize.com*), which mainly caters to student groups (see *Best Sleeps*).

Thatch Caye

My favorite Belizean island lodge is on its own tiny island just north of Southwater Caye. This eco-friendly resort offers first-class accommodations (camping is also available), a small but excellent dive operation, guided fly-fishing and other water sports (see *Best Sleeps*).

Tobacco Caye

Just north of Southwater Caye, this tiny dot of sand is also smack-dab on top of the barrier reef. There's fantastic snorkeling and diving right from the shore – a spectacular wall is just a few hundred feet out. Tobacco Caye has a little more action going on than the other cayes in the area. There's regular boat service from Dangriga, and half a dozen rustic lodges. In fact, things can get a little crowded here during high season, as it's quite a popular destination, and only a small island.

The accommodations here are fairly backpacker-style, but some do not have backpacker prices, and all have received mixed reviews. You can try your luck at **Tobacco Caye Diving** (*www.tobaccocayediving.com*), **Tobacco Caye Lodge** (*www.tclodgebelize.com*) or **Reef's End Lodge** (*www.reefsendlodge.com*), but nearby Thatch Caye (see *Best Sleeps*) offers a better class of lodging, and you may end up going diving with their crew anyway.

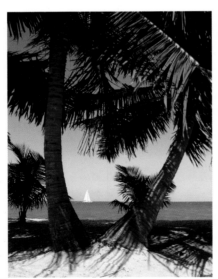

Placencia

Once an off-the-beaten-path spot known only to a few divers and backpackers, the **Placencia** area is slowly but surely evolving into a major resort (the same is true of Belize as a whole). However, it still has a low-key, island-time sort of vibe. Beachfront resorts, including luxury complexes and backpacker shacks, are strung out along a long, narrow peninsula. The villages of **Maya Beach** and **Seine Bight** are towards the north, and **Placencia Town** itself is at the southern end.

The **beaches** here are beautiful but, typical for Belize, there's lots of seagrass and few waves. Between the peninsula and the mainland, Placencia Lagoon is a peaceful waterway where nature-lovers take canoe trips to see manatees and a wealth of birds, and anglers tangle with huge snook. Just off-shore are world-class diving and snorkeling on the barrier reef and **Glover's Reef Atoll** (see above), and the rain forest preserves of

To & From Honduras

The **D-Express boat** makes weekly trips to Puerto Cortés in Honduras, stopping at Big Creek and Placencia. The boat leaves from Placencia every Friday at 9:30am, and from Puerto Cortés every Monday at 11am. Cost is $63. *Info: www.belizeferry.com; Tel. 624-6509 or 523-4045.*

Cockscomb Basin and **Mayflower Bocawina** are a short ride inland. From the tourist's standpoint, Placencia has everything Ambergris has, and then some.

Placencia town itself is quite small (about 600 residents), and far from urban – a few clusters of buildings among the palms. There's one dreadful dirt road, and a long pedestrian sidewalk ("the narrowest main street in the world") that passes by most of the hotels, restaurants and other points of interest. The airstrip, just north of town, is served by several daily flights from Belize City on both Maya Island Air and Tropic Air. At the southern tip of the peninsula are the docks, where you can catch a boat out to one of the Cayes, or south to Honduras.

Placencia is one of the oldest communities in Belize. The ancient Mayans came here for fish and salt. British buccaneers founded the village in the 1600s, and it changed hands between the Spanish and the English a time or two. Today's residents are a broad mix of Creoles, Garifuna, Mestizos and plenty of Anglo expats.

There are a few resorts in the area that have their own dive shops, including **Robert's Grove** (*www.robertsgrove.com*) and **Blancaneaux's Turtle Inn** (*www.blancaneaux.com*). See *Best Sleeps* for more information on these. There are also a few dive shops in Placencia Town, including the **Seahorse Dive Shop** (*www.belizescuba.com*), Avadon Divers (*www.avadondiversbelize.com*) and **Splash Dive Shop** (*www.splashbelize.com*). See *Best Sports & Recreation* for more information on Placencia diving. *Info: www.placencia.com.*

Monkey River

The **Monkey River**, one of Belize's major rivers with its headwaters high in the Maya Mountains, meets the Caribbean Sea about a half hour's boat ride south of the Placencia peninsula. A boat trip up the river is an excellent way to spend a day. A jungle river cruise is my favorite way to observe wildlife. You sit in (relative) comfort, instead of trudging through the mud, and your chances of seeing birds and animals are better than on a hike, because the river provides an opening in the thick forest.

South of the river is the large protected area of **Payne's Creek National Park**. Most of the park is impenetrable jungle, and there are no facilities for visitors, although there are a few hiking trails right around Monkey River Village. There are many troops of black howler monkeys in the area, as well as deer, armadillos, tapirs, ocelots and jaguars. The river is slap-full of crocodiles and manatees (to say nothing of tarpon and snook). Huge colonies of tiger heron and ibis live and breed in the area, and hawksbill sea turtles nest on the beaches.

At the mouth of the river is **Monkey River Town**, a very funky little village of about 200 people. There's no proper road to the village, so almost all access is by boat. Back in the bad old days of the banana industry, Monkey River was a sizable town, but as the banana industry declined, so did the town, and today the few villagers make their living from fishing and guiding eco-tourists on trips to the river and the jungle. There are several local families with boats who run day trips, and you can contact them through any of the lodges in the area.

If you really want to experience the jungle, spend the night in Monkey River Town, so that you can be on the river at dawn. This will give you your best chance of seeing birds and wildlife, and your only realistic chance of a trophy sighting such as a cat or a tapir. A few of the villagers offer rooms and meals, but the only thing that approximates a hotel is Clive's Place, also known as the **Sunset Inn**. Clive Garbutt is the best-known of the local guides. He and his family run wildlife and fishing trips. The inn has eight rooms with private bath, hot water and 24-hour electricity (a real luxury around here) as well as a restaurant and bar. *Info: www.monkeyriverbelize.com; Tel. 709-2028 or 720-2025.*

Punta Gorda & The Toledo District

Punta Gorda ("PG" for short) is the southernmost town of any size in

Belize and the capital of the Toledo district, about four hours by car (closer to six on the bus) from Belize City. The population of around 6,000 people is a mixture of Maya, Garifuna and Creoles.

PG has a pleasant waterfront promenade (though the beach is not very nice for swimming), an active morning street market four days a week, and some lively drumming and other local music going on in the bars. Sleepy, hot, humid and not terribly clean, the town has a friendly, relaxed vibe – some love it, some hate it. Its main attraction is as a gateway to the various sights in the region, including the Mayan site of **Lubaantun**, the nearby Mayan villages, wildlife reserves and boat trips to Guatemala.

There are several tour operators in town. I highly recommend **Tide Tours**, which is associated with TIDE, a conservation group that manages several local national parks and reserves. They offer a wide range of tours from half a day to a week or more. Hiking, horseback riding and canoeing are all fine ways to see the jungle, the Mayan villages, and the many waterfalls and caves. Fishing, diving, snorkeling, kayaking and river cruises are also on the menu. *Info: www.tidetours.org; Tel. 722-2129.*

The Toledo District has several easily-accessible attractions for day trips, including the Agua Caliente hot springs at Big Falls, the Hokeb Ha Cave at Blue Creek and the small but fascinating Mayan site of **Nim Li Punit**, which has over 25 elaborately-carved stelae.

There are also several large nature reserves, including some of the country's most remote and pristine rain forest areas: the **Columbia River Forest Reserve**, **Río Blanco National Park** with its splendid waterfalls, and **Payne's Creek National Park**, 39,000 acres of broadleaf forest, pine savannah and mangrove lagoons, a major breeding area for the West Indian manatee and home to over 300 species of birds.

Offshore are the 500-square-mile **Port Honduras Marine Reserve** and the **Sapodilla Cayes Marine Reserve**, which protects the south-ernmost set of islands in Belize. These parks have few or no facili-

To & From Guatemala

Requena's Charters offers daily boat service from Punta Gorda to Puerto Barrios, Guatemala. The boat leaves PG at 9am, and returns from Puerto Barrios at 2pm. The crossing takes about an hour. *Info: www.belizenet.com/requena; Tel. 722-2070.*

ties for visitors, but can be explored in the company of a local guide. If you like visiting marine reserves, these are are both worthy trips.

If you'd like to venture off the usual tourist trail for a real cultural experience, visit one of the small Mayan villages in the region. The **Toledo Ecotourism Association** has developed a program to bring visitors to ten local villages, with a focus on cultural exchange and environmental conservation. The TEA guesthouses are clean but very basic: bunk beds with mosquito netting, and a bucket outdoors for showering. *Info: www.southernbelize.com/tea.html; Tel. 722-2096.*

Residents sleep in simple thatched huts, and eat beans and tortillas made from the corn they grow in their *milpas*. Electricity and running water are newfangled innovations. Most of the people are friendly but a bit shy. As usual, you'll find the children the best cultural ambassadors. This would be an excellent trip to take with your kids, if they (and you) can handle roughing it a bit.

Each of the villages has various points of interest nearby that you can hike to, including caves, waterfalls, Mayan ruins and nature reserves. Local guides will show you the medicinal plants that the villagers harvest from the jungle, and demonstrate traditional crafts. Getting to the villages by public transport is not so easy, as buses generally run from Punta Gorda only once per week, on market days.

Lubaantun

The largest Mayan site in Southern Belize is about 26 miles northwest of Punta Gorda, near the village of San Pedro Columbia. **Lubaantun** dates from the Mayan Classic era, and was a prosperous commercial center around 700-900 AD. The five plazas are surrounded by 14 major structures, including three ball courts, on a lovely site between two small rivers.

Lubaantun has some architectural features that are unique among Belizean Mayan sites. Most of the structures were built of large stones laid without mortar (perhaps inspiring the modern name, which means "Place of Fallen Stones"), and some of the pyramids have unusual rounded corners.

The modern history of the site is quite colorful. One early explorer is believed to have dynamited a couple of the temples, and another apparently planted a fabulous (but fake) crystal skull at the site in 1926, causing a controversy that went on for years.

Lubaantun is easy to get to by car, or on a guided tour from Punta Gorda. You can also hire a local guide at the small visitors' center, which has a small display of ceramic figurines and pottery found at the site. *Info: www.southernbelize.com/lubaantun.html. Open daily 8am-5pm. Entry $5.*

BEST SLEEPS & EATS

GALES POINT
Manatee Lodge $$$
This remote little lodge has a spectacular location, right on the lagoon, adjacent to miles of deserted beach. The staff are nice and the activities are great, but the eight rooms are a bit run down and overdue for renovation. Hang around with the manatees, look for sea turtles on the beach, or fish in the lagoon for snook and tarpon. *Info: www.manateelodge.com; Tel 220-8040 or 877/462-6283 US.*

DANGRIGA
Dangriga, the largest town in Southern Belize, has several mostly budget lodgings right in town, and there are some splendid resorts in the surrounding countryside and on the nearby cayes. As I discussed in Chapter 4, the remote island getaways aren't for everyone. The only access is by private boat, which usually runs only once or twice per week, so once you're there, you're there.

Thatch Caye Resort $$$$
This place opened in 2008, and has already earned several prestigious awards, as well as rave reviews from guests. Owners Steve and Travis took eight years to build it by hand, bringing everything by boat. On my visit, I found a very well-run upscale resort that ranks as one of the best island lodges in the country. Casitas have every amenity you could want, including refrigerators, ceiling fans and rooftop hammocks. They also have AC, but to date, no one has needed to use it. The main lodge features beautiful woodwork and amazing artistry in rattan. Divemasters Ian, Emily and Chico (who has been diving in these

waters for 17 years) lead snorkeling and diving trips to the barrier reef, a short boat ride away, or only slightly farther, to Glover's Reef, perhaps the most pristine dive site in Belize. Flats fishing for bones, tarpon and permit is also on offer. This is a very eco-friendly lodge – sun and wind provide electricity, and rainwater fills the cisterns for showers. But every luxury is here, including wi-fi. *Info: www.thatchcaye.com; Tel. 532-2414 or 800/ 435-3145 US.*

Isla Marisol $$$$
Located on a tiny caye on Glover's Reef just off Dangriga, this resort draws high praise from serious divers and fishers, who come on weeklong packages. The reefs in the area are spectacular and pristine, and there's excellent fly fishing on the flats. The bungalows are no luxury chalets, but they are clean and comfortable enough, with private bathrooms and AC (which seems to run only at night). *Info: www.islamarisolresort.com; Tel. 522-0235, 610-4204 or 866/990-9904 US.*

Coco Plum Island Resort $$$$
This island lodge has 14 brightly-painted wooden cabanas, each with a

veranda (with hammock, of course) as well as AC and all the mod cons that you'd expect on a tiny tropical island. Diving and fishing are the main attractions of course, but Coco Plum also specializes in honeymoon and wedding packages. Everyone loves the attentive staff. *Info: www.cocoplumcay.com; Tel. 800/763-7360 US.*

Blue Marlin Lodge $$$$
This lodge on South Water Caye, near Dangriga, has a couple of lodging options – the best are the newer beach cabins, which have AC and nice Caribbean décor. A variety of weekly diving and fishing packages are on offer. This place is nothing fancy (the management themselves describe it as "rustic" and "funky"), but it's comfortable, and the staff are great (don't

believe them when they say there are no sand fleas, though). *Info: www.bluemarlinlodge.com; Tel. 522-2243 or 800/798-1558 US.*

Mama Noots Eco Resort $$$

This relaxed jungle lodge is located in Mayflower Bocawina National Park. Millions of birds race about, and hiking trails lead to picture-perfect waterfalls surrounded by greenery. The cabins are on the rustic side (management says they have a "rugged outdoors feel"), but they are clean and comfortable enough, with private bath and fans but no AC. New owners recently took over, ditched the old name "Backabush," and spruced things up a bit. This is a very eco-friendly lodge, powered by hydro and solar electricity. *Info: www.mamanoots.com; Tel. 670-8019 or 928/300-1969 US.*

The **Riverside Café**, right by the boat docks in Dangriga, is about the only sit-down restaurant in town, and serves good seafood and Belizean fare. There are a few little thatched beach spots that serve grilled fish and other Garifuna goodies. For a super-cheap and tasty meal, hit one of the little improvised streetside barbecue stands.

HOPKINS

This peaceful little Garifuna village is not known as a tourist hotspot – yet. But the area does have a wide variety of accommodations, including a couple of luxury lodges and several decent low-budget spots.

Hamanasi Adventure and Dive Resort $$$$$

Everyone loves this small and intimate resort. The staff remembers your name, and goes above and beyond to make sure you have a great vacation. From the shady, bird-infested grounds to the flowers strewn on your bed, to the candlelit dinners of seafood fresh from the dock, all the elements of a dream vacation or honeymoon are here. The rooms are spacious and luxurious, with AC, private porches, elegant hardwood furniture and comfortable beds. Phones? TVs? Bah! Don't need 'em. The beachfront rooms are nice, but the most popular are the treehouses, freestanding cabanas 12 feet up in the air, with colorful birdies to sing right outside your window in the morning. Naturally, a full range of diving and other tours can be arranged, but this isn't a hard-core dive lodge. *Info: www.hamanasi.com; Tel. 533-7073 or 877/552-3483 US.*

Jaguar Reef Lodge $$$$$
This resort does a great job of delivering that relaxing Caribbean vacation. It's especially popular for weddings and honeymoons. The highlights are the long and lovely sandy beach, and spectacular fishing and diving. Beachfront cabanas and poolside suites are spacious, clean and attractive, with tile floors and local art on the walls. Fishing opportunities include snook and tarpon on the Sittee River; flats fishing for bonefish and permit; and reef trips for barracuda, kingfish and wahoo. Amenities include two swimming pools and a Jacuzzi, a restaurant and bar on a pleasant beachfront patio, high-speed internet access, and free use of sea kayaks and mountain bikes. *Info: www.jaguarreef.com; Tel. 533-7040 or 888/731-1132 US.*

Villa Verano $$$$$
This new luxury resort next to the Jaguar Reef is already collecting a string of rave reviews. All the rooms are sumptuously furnished, and have everything, including AC, TV, wi-fi, small fridges, hair dryers, etc. Large parties can rent a four- or five-bedroom condo or an entire villa. There's a huge beachfront pool, a fitness center, a game room with a pool table for rainy days, and kayaks and catamarans for nicer weather. *Info: www.villaveranobelize.com; Tel. 533-7016 or 877/646-2317 US.*

Kanantik $$$$$
This remote luxury resort, midway between Hopkins and Placencia, offers a bit of European flair in the Central American jungle. The 25 air-conditioned cabanas are spacious, private and lovely, with rich wood floors and Mayan-themed décor. The beach is long, sandy and palm-shaded, and the pool is cool. There's a complete dive operation on site. The dining is a highlight. Everyone enjoys the pizzas made in a real wood oven, and

the coffee from a real Italian espresso machine. Garifuna dancers entertain weekly. The owner is a real character – most guests love him. *Info: www.kanantik.com; Tel. 533-7048 or 877/759-8834.*

Belizean Dreams $$$$ These luxurious oceanfront villas have beautiful kitchens and large verandahs overlooking the sea. The immaculate grounds include an infinity pool and a beautiful beach. A friendly concierge is on hand to book tours and see to your every need. The poolside Woven Palm restaurant serves up a gourmet fusion of Belizean and Mediterranean cuisine. *Info: www.belizeandreams.com; Tel. 523-7271 or 800/456-7150 US.*

Hopkins Bay Resort $$$$

The sister property to Belizean Dreams offers the same level of luxury, with an infinity pool, concierge service and even in-room massages. The villas have one, two or three bedrooms, each with full kitchens, AC, wi-fi and every luxury amenity. The Orange Grove Caribbean Café presents trendy island fare. *Info: www.hopkinsbayresort.com; Tel. 523-7284 or 800/785-1721 US.*

Beaches and Dreams Seafront Inn $$$

This basic but friendly little resort is on the beach in Hopkins. There are only four cabanas, all with private bath, clad in hardwood with cheerful Caribbean décor. Great fishing trips leave from the private dock. The restaurant is a local favorite. *Info: www.beachesanddreams.com; Tel. 523-7259.*

Sir Thomas' at Toucan Sittee $$$

This lodge is on 18 acres of jungle on the banks of the Sittee River. The quaint bungalows put you right in the middle of the forest, but have mod cons including fridges and wi-fi. Birders and wildlife enthusiasts will love this place. *Info: www.sir-thomas-at-toucan-sittee.com; Tel. 523-7039 or 669-7480.*

Hopkins Inn $$
Right in Hopkins, this modest inn has beachfront cabanas with private bath, refrigerators, coffee makers, fans and small verandahs. Nothing fancy, but spotlessly clean, and the owners are wonderful. You can have breakfast in your room, and other meals at one of the nearby restaurants. The beach bar next door is a blast. *Info: www.hopkinsinn.com; Tel. 523-7283.*

Glover's Atoll Resort $$
This tiny island on Glover's Reef has cheap, basic accommodations for every (low) budget: quaint thatched cabins over the water, dorm beds and a campground. There's limited electricity and no running water, but there is a dive center and a little restaurant, and all the coconuts you can eat or drink are free! The boat goes every Sunday from Sittee River, and is included in the price of a week's stay. *Info: www.glovers.com.bz; Tel. 532-2916.*

Hopkins is becoming a bit of a hip backpacker spot, and budget lodgings are sprouting up. Two nice beachfront ones are **Tipple Tree Beya** (*www.tippletree.com; Tel. 520-7006*) and **The Funky Dodo** (*www.thefunkydodo.com; Tel. 667-0558*).

The main hangout in Hopkins is **King Kassava**, a restaurant and bar located right in the center of town where the buses stop. Cheap meals, stout drinks and colorful characters. **Lebeha** is a drum school that also has some beachfront cabanas, a restaurant and bar, where the locals slap the skins until the wee hours.

BEST SLEEPS IN PLACENCIA
Placencia town is located at the end of a long peninsula, an hour's drive on a bone-rattling dirt road from the Southern Highway. Right in town, there are lots of budget and midrange lodgings, perfect for those who want to be part of the scene. The upscale resorts are located just north of town, most of them a medium walk or a short taxi ride away. Farther north, around the village of Maya Beach, are a few more resorts in various price ranges. Some guests like the seclusion up there, but others feel trapped, and don't dig the tedious (and expensive) ride into town.

Chabil Mar Villas $$$$$
These luxurious bougainvillea-wreathed villas draw consistent rave reviews from guests. Most are two-bedroom units, and all have full kitchens with

all the modern gadgets, dishwashers, washer/dryers, TV with DVD player, free wireless internet, and on and on. There are beautiful tile bathrooms and colorful local art on the walls (including a jaguar mural in my room – a sure way to guarantee a good re-

view). There's no dining room, but there's a full menu and bar – all delivered wherever you like – in your room, on the beach, by the pool…in fact everything can be handled right in your room, even checking in and out. Iguanas roam the lush grounds, the two infinity pools are refreshing, and the sandy beach is neatly raked. The staff know their jobs well, and always have a friendly hello. Luxury and privacy are the watchwords here (although it's a short walk into Placencia). For a romantic getaway or a family trip, this is my top choice. *Info: www.chabilmarvillas.com; Tel. 523-3606 or 866/417-2377 US.*

Blancaneaux's Turtle Inn $$$$$

One of Francis Ford Coppola's two properties in Belize, this beachfront resort is known as one of the most luxurious in the country. There's a variety of accommodations, from seaview cottages to huge seafront villas. All are spacious, sumptuously appointed and decorated in Asian style.

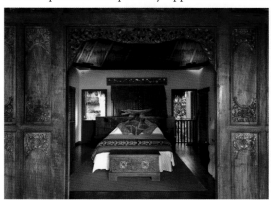

Some have large private verandahs and outdoor garden showers. Get one directly on the beach if possible. The two restaurants serve Italian and Belizean cuisine, elegantly presented and very pricey, as you'd expect. The wine list and the coffee are superb. *Info: www.coppolaresorts.com/turtleinn; Tel. 523-3244, 824-4912 or 800/746-3743 US.*

Hatchet Caye $$$$$

This new island resort (it opened in June 2011) is located on a tiny spit of sand a few miles east of Placencia. The rooms are large and luxurious, with attractive furnishings and all the modern goodies, including AC, TV, wi-fi, safes and hair dryers. The Lionfish Grill offers a full array of local seafood, and the exotic fish it's named for, an imported threat to the local ecosystem, is a specialty of the house. Naturally there's a fully-equipped diving operation on site – fantastic dive sites are right off the beach. There's a freshwater pool, and kayaks and other beach toys are available. *Info: www.hatchetcaye.com; Tel. 533-4446 or 523-3337.*

Robert's Grove Beach Resort $$$$

This is my favorite place in Placencia, a true luxury resort located just north of the airstrip. There's a lovely beach, kayaks and windsurfers, an in-house 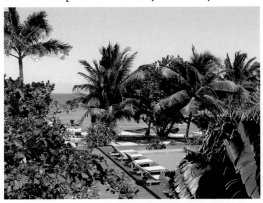 dive shop, two restaurants, three pools, rooftop Jacuzzis, a tennis court, a full-service spa and a well stocked gift shop. The 42 rooms and suites have attractive décor, large comfortable beds and every luxury amenity – AC, TV, fridge, hair dryer – the works. Those who are tired of beans and rice will delight in the excellent dining. The Seaside Restaurant offers a large selection of local and American favorites, while over on the lagoon side, the more casual Habanero serves great Mexican food. Start the day with the wonderful (included) Continental breakfast, or peruse the menu for the full complement of bacon and egg dishes. Saturday night is the famous poolside barbecue. The staff are very professional and very friendly, and there are even two dogs and a cat. *Info: www.robertsgrove.com; Tel. 523-3565 or 800/565-9757 US.*

Laru Beya Resort $$$$
This beachfront resort is next to Robert's Grove, and it also offers private luxury. There's a variety of rooms and villas, all with ceiling fans, AC and full kitchens. The nicest ones, such as the Penthouse Villa, which features a private rooftop Jacuzzi, are predictably pricey, but if you choose one of the cheaper rooms, you can stay here at a very good price for a first-class resort. There's a large pool with a wooden deck, and the beach is nice for swimming or for messing about in one of the complimentary catamarans, windsurfers or kayaks. *Info: www.larubeya.com; Tel. 523-3476 or 800/890-8010 US.*

Maya Beach Hotel $$$
If you don't mind staying at Maya Beach, a good ride north of Placencia, check out this popular mid-price spot. Simple but nice rooms, all with private bath, AC and ceiling fans. Guests rave about the service and the peaceful vibe. *Info: www.mayabeach.com; Tel. 520-8040 or 800/503-5124 US.*

Singing Sands $$$
This is another Maya Beach hotel that gets wonderful reviews. There are six thatched cabanas and four apartments, all furnished in an attractive woody style, all with AC, coffee makers, hair dryers and wi-fi. With a pool, a dock, a restaurant and a bar, this place has what it takes to keep most tropical fun-seekers happy for a few days (or longer). *Info: www.singingsands.com; Tel. 533-3022 or 888/201-6425 US.*

Green Parrot Beach Houses And Resort $$$
Also in Maya Beach, here are a couple of thatched cabanas and six larger beach houses with kitchenettes, good value for families. There's a restaurant and bar, and the usual beach toys. *Info: www.greenparrot-belize.com; Tel. 533-8188.*

The Placencia? Perhaps

When the previous edition of this book was published, the **Placencia Hotel and Residences** (*www.theplacencia.com*) was just a couple of years old. Located a good ride north of Placencia, it's a large, modern hotel, part of a development that also includes condos and houses for sale. There's a huge pool, tennis courts, three restaurants and all that you'd expect at a major luxury resort. Alas, some guests that we've heard from recently were disappointed, and described a sterile vibe, mediocre food and inattentive staff.

Ranguana Lodge $$

Right in Placencia Town, five cozy cabanas on the beach, with private bath, AC, ceiling fans, fridges, coffee makers and microwaves, as well as nice little porches with hammocks. *Info: www.ranguanabelize.com; Tel. 523-3112.*

Sea Spray Hotel $$

Another nice little budget hotel on the beach in the middle of the village. All rooms have private bath and ceiling fans. Some have AC and kitchenettes. *Info: www.seasprayhotel.com; Tel. 523-3148.*

One World $$

This guest house is run by a Swiss lady and, not surprisingly, is neat as a pin. It's one of the few lodgings that isn't on the beach, but the amenities, including AC, TV and fridges, make it a bargain for the price. There are a gift shop and laundromat on site. *Info: www.oneworldplacencia.com; Tel. 523-3103 or 620-9975.*

Manatee Inn $$

This newer two-story inn has nice wood furnishings and a verandah with an ocean view. *Info: www.manateeinn.com; Tel. 523-4083 or 607-0202.*

Paradise Resort $$

Located at the southern tip of the peninsula, this pleasant place has 12 rooms and a two-bedroom suite, all renovated just a few years ago, with private bath and AC. *Info: www.paradisevacationbelize.com; Tel. 523-3179 or 904/564-9400 US.*

There are lots of apartments and small guest houses for rent, and this is a more economical way to go if you're staying more than a few days, or if you're with a larger group. See *www.placencia.com* for a comprehensive listing of lodgings in all categories.

BEST EATS IN PLACENCIA

The area has a great selection of eating places in all price ranges. Most of the hotels have restaurants, some of them quite good. **Robert's Grove Resort** offers elegant dining at the Seaside Restaurant, and Mexican fare with a nice water view at Habanero. For a luxurious fusion of Continental and Caribbean cuisine, make a reservation at **Blancaneaux's Turtle Inn**

It's worth the trouble to find **The Secret Garden** (*Tel. 634-9789*), a peaceful place that serves a Caribbean/Asian fusion, including some vegetarian items. **De Barcelona Beach Tapas Bar** (*Tel. 660-0837*), a new place next to the police station, serves vaguely Spanish-style food in friendly fashion.

There are several casual sand-floor-and-thatched-roof joints on the beach, serving up Caribbean-style seafood dishes and umbrella drinks. Two of the most popular are **De Tatch** (*Tel. 503-3385*) and the **Cozy Corner** (*Tel. 523-3540*). For authentic Belizean food, visit **Wendy's**, down by the docks (no relation to the barfsome chain of the same name).

For a great cup of coffee and an organic muffin, go to **Above Grounds Coffee** (*www.abovegroundscoffee.com*).

If you're staying in Maya Beach, you won't go hungry. The beachfront restaurants at **Singing Sands**, the **Green Parrot**, and the **Maya Beach Hotel** all serve nice Belizean/international fusion with fresh local ingredients.

There are plenty of little bars where locals and tourists mingle, and expats go to seed. The **Pickled Parrot** serves American bar food, cold beer and the dreaded "parrot piss." The **Barefoot Bar at the Tipsy Tuna** is a fun beachfront spot that has a weekly schedule of live music.

PUNTA GORDA AREA
Belcampo Lodge $$$$$
This upscale ecolodge (formerly Machaca Hill) sits on a breezy hilltop within the 11,000 acre Laughing Falcon Reserve. The location offers wonderful views of the rain forest canopy. The 12 cabanas are first-class, with screened verandas, AC, ceiling fans, mini-fridges, hair dryers and wi-fi. The restaurant features vegetables grown at the adjacent farm, where you can take a full-day course in coffee or cacao. There's a pool, a small spa and

a riverside deck, and all kinds of tours to the local wonders are on offer. *Info: www.belcampoinc.com/bz; Tel. 722-0050.*

Cotton Tree Lodge $$$$

This is a special place, loved by all who visit. It's located on the lovely Moho River – they'll pick you up by boat from the airstrip. The cabanas are

 elegantly rustic, and tightly screened. You'll be serenaded to sleep by the crickets, and wake up to a symphony of birdsong – partially cleared jungle sites like this support an incredible variety of bird species. There's also a jungle house, way back in the forest, where you may see howler monkeys from the porch. Owner Chris is very environmentally conscious – solar cells provide electricity, and composting toilets fertilize the bananas. Vegetables and eggs come from the on-site organic gardens, and there's a vast variety of tropical fruit trees, including cacao. You can watch how they turn these into delicious chocolate, and even have a go yourself. There are plenty of activities in the immediate area – kayak on the river, hike or ride a horse through the forest, swim by a lovely waterfall, or visit one of the nearby Mayan villages for a fascinating cultural experience. Meals are served in the central lodge, where Buddy the dog and Mister Miss the cat entertain. *Info: www.cottontreelodge.com; Tel. 670-0557 or 866/480-4534 US.*

The Lodge at Big Falls $$$$

About 20 minutes from town, on the Rio Grande River, this excellent lodge has comfortable cabanas, great food and an especially helpful staff. The cabanas have river views and nice décor with tile floors and verandahs with hammocks. Swim in the pool or the river, or take a kayak or a mountain bike for a ride. The food here is especially good. *Info: www.thelodgeatbigfalls.com; Tel. 732-4444 or 610-0126.*

Coral House Inn $$$

The nicest of the places right in town, this remodeled old house is on the beach at the very southern end. The four rooms have private bath, AC and wireless internet, and there's a nice little pool. *Info: www.coralhouseinn.net; Tel. 722-2878.*

Sea Front Inn $$$
Another pretty nice seaside inn with good prices, located at the north end of town. This family-run inn has 14 hotel rooms and six apartments, all with private bath and AC. Some have large verandahs with fine views. *Info: www.seafrontinn.com; Tel. 722-2300.*

Hickatee Cottages $$
These three pleasantly-furnished little cottages are set in a nice jungle area about a mile south of Punta Gorda. There's a well-maintained hiking trail for you to check out the orchids, toucans, hummingbirds and a resident troop of howler monkeys. Owned by a British couple, this humble establishment gets consistent rave reviews. The low prices include transfers from the airstrip or bus station, internet access and bikes. *Info: www.hickatee.com; Tel. 662-4475.*

Punta Gorda watering holes include Earth Runnins' Café, an internet café with a Reggae vibe, and beachfront Waluco's, where you're likely to catch some local Garifuna drumming and partying.

BEST SHOPPING
At Maya Center, on the Southern Highway just south of the turnoff to Hopkins, you'll find the **Maya Center Women's Group Gift Shop**, run by a cooperative of village women. This is big cat country – the local men guide tours in the nearby Jaguar Reserve, and the women make nice wood and stone carvings, woven apparel and jewelry, most with the obligatory jaguar and/or ancient Mayan imagery. By buying here, you'll be helping the locals to preserve their beautiful forest and its inhabitants.

BEST NIGHT-LIFE & ENTER-TAINMENT
PUNTA & GARIFUNA MUSIC

Most traditional folk music in Belize comes from the Garifuna. The **Garifuna** (or Garinagu)

live all along the Caribbean coast from Belize down to Nicaragua, and their music is beloved throughout the region.

The most popular genre of Garifuna music is called **Punta**. As are other Afro-Caribbean styles such as Reggae, Calypso and Salsa, Punta is descended from a mixture of African and European influences, with a uniquely Caribbean flavor. Drums and other percussion instruments are central to the sound. Traditional Punta is played on locally-made instruments such as the *garawon* drum, rattles, turtle shells and sometimes wind instruments made of conch shells. A typical Punta song pits male against female, with sexually-charged dialogue and energetic dancing that involves shaking the buttocks at incredible speeds! Popular Punta artists include Andy Palacio, Chico Ramos, Mohobub and Supa G. A related musical genre is **Paranda**. The most famous Paranda artist is **Paul Nabor**, who hails from Punta Gorda. Many call his song *Naguya Nei* the unofficial Garifuna national anthem.

Punta Rock is a modern version of Punta music that adds electric guitars and synthesizers to the traditional instrumentation, and often has socially-conscious lyrics. The acknowledged founder of Punta Rock is **Pen Cayetano**, from Dangriga. Since its origins in the early 1980s, Punta Rock has grown to become the most popular musical style on the Caribbean coast of Central America. Cayetano is also a talented painter, and he has a studio in Dangriga that you can visit, but it's usually open only in November, during the festivities around Garifuna Settlement Day. You're likely to hear the infectious rhythms of Punta at any nightclub or disco in coastal Belize, but if you really want to get into the music, head for Dangriga or Punta Gorda. *Info: www.cayetano.de; www.stonetreerecords.com.*

In Placencia, the **Barefoot Bar at the Tipsy Tuna** is the place to go after dinner, with live music every week. On my last visit, a punta rock band was playing, the *panty rippaz* were flowing, and hips were shaking. Several of the resorts have a weekly beach barbecue, sometimes with live bands.

BEST SPORTS & RECREATION
DIVING & SNORKELING
There's excellent diving on the barrier reef and the atolls offshore, and this region sees far fewer divers than the reefs around Ambergris and Caulker. Some resorts have their own dive operations, but local dive shops will pick you up and drop you off wherever you're staying.

Whale Sharks

The largest fish on the planet are members of the shark family but, unlike their more rapacious relatives, they are filter feeders, eating a variety of tiny fish and other sea life, and therefore not dangerous to humans (but I wouldn't advise getting too close). Whale sharks frequent Southern Belize from March-June, especially around full moon nights. Snapper spawn around Glover's Reef Atoll in vast numbers around that time, and the whale sharks come to feed on the eggs. The sight of thousands of snappers spawning in a huge ball while giant whale sharks swim overhead slurping up the eggs could be the dive experience of a lifetime.

Whale shark encounters are much like dolphin encounters – your boat cruises around in likely-looking areas while your eagle-eyed skipper looks for the tell-tale boil in the water that indicates the presence of whale sharks and the small fish that accompany them. When they are located, snorkelers and scuba divers plop over the side and, hopefully, swim quietly while the giant fish lurk around.

Whale sharks are usually slow swimmers, but may not show much interest in visitors. Sometimes they'll circle around a little, but often they will just keep on swimming in the direction they were going. The trick is to observe the whale sharks from the boat to determine which direction they are swimming in and then drop the tourists in the water a little ahead of their path. Be sure to take an underwater camera along on this outing.

Dangriga Area Diving

Isla Marisol
Located on a tiny caye on Glover's Reef just off Dangriga, this resort does a wonderful job with their weeklong diving and fishing packages. The reefs in the area are spectacular and pristine, and there's excellent fly fishing on the flats. *Info: www.islamarisolresort.com; Tel. 522-0235, 610-4204 or 866/990-9904 US.*

Thatch Caye Resort
This fairly new place is an upscale resort with a small but excellent dive

operation. Divemasters Ian, Emily and Chico (who has been diving in these waters for 17 years) lead snorkeling and diving trips to the barrier reef, a short boat ride away, or only slightly farther, to Glover's Reef, perhaps the most pristine dive site in Belize. *Info: www.thatchcaye.com; Tel. 532-2414 or 800/435-3145 US.*

Blue Marlin Lodge
This rustic lodge on South Water Caye, near Dangriga, has a couple of lodging options and a variety of weekly diving and fishing packages. *Info: www.bluemarlinlodge.com; Tel. 522-2243 or 800/798-1558 US.*

Placencia Area Diving
Seahorse Dive Shop
Located in the center of Placencia, this full-service dive operator specializes in whale shark dives. *Info: www.belizescuba.com; Tel. 523-3166, 523-3356 or 800/991-1969 US.*

Splash Dive Shop
This shop, established in 2000, does dive and snorkeling trips, as well as inland tours. *Info: www.splashbelize.com; Tel. 523-3058, 523-3080 or 620-6649.*

Avadon Divers
This outfit has three boats, offers a full roster of trips and training, and gets a lot of rave reviews. They also offer fishing and sailing excursions. *Info: www.avadondiversbelize.com; Tel. 503-3377, 523-3577 or 888/509-5617 US.*

There are also a couple of resorts in the area that have their own in-house dive operations:

Robert's Grove Beach Resort
This upscale resort has a good dive and snorkeling outfit with several boats (see photo above). *Info: www.robertsgrove.com; Tel. 523-3565 or 800/565-9757 US.*

Blancaneaux's Turtle Inn
This luxury resort has its own dive operation. *Info: www.blancaneaux.com; Tel. 523-3244, 824-4912 or 800/746-3743 US.*

FISHING
Placencia Area Fishing
Whipray Caye Lodge
A place for the serious angler, this lodge offers basic accommodations on a tiny island 11 miles off Placencia. Owner Julian Cabral is an expert at wade-fishing for permit on the flats. Tarpon, bonefish, snapper and grouper are also around. *Info: www.whipraycayelodge.com; Tel. 610-1068 or 608-8130.*

Tarpon Caye Lodge
At this island lodge near Placencia, another of the numerous Cabral clan guides anglers to 30-pound permit, baby (up to 100 pound) tarpon, bonefish and snook. *Info: www.tarponcayelodge.com; Tel. 523-3323 or 664-2096.*

Punta Gorda Area Fishing
The Punta Gorda area is one of the hottest spots in the world for permit. Look up local guide Dennis Garbut to pursue the permit.

OTHER WATER SPORTS
Slickrock Adventures
This tour operator specializes in sea kayaking (see photo at right), and has a private island off Glover's Reef. *Info: www.slickrock.com; Tel. 800/390-5715 US.*

Island Expeditions
This company offers a variety of sea kayaking, sailing and snorkeling trips to Glover's Reef and Lighthouse Reef. *Info: www.islandexpeditions.com; Tel. 800/667-1630 US.*

Sea Kunga
This outfit is based in Placencia, where they offer lodging in rustic

beach cabanas, They do adventure kayak tours at several locations. *Info: www.seakunga.com; Tel. 800/781-2269 US.*

Toadal Adventure
Also in Placencia, Toadal does both reef and jungle trips. *Info: www.toadaladventure.com; Tel. 523-3207.*

Sailors should check out *www.belize-sailing-charters.com.* They offer all sorts of sailing and land-sea packages (see photo below).

8. PRACTICAL MATTERS

AIRPORTS/ARRIVALS

Belize's only international airport is **Philip Goldson International Airport** at Belize City (BZE). Several US carriers fly there from hubs such as Atlanta, Charlotte and Houston. Belize City also has a smaller airport, known as the **Municipal Airstrip**, which is used for some domestic flights.

If you can find a knowledgeable travel agent, she or he may be able to find you a better deal than you'd get directly from the airlines. It's also well worth considering buying your airfare as part of a package tour (see below).

All departing air passengers are required to pay a departure tax of US $40 per person, which some airlines now include in ticket prices.

CRUISES

Over a dozen major cruise lines now visit Belize. They do not dock in the country, but anchor out in the channel, and use tenders to ferry passengers to the new cruise terminal in Belize City (see Chapter 5) and other locations. A wide variety of shore excursions and tours is offered to cruise passengers.

The major cruise lines are offering ever-more-ambitious day trips in Belize, from snorkeling and diving to lounging on "private islands" to inland visits to the Mayan ruins and nature reserves. However (inevitable with thousands of passengers on a ship) mainstream cruise ship tours are rushed and impersonal, with little chance to really get the flavor of the country. For a more Belizean cruising experience, try **Blount Small Ship Adventures**, which offers 11- and 14-night itineraries that visit several of Belize's isolated cayes, as well as Guatemala and the Bay Islands of Honduras. *Info: www.blountsmallshipadventures.com; Tel. 800/556-7450 US.*

TOUR OPERATORS

Guided tours are a big part of the scene in Belize. On the coast it's diving, fishing and boat rides, inland it's trips to the nature reserves (by foot, horseback or boat) and the Mayan ruins. Spelunking and cave tubing are also popular activities. The tour business is a complex web of larger and smaller operators. Wholesale tour companies subcontract with local tour guides, hotels, van drivers, etc. A tour can mean anything from hiring a local fisherman for a boat ride to a door-to-door package that includes airfare, hotels, ground transport…and a boat ride with that same local fisherman.

If you're the independent type, you can get around perfectly well on your own by bus, small plane or rented car. However, you will probably still want to hire a guide at one point or another. I highly recommend visiting the forests and Mayan ruins in the company of a local guide. You'll see much more, and learn more about the area, than you would on your own.

There are several other reasons why **using a local guide is a good idea.** Although traveling in Belize is safer, and public transport more reliable, than in neighboring countries, it's still the developing world, and all kinds of unexpected delays can rob you of your hard-earned vacation time. A good tour operator can meet you at the plane with a nice new air-conditioned van, and take you where you want to go quickly and comfortably.

Perhaps most importantly, hiring local guides is a good way to help the local economy. If the rain forests and coral reefs of Belize are to survive, the locals need to be able to make more money showing them to wildlife lovers than they would by clear-cutting the trees and stripping the reefs of fish. The struggle to protect the world's natural wonders for future generations is an ongoing battle, and your dollars can help support the right side.

There are three ways to go about arranging tours:

1) You can book tours over the web with a Belizean tour operator, or through your local travel agency, before you even leave home. If you wish,

you can get a package that includes flights, hotels, meals and guides. If you want to visit one of the more remote regions, and have limited time, this is a good option, though it won't be the cheapest. The more independent-minded can simply book a tour with a local operator in each place that they visit.

2) Most hotels are familiar with the local tours that are on offer, and will be happy to help you make arrangements (although they may tack on an extra fee). Quite a few have their own in-house tour agencies. Some hotels and restaurants are well-known clearinghouses for local tour guides, and are excellent places to find reputable guides.

3) In the more touristed areas, freelance tour operators hang around the beach or the main street and offer their services. The best guides are licensed by the Belize Tourism Board (see below). Use your judgment.

Note that all of the larger hotels, and most dive operators, can arrange tours to any part of the country, and most will let you put together a custom package of tours, transportation and lodging. Because the country is small, and tour services are well-developed, it's quite feasible to stay in one location and take tours to different areas. For example, if you'd like to stay on Ambergris Caye and go diving one day and take a mainland jungle tour the next, it's no problem, man.

The **Belize Tourism Board** (*www.travelbelize.org*) and **Belize Tourism Industry Association** (*www.btia.org*) both have information about tours on their web sites, and the latter has a member directory arranged by location.

Here are the best of Belize's tour companies:

International Zoological Expeditions offers ecotourism, educational and adventure travel. Highly recommended. *Info: www.ize2belize.com; Tel. 508/655-1461 US.*

To See Belize is a very good tour company owned by Ellen Howells, an old Belize hand whose family runs the Lamanai Outpost Lodge. *Info: www.toseebelize.com; Tel. 877/222-3549 US.*

Island Expeditions specializes in kayaking and snorkeling trips to Glover's Reef and Lighthouse Reef. *Info: www.islandexpeditions.com; Tel. 800/667-1630 US.*

Paradise Expeditions specializes in birding tours. *Info: www.birdinginbelize.com; Tel. 824-2772.*

Victor Emmanuel Nature Tours specializes in birding tours. *Info: www.ventbird.com; Tel. 800/328-VENT.*

Star Tours, on Caye Caulker, does snorkeling tours and runs two budget lodgings. *Info: www.startoursbelize.com; Tel. 226-0374 or 226-0124.*

Ian Anderson's Adventures in Belize. Mr. Caves now runs a travel agency and tour company. *Info: www.adventuresinbelize.com; Tel. 610-3451 or 866/822-2278 US.*

DuPlooy Travel is a package tour operator located at DuPlooy's Resort in Cayo. *Info: www.belize-vacation.com; Tel. 824-3101.*

Yute Expeditions, based in Cayo, has twelve modern vans and 4x4s, and offers tours throughout the country. *Info: www.inlandbelize.com; Tel. 824-2076.*

C&G Tours, based in Dangriga, runs tours all over the country, especially Cockscomb and Mayflower. *Info: www.cgtourscharters.com; Tel. 532-3641.*

Caribbean Tours is based in Placencia, and offers tours and vacation rentals throughout Southern Belize. *Info: www.ctbelize.com; Tel. 523-3481.*

Tide Tours, in Punta Gorda, is associated with TIDE, a conservation group that manages several local national parks and reserves. Hiking, horseback riding, canoeing, fishing, diving, snorkeling, kayaking, you name it. *Info: www.tidetours.org; Tel. 722-2129.*

S&L Travel and Tours is located in Belize City, and offers half-day to weeklong tours all over the country. *Info: www.sltravelbelize.com; Tel. 227-7593.*

GETTING AROUND BELIZE

By Air

There are two domestic airlines: **Maya Island Air** (*www.mayaislandair.com; Tel. 223-1140)*, and **Tropic Air** (*www.tropicair.com*). Both offer several flights per day from Belize City to San Pedro, Caye Caulker and Corozal in the north; and Dangriga, Placencia, and Punta Gorda in the south. Charter flights are also available from both Goldson International Airport and the Municipal Airstrip. Flights are frequent enough that it's easy to connect with international flights and avoid spending a night in Belize City.

Other than Goldson International in Belize City, the country's airports are little more than landing strips with few or no facilities. Some of the smallest are nothing but a reasonably level field of grass. Little boys with sticks drive the cows off before each landing.

By Car & Car Rental

Renting a car offers the maximum in flexibility, and driving in Belize is generally safe and easy. Well-maintained paved highways connect the major regions of the country, and decent dirt roads lead to most of the places you'll want to go. Some of the smaller roads are dodgy, especially in the rainy season, so if you plan to get off the beaten track, choose something with high ground clearance, and perhaps four-wheel drive. Most rental agencies have a good selection of 4WD vehicles, from cute little Subarus to hulking SUVs.

Driving in Belize is not the death-defying adventure that it is in other Central American countries, but do use extra caution. Many locals are terrible drivers, and are especially fond of passing on blind curves. Because of unlit vehicles and animals on the roads, you may want to think twice about driving after dark. Never leave anything of value in a parked car, and be very careful where you park in cities. In fact, I strongly recommend that you don't drive in Belize City at all.

The only real possibility is to rent your car at the international airport, where a large selection of companies (international chains and small local agencies) competes for your custom, offering nice new vehicles. There is one agency in Placencia, Barefoot Rentals, which I emphatically do not recommend (decrepit cars, snotty staff).

If you plan to rent from a chain, it's more convenient, and much cheaper, to reserve a car online before leaving home. A small local outfit may just give you a better price however, especially if you want to rent for a longer period, or if you want to hire a car and driver. Rentals in Belize are overpriced. Prices start around $60 per day and go up.

Crystal Auto Rental. This is the largest of the local companies, with a fleet of over 150 vehicles, including vans and pickups, and has been in business since 1989. *Info: www.crystal-belize.com; Tel. 223-1600.*

Pancho's, one of the oldest outfits in Belize, has a nice range of SUVs and vans. *Info: www.panchosrentalbelize.com; Tel. 225-2540.*

Budget Rent a Car. *Info: www.budget-belize.com; Tel. 223-2435 or 223-3986.*

Vista Auto Rentals. *Info: www.vistarentalsbelize.com; Tel. 225-2292.*

Euphrates Auto Rental. *Info: www.ears.bz; Tel. 227-5752.*

Jabiru Auto Rental. *Info: www.jabiruautorental.bz; Tel. 225-3630 or 610-2454.*

Hertz Auto Rental. *Info: www.hertz.com.*

Thrifty. *Info: www.thrifty.com.*

By Taxi

Taxis are reasonably priced, convenient and easily recognized by their green license plates. After dark in Belize City, a taxi is the only safe way to get around. A taxi can also be an affordable way to get to rural destinations, or just to take a tour around the countryside, especially if you're with a group. Fares to the most common destinations are fixed, but elsewhere they may be negotiable. A word to the wise: any time you take a taxi in the developing world, be sure to agree on a fare *before* riding anywhere.

By Bus

Buses run hourly from Belize City along all the major highways, with service to major towns in Belize, as well as Chetumal, Mexico and Melchor, Guatemala. There are also less frequent express buses. The former monolith, **Novelo's Bus Line**, has recently split up into smaller regional companies. Finding the right spot to catch a bus to your destination can be a project, so ask for the latest at your hotel.

Many buses are old American school buses, and are less than comfortable. The regular buses also make frequent stops, so it's well worth paying the extra price for an express bus. Belize's buses are reasonably punctual and reasonably safe, but do try to keep your eye on your luggage.

If traveling to or from Mexico, you'll find a wealth of information on bus services at *www.travelyucatan.com/trans-4.htm*. Current bus schedules are available at *www.ticketbus.com.mx*.

By Boat
Caye Caulker and Ambergris Caye are served by scheduled passenger boats operated by the **Caye Caulker Water Taxi Association**. They depart from the Belize Marine Terminal, located at the north end of the Swing Bridge in Belize City. The fare to San Pedro is $27.50 round trip for adults, $15 for kids. The fare to Caulker is $17.50 round trip for adults, $10 for kids. Boats can drop passengers at other islands on the way, such as Long Caye and St. George's Caye, and you can arrange for pickup by phone. *Info: www.cayecaulkerwatertaxi.com; Tel. 223-5752 or 226-0992.*

International ferries run from Punta Gorda to Puerto Barrios, Guatemala (*daily; www.belizenet.com/requena; Tel. 722-2070*), and from Placencia and Belize City to Puerto Cortés, Honduras (*weekly; www.belizeferry.com; Tel. 624-6509 or 523-4045*).

If you go to a lodge on a remote caye, they will arrange for a boat to take you to and from the mainland.

LODGING
Belize has a wide range of different types of lodgings, from

Lodging Prices

Prices quoted are for one double room.

$ Backpacker: $25 or less
$$ Budget: $25-60
$$$ Midrange: $60-125
$$$$ First-class: $125-200
$$$$$ Luxury: $200 and up

luxurious resort complexes to funky backpacker crash pads. There are colorful jungle and oceanfront lodges dotted throughout the country, some of them very special places indeed. Lovely settings and friendly service are the norm, but there are a few issues to warn you about.

Belize is not exactly a budget travel destination. More upscale lodgings can be expensive, and some fail to come up to US/European standards, leading many visitors to call them overpriced. Remember that this is the tropics – you'll find the occasional bug or mildewy smell at even the best establishments. Hot water is often a problem, even at expensive places, and air conditioners may be old and cranky.

Quoted prices may sound like great deals, but Belizean hoteliers are masters at tacking on nickels and dimes that can almost double the cost of a room. There's a government hotel tax of 9%, and many hotels add a 10-16% "service charge" or other mysterious fees. Upscale hotels accept major credit cards (sometimes with extra fees), but some cheap local places do not. Most places will gladly arrange transportation to and from the airport and tours of local attractions, but some will add extra charges for these services.

Many hotels require payment in advance and, as many travelers have reported, may not gracefully refund your money if your plans change, so choose carefully. Don't believe everything you read on a hotel's web site.

EATING OUT
Belizean food is like the Belizean people: a mixture of influences in every possible combination. In addition to "traditional" Belizean fare, you'll find excellent Mexican food, good Chinese, and (in tourist areas), American favorites such as burgers and chicken wings. You'll also find plenty of the Caribbean/Latin American staple: beans and rice, more beans and more rice. By far the best thing going is the wide variety of **fresh fish and seafood**.

Vegetarian fare is easily available in tourist areas, but less so in local eateries. The rice and beans are sometimes cooked with lard, sometimes with more appetizing coconut milk.

A **Belizean breakfast** consists of refried beans, scrambled eggs, and fry jacks (something like a deep-fried piece of pita bread) and maybe a piece of fried fish. A fruit plate, with fresh papaya, pineapple and watermelon, is often a good choice in the morning.

Belize City, San Pedro, Cayo and other tourist areas boast a good variety of restaurants, many of the best of them in the upscale hotels. On the cayes, seafood is fresh and served in an interesting variety of ways (how about fish fajitas, or lobster marinara?), although it's not always cheap. Caye Caulker is the place to go to gorge on **lobster** at a reasonable price.

At the various island and jungle lodges, the cuisine tends to be a mix of local and international, geared to the tastes of sophisticated travelers, and is often excellent. In Southern Belize, be sure to sample some **Garifuna** cuisine at a thatched beach restaurant. A typical meal includes cassava bread, conch soup and fresh fish grilled or cooked in coconut milk, with a side of *hudut*, a savory dish made of mashed plantains.

The most common local **beer** is Belikin, which comes in regular (lager) and stout varieties. **Wine** is, of course, not produced in the tropics, so Belize has no real wine-drinking tradition. Some of the finer eateries, however, have decent wine lists. Chilean wines are common, and may be the best value.

Throughout the tropics, the local liquor is **rum**, which is made from sugar cane. Belize produces a variety of rums, which run the gamut from cheap rotgut to fine sipping rums. By most accounts, the best is a brand called One Barrel. The drink to have on the islands is a **panty ripper** (One Barrel and pineapple juice). Even the finest Belizean brands are inexpensive, at least if you buy them at a supermarket. Other liquors from around the world are available at higher prices. Another interesting local tipple is **cashew wine**.

Belize grows very good **coffee**, and some establishments serve an excellent brew. Alas, not all Belizeans appreciate a good cuppa – some cheaper places may serve you a generic cup of instant. At one of the resorts I recommend in this book, **Belcampo Lodge** (see pages 185-186; *www.belcampoinc.com/bz)*, you can learn all about the coffee-making process and sample terrific coffee onsite in beautiful, lush surroundings.

Whatever you eat in Belize, be sure to sample some of whatever **fruits** are in season. The mangos, pineapples, papayas, bananas, citrus and other tropical delights that grow down here are simply different fruits from the ones you buy at the supermarket back home: sweet, juicy and cheap. Quench your thirst with a *pipa*, a chilled green coconut with a straw inserted so you can sip the sweet milk. Kids love to chew on a stalk of sugar cane. Fresh-squeezed **juices** from a rainbow of exotic fruits are available everywhere. Don't be afraid to experiment.

BANKING & CHANGING MONEY

The Belizean dollar is fixed at an exchange rate of **two Belizean dollars to one US dollar.** Both US and Belizean currency are accepted interchangeably, so there's no reason to change money. Belizean dollars are not convertible outside the country, so remember to change any leftover cash back to greenbacks before leaving, or squander it in Jet's Bar at the airport.

Most towns have at least one ATM, but some accept only Belizean bank cards, and will not work with your ATM card from home. As of this writing, there are several usable ATMs on Ambergris, and one on Caye Caulker (Atlantic Bank). Credit cards are now pretty widely accepted, at least in tourist areas. Some places tack on an extra fee for using cards (this is technically against the rules, but they do it anyway). Most banks will do cash advances on credit cards.

BUSINESS HOURS

Most businesses are open from around **9am to 5 or 6pm Monday through Friday**, and perhaps Saturday morning. Hours tend to be longer in larger cities and tourist areas. Many businesses and offices close for two hours at lunchtime. Most banks are open Mon-Fri 9am-4pm, but banks in small towns may have more limited hours. Most non-tourist-oriented businesses are closed on Sunday.

Prices in this Book

In Belize, **prices may be quoted in Belizean or US dollars.** In order to make it easy for you to see how much things cost, this book quotes all prices in US dollars.

CLIMATE & WEATHER

Belize has two main seasons. The **dry season** lasts from November through May, and is the main tourist season. The **rainy season** lasts from June through October, and sees far fewer tourists. Most areas of the country do get a lot of rain during this season, and some remote regions can become almost inaccessible by road. However, prices can be lower, and the crowds are gone.

CONSULATES & EMBASSIES

The **US embassy** is in Belmopan. *Info: www.belize.usembassy.gov.* The **British High Commission** is in Belmopan. *Info: www.britishhighcommission.gov.uk.* The **Belize Embassy** to the US is in Washington DC. *Info: Tel. 202/332-9636 US.*

ELECTRICITY

Belize uses **110-volt AC, the same as in the US**, and the plugs are the same. Grounded (three-prong) plugs are not common, and the general level of electrical safety is low. Cheaper lodgings may feature "suicide showers," little electric heaters attached to the showerhead, sometimes with poorly insulated connectors (we've heard no reports of anyone actually being killed by one of these contraptions, which are also known as "widow makers," but *do not touch them*). Remote lodges get their power from generators, which may be turned off at night, and may deliver dodgy voltage.

EMERGENCIES & SAFETY

Crime

Belize is more prosperous than her Central American neighbors, and enjoys a far lower crime rate. Muggings and violent crime against tourists are rare here. However, you do need to be on your guard. Thieves target tourists everywhere in the world, just as surely as cats target mice. Belize City in particular has a high crime rate. **Follow these rules** and you should be fine:

• It is absolutely, positively not safe to walk around the streets of Belize City after dark. *Always take a taxi.* Some areas are dodgy during the day as well, so don't wander aimlessly.

• Never, ever leave any valuables in parked cars. In fact, it's probably unwise to park anywhere other than a watched hotel parking lot.

- Be on the alert for pickpockets in any crowded situation, especially at airports, bus stations and such places. Not only cities, but heavily-touristed parks and attractions have their share of thieves.

- In some parks, walking alone on isolated trails is not recommended. Always check in at the ranger station, and hike in groups, preferably with a local guide. Also be careful about walking alone on isolated beaches.

- In crowded tourist areas, be on the alert for common scams: the "fellow American" who's been robbed and needs some money to get home, the fake fight or other disturbance, the "accidentally" spilled drink, the friendly stranger who offers you food (which may be drugged), the crowd of cute little kids who mob you and lighten your pocket, etc etc *ad infinitum.*

- Petty theft is not the only type of crime to watch out for. **Con men** run various investment scams on tourists and retirees. If you're doing any kind of business, buying real estate or investing in the country, be extra careful to deal only with reputable firms, and, most definitely, seek advice from a local third party such as a lawyer or accountant before signing anything or parting with any dough.

One of the saddest things about crime is that it can discourage you from making friends with locals. So remember, not every Belizean who approaches you is out to rip you off. They're friendly people in general, and many are simply eager to speak with a foreigner. It would be a terrible shame if you allowed your fear of crooks to make you keep every local you encounter at arm's length. You must use your own judgment about the people whom you meet on your travels.

I highly recommend a **money belt.** *Not* the external "fanny-pack," but a small flat belt that goes around your waist (there are similar things that go around your neck) *under your clothes.* With your passport, plane ticket and main cash stash zipped up out of sight, you can relax and enjoy your trip (keep a small roll of walking-around money in a pocket, so you never have to pull out your money belt in public). Money belts are available at any good luggage shop or (much cheaper) at discount stores.

As for those fanny-packs, they're famous around the world as magnets for thieves and con artists. Even if you don't plan to keep any valuables in it, I strongly urge you to leave it at home. A fanny pack shouts "opportunity!" to people whom you'd rather not meet. The sight of a fanny pack to a street hustler is like the sound of a can opener to a hungry cat.

Unlike some tropical vacation destinations, Belize is not particularly tolerant of **marijuana** or **drugs**. While the cops are not zealous about busting joint-smokers, they can and will put you in jail if you get on the wrong side of them. You will be offered *ganja*, especially in party-hearty centers such as Ambergris and Caye Caulker, but buying on the street exposes you to many dangers, including being ripped off or turned over to the authorities. I advise against buying grass (or anything else) from street hustlers. As for coke and other drugs: Don't!

On the roads, you may occasionally pass through a police checkpoint. Have your passport and the car's papers available.

Prostitution is technically illegal in Belize, and therefore unregulated. The business is quite sleazy, with muggings and druggings a regular part of the scene. AIDS is quite common. Having sex with anyone under 18 is strictly illegal.

You can check the latest Consular Information Sheets and Travel Warnings from the US State Department at *www.travel.state.gov*.

HEALTH
Belize's health care system is not so great. Larger cities have public hospitals and clinics, but you'll get better and quicker service from a private doctor or clinic, which you can find in the phone book. **In an emergency, dial 90 or 911 for the police.**

The health hazards here are the same ones you'll encounter in any tropical country. Be very careful about exposure to the sun: it can hurt you even on cloudy days. Some tap water is safe, some isn't. The folks at your hotel will tell you if the water in the bathroom is for washing only (and provide a jug of nice clean drinking water, as well). No matter how careful you are, it's not unlikely that a bit of Montezuma's revenge will be part of your Belizean adventure. Experienced travelers swear by Imodium AD, so bring some with you.

Malaria, a nasty disease that's spread by mosquitoes, is present in the southern regions, though it's usually a threat only to those who spend a long time in remote areas. Chloroquine drugs are effective preventives. These are prescription drugs that you should start taking before your trip. These are very strong drugs, and some people report side effects such as digestive problems, headaches and very bizarre dreams. Some recommend a drug called Malarone, which is bit more expensive but is said not to have any of the unpleasant side effects.

Take stringent precautions against mosquitoes. Cover up with socks and long-sleeved pants and shirts (mosquitoes' favorite place to bite is your ankles). Light long pants such as linens or khakis really are the best choice for tropical travel. Skeeters, fleas and other insects are most active right around dawn and dusk. Some ecolodges have mosquito nets to drape over the beds at night – use them! If you do get sick, chloroquine drugs are also available at pharmacies in Belize.

Tiny little insects called **sand fleas** are a problem in beach areas. Different people have different reactions to the little buggers: some people aren't bothered at all, some are mercilessly bitten, and some have dangerous allergic reactions. Most travelers agree that a liberal coating of Avon's Skin-So-Soft is effective against the sand fleas. It won't impress the mosquitoes however, so pack *plenty* of maximum-strength **insect repellent**, with DEET, for them. A tube or two of cortisone-based anti-itch cream is also a good thing to have.

No shots are required for travel to Belize, but you should definitely be up to date on your routine vaccinations. The **US Centers for Disease Control** recommend malaria pills if you're going to a high-risk area. Dysentery, cholera and other diseases caused by poor sanitation are present. You can check with the CDC (*www.cdc.gov/travel; Tel. 800/232-4636 US*) for the most recent health advisories and immunization recommendations.

AIDs is common in Belize. If you choose to have sex with a prostitute or anyone else, be absolutely sure to use a condom.

Poisonous snakes are common throughout the country, but snakebites are rare. When hiking in the forest, watch your step at all times, and don't stick your hand in anywhere it doesn't belong. A stout pair of hiking boots is a very good idea for several reasons. Slipping in the mud and spraining your ankle is more likely than getting bit by a *tommygoff*, and it could ruin your holiday.

Travelers with special health concerns should note that remote jungle lodges have limited ability to evacuate you in a medical emergency. If something happens to you, it could be hours before you get to a hospital.

ETIQUETTE

Belizeans are great ones for politeness – when they meet, there's a great deal of handshaking, "How's the family?" and so forth, before any business gets discussed. Peoples' concept of time is different in Central America than it is in the US and Northern Europe. In Belize, public transport and other services are generally quite punctual, but individuals are not. Don't get too upset when people show up fashionably late.

Even though you're in the tropics, please don't dress as if the whole country is a beach. At coastal resorts and tourist towns, beach bum attire is fine, but in places like banks and stores, you'll notice that the locals wear long pants, shirts, and even jackets and ties, just as we do at home. Walking around in shorts, flip-flops and a baseball cap marks you instantly as a tourist.

A SHORT HISTORY

Belize's recorded history begins with the **Maya**, who built an advanced civilization of independent city-states that stretched from Mexico to Honduras. Their knowledge of astronomy, their calendar and their written language were unparalleled among ancient peoples. Scholars divide the Mayan era into three periods. Most of their cities were built during the Classic Period, which lasted from around 300-900 AD.

Belize has many important Mayan sites, including the earliest known community in the Maya world, Cuello in the Orange Walk District, which is believed to have been settled as long ago as 2000 BC. The Mayans built enormous cities – the largest in Belize, Caracol, had more residents than

Who's a Creole?

The word Creole has many different meanings, and it means different things in different parts of the world. In Belize, the term (also spelled *Kriol*) refers to the people who form the largest of the country's ethnic groups and to the dialect of English that they speak. The Creoles of Belize have a mixed ancestry of indigenous peoples, African slaves and British settlers.

Belize City does today – with majestic temples, palaces and plazas. They recorded significant events in their history on pillars of stone called *stelae*. Around 900 AD, the construction of monuments and stelae stopped, the cities were abandoned, and the Mayan people reverted to a scattered race of subsistence farmers. Today there are several distinct groups of Mayan people living in Belize, speaking their own indigenous languages. See Chapter 6 for more about the ancient Maya.

After 1492, the Spanish began settling Central America, but they didn't have a monopoly on the area for long. With its many islands, reefs and shallow sand flats, Belize proved a perfect place for British privateers ("pirates" to the Spanish) to hide out and launch raids against the Spanish treasure ships that carried the riches of the New World back to Spain. Later, as the era of piracy wound down, some of these swashbucklers settled on the mainland and set about cutting logwood and mahogany. As you may imagine, these settlers, who became known as the **Baymen**, were a rowdy, hard-drinking bunch. According to popular legend, they built Belize City on a base of wood chips and rum bottles.

Conflict between the Baymen and the Spanish went on throughout the 1700s, culminating in the 1798 Battle of St. George's Caye, in which the Spanish were defeated and ceded control of the region to Britain. In 1871 it became the Crown Colony of **British Honduras**.

Logging was the mainstay of Belize's economy for many years. Unlike in other colonies in the region, large-scale sugar cultivation never developed here. The British began to import African slaves in the 1720s. However, the need for labor in the forests was far less than on the sugar plantations, one

of the reasons why Belize today has a far lower population density than neighboring countries.

Over the years, several other ethnic groups joined the British and the Africans to create the diverse patchwork of today's Belize. In 1832, a large number of **Garifuna** arrived in Southern Belize from the island of Roatan, where they had been exiled by the British (see Chapter 7). Around 1847, the Caste War in neighboring Yucatan, in which the native Mayans revolted against their Spanish and Mestizo overlords, sent thousands of refugees (**Mestizo** and **Maya**) into Northern Belize. Beginning in 1958, small groups of **Mennonites**, members of a pacifist Anabaptist sect, began to settle in the Orange Walk and Cayo districts (see Chapter 5).

In 1961, Hurricane Hattie caused a lot of damage in coastal areas, so the government decided to move the capital from low-lying Belize City to a new site at the geographic center of the country. Construction of the planned city of **Belmopan** began in 1970, and today it is the country's capital, although Belize City remains the business and economic center. British Honduras became a self-governing colony in 1964. It gained full independence, and changed its name to Belize, in 1981.

LAND & PEOPLE
Belize is located in Central America, on the Caribbean Sea. Her neighbors are Mexico to the north and Guatemala to the west and south. Much of the country is flat, swampy coastal plain, rising to the Maya Mountains in the west and south. The country is divided into six districts: Corozal, Orange Walk, Belize, Cayo, Stann Creek and Toledo.

Belize is one of the most prosperous countries in Central America, but it is still poor compared to the US, with a per-capita Gross Domestic Product of $8,400 (compared with $41,600 for the US). Some 43% of the people live below the poverty line. Rates of literacy (77%) and life expectancy (69 years) are only fair.

Belize is a very ethnically diverse country. About 49% of the people are **Mestizos** (of mixed Spanish and Native American descent), 25% are **Creoles** (of mixed British and African descent), 11% are **Maya**, and 6% are **Garifuna** (descendents of Caribs and African slaves, most of whom live along the southern coast). The remaining 10% includes East Indians, Chinese, Lebanese, Europeans and North Americans. About 50% of Belizeans are Roman Catholic and 27% are Protestant.

Tourism is Belize's main economic activity, followed by industry (20% of GDP), which mostly consists of clothing production and food processing, and agriculture (10% of GDP), especially bananas, cacao, citrus, sugar and farm-raised shrimp.

INTERNET ACCESS
Belize is getting wired up rapidly. Internet cafés are common in cities and tourist areas. Most hotels offer internet service, and many now have wi-fi (with the exception of the more remote wilderness lodges, which may be out of reach of the telephone network). See the list of Belize-oriented internet directories and search engines at the end of this chapter. Belize's internet suffix is .bz.

LANGUAGE
Belize was a British colony until 1981, and the official language is **English**. Most locals speak a melodious local dialect, which is called **Creole** (or Kriol). **Spanish** is also widely spoken, especially in certain areas, including San Pedro and the area around San Ignacio. Many Belizeans are bilingual. There are several ethnic groups that speak their own indigenous languages, including **Garifuna** and three different **Mayan** dialects. Some of the traditional Mennonite groups speak **German** among themselves.

NEWS MEDIA
Belizeans are a literate lot. I highly recommend a look at some of the national and local papers to get a feel for the country before your visit. Check out *www.belizenews.com,* which has links to all the country's major news media.

National
- *www.amandala.com.bz*
- *www.reporter.bz*
- *www.belizean.com*
- *www.guardian.bz*
- *www.channel5belize.com*
- *www.7newsbelize.com*
- *www.belizefirst.com*
- *www.belizemagazine.com*

Regional
- *www.sanpedrosun.net*
- *www.ambergristoday.com*

- *www.sanpedrodaily.com*
- *www.placenciabreeze.com*

PASSPORT REGULATIONS

Except for cruise ship passengers, all visitors to Belize need a passport to enter the country (drivers' licenses, etc, are no longer valid). Visas are not required for citizens of the US, Canada, British Commonwealth or European Union.

Visitors are permitted to stay in Belize for up to 30 days. To stay longer, you must get a visitor's extension from one of the district offices, and pay $50 per month. For more information, contact the **Belize Immigration and Nationality Department** (*Tel. 822-2423*) or the **Belize Embassy in Washington DC** (*Tel. 202/332-9636 US*).

All visitors must pay a departure tax at the airport, currently $40 US per person (this is often included in ticket prices).

POSTAL SERVICES

Belize's postal service is less than efficient (although some of the stamps are very pretty). You can expect mail from Belize to the States or Europe to take at least two weeks, if it arrives at all. When contacting hotels or tour operators in Belize, use email or fax if at all possible.

TELEPHONES

The telephone system is also a little on the crummy side, but serviceable. Cell phones are common, and you can even rent one for your visit – try the car rental agencies.

The country code is 501. To call Belize from the US, dial: 011 501 [local number].

To call the US or Canada from Belize, dial: 001 [area code and number].

Most phone booths use **phone cards**, which you can buy at grocery stores and newsstands. Phone cards are a bargain, and offer the cheapest way to call North America. Try to avoid making calls from hotels, which love to add a hefty markup to the price.

Another good way to call home is by calling the direct access number for your long-distance company, and using your calling card:

- **AT&T Direct**: 555 (hotels) 811 (pay phones)
- **MCI**: 557 (hotels) 815 (pay phones)
- **Sprint**: 556 (hotels) 812 (pay phones)

Many remote lodges are far from phone lines or cellular coverage, so the only option may be to use a satellite phone, which is quite expensive.

You can send faxes at most post offices and hotels.

TIME
The time in Belize is equal to US Central Standard Time (six hours behind Greenwich Mean Time, one hour behind Eastern Time). However, they do not recognize Daylight Savings Time. The length of the days and nights doesn't vary much here in the tropics. It gets dark about 6pm every day, year round.

TIPPING
Restaurants often add a "service charge" automatically, so examine your bill. If a service charge has been included, there's no need to do more than round up to the next even amount, unless service is exceptional. Taxi drivers don't usually expect tips. Porters should receive a little something. Many tour guides have come to expect tips, especially in tourist-swamped regions, but you really needn't give them anything extra unless they go above and beyond the call of duty.

When checking out of a hotel, I always leave a buck or two in the room for the housekeeping staff. Remember, that loose change that seems like a nuisance to you is a substantial amount of money to them.

You may occasionally be approached by freelance porters, usually young kids (in a former age, they would have been called "blackguard boys"), who hang around tourist areas and offer to carry your bags, guard your car while you're away, help you through the intricacies of buying a bus ticket, or other small services. Use your discretion as to whether they are to be trusted. If your tip is too small, they'll let you know.

TOURIST INFORMATION
The **Belize Tourism Board** (www.travelbelize.org) and Belize Tourism Industry Association (www.btia.org) both have good general information on their web sites. Brochures and tourist maps are available at pretty much every hotel.

WATER
Tap water is said to be safe to drink, especially at upscale hotels, which have their own large-scale filters. I drank the stuff on my last trip with no problems, but bottled water is easily available in case you're worried. Cheap lodgings may have dodgy water supplies, with low pressure and little or no hot water.

WEIGHTS & MEASURES
Belize and the US are the only two countries in the world that do not officially use the metric system. You'll find the same familiar feet, miles, pounds and gallons that you're used to at home. However, as the metric system is used by all the neighboring countries, and by the large number of European visitors, Belizeans are familiar with metric measurements, and you'll sometimes see both systems used side-by-side.

WEB SITES
Be very wary of information you find on the web. Many companies never update their sites. You'll find sites for hotels and tour operators that closed years ago. Always call for the latest schedules and prices.

The **Belize Tourism Board** (*www.travelbelize.org*) and **Belize Tourism Industry Association** (*www.btia.org*) both have good general information on their web sites.

The **Belize Chamber of Commerce** (*www.belize.org*) has info about doing business in Belize.

Amandala (*www.amandala.com.bz*) is a weekly newspaper covering the whole country.

This site, *www.belizenews.com*, has links to all the country's major newspapers.

Belize-based Search Engines
• *www.belize.net*
• *www.belizesearch.com*
• *www.belizegateway.com*

Regional Sites
• *www.ambergriscaye.com* has a great collection of info and links, not just about Ambergris Caye, but all over the country.
• *www.sanpedrosun.net* is the site of the San Pedro Sun, Ambergris Caye's local newspaper.
• *www.goambergriscaye.com*
• *www.gocayecaulker.com*
• *www.belizedistrict.com* has lots of info about Belize City and the north, including a searchable database of hotels.
• *www.northernbelize.com*
• *www.sanignaciotown.com*
• *www.southernbelize.com*
• *www.stanncreek.com*
• *www.placencia.com*

To learn more about Garifuna culture, see the web hub *www.garinet.com* and the site of the **National Garifuna Council** at *www.ngcbelize.org*.

Ecotourism
• *www.ecotourism.org* is the site of the International Ecotourism Society, and includes lists of environmentally friendly lodges and tour operators.
• *www.planeta.com* has lots of information about ecotourism in Belize and the world.
• *www.ran.org* is the site of the Rainforest Action Network, which has several projects in Belize.

General Info
• *www.belizetourism.net*
• *www.belizeexplorer.com*
• *www.belizenet.com*
• *www.belizeit.com*
• *www.belizemagazine.com*
• *www.mybelizeadventure.com*

- *www.planetbelize.com*
- *www.tripadvisor.com* and *www.virtualtourist.com* have comments from fellow tourists about various attractions, lodgings and restaurants.

216

INDEX

PHOTO CREDITS

The following photos are from Charlie Morris: pp. 175, 181, 182, 186. *The following photos are from wikimedia commons*: p. 20: Linda de Volder; p. 157: Bjorn Christian Torrissen; p. 163: Pgbk87. *The following photos are from Laura L Fellows*: p. 50, 167, 218. *The following photos are from Sharon K. Andrews*: pp. 137. *The following photos are from Lamanai Outpost*: pp. 117, 149, 150, 221 bottom. *The following images are from The Lodge at Chaa Creek*: p. 144. *The following images are from Chan Chich Lodge*: p. 116. *The following images are from Mata Chica Beach Resort*: p. 64. *The following images is from Randy Green*: back cover, p. 219. *The following image is from Belize River Lodge*: p. 119. *The following photos are from Jennifer Sharp (aqualandphotos.com)*: pp. 3 bottom, 23 top, 24, 27, 34, 44, 46, 52, 99, 106, 168, 220 top, 222 bottom. *The following photos are from Marty Casado (ambergriscaye.com)*: pp. 1, 21, 23 bottom, 25, 26, 32, 35, 38, 45, 48, 59, 60, 101, 102, 108, 110, 123, 124, 133, 201, 220 bottom, 222 top.

The following images are from flickr.com: front cover: Serge Melki; p. 1: Navin75; p. 3 top: V31S70; p. 3 middle: Victoria Reay; p. 3 bottom: Captain DJ; p. 10: ipeterson; p. 11: Jeff Fennell; p. 12: laszlo-photo; p. 15: Clearly Ambiguous; p. 16: cpchannel; p. 18: tacogirl; p. 22: FuriousGeorge1; pp. 28, 30: ambergriscaye; pp. 39, 128: lbeefus; p. 42: jonrawlinson; pp. 91, 92: cloud2013; p. 98: Adalberto.H.Vega; p. 83: satemkemet; p. 85: jayhem; p. 120: clurr; p. 126: malias; p. 130: Saucy Salad; pp. 145, 152, 199: Jonathan E. Burger; p. 153: Semio; pp. 159, 170: Marco Heidelberger and Christine Ebert; p. 160: DrewAndMerissa; p. 161: puroticorico; p. 187: Yorkaholic; p. 208: Rick's Pics; p. 215: mikebaird; pp. 221 top: Shellius.

Note: the use of these photos does not represent an endorsement of this book or any services listed within by any of the photographers listed above.

Open Road Publishing

Open Road has launched a greatl new concept in travel guides that we call our *Best Of* guides: matching the time you *really* have for your vacation with the right amount of information you need for your perfect trip! No fluff, just the best things to do and see, the best places to stay and eat. Includes one-day, weekend, one-week and two-week trip ideas. Now what could be more perfect than that?

Best Of Guides

Open Road's Best of Arizona, $12.95
Open Road's Best of The Florida Keys & Everglades, $12.95
Open Road's Best of Las Vegas, $14.95
Open Road's Best of New York City, $14.95
Open Road's Best of Southern California, $14.95
Open Road's Best of Northern California, $14.95
Open Road's Best of The Bahamas, $14.95
Open Road's Best of Bermuda, $14.95
Open Road's Best of Belize, $12.95
Open Road's Best of Cuba, $12.95
Open Road's Best of Costa Rica, $12.95
Open Road's Best of Panama, $12.95
Open Road's Best of Guatemala, $9.95
Open Road's Best of Italy, $14.95
Open Road's Best of Paris, $12.95
Open Road's Best of Provence & The French Riviera, $12.95
Open Road's Best of Spain, $14.95

Family Travel Guides

Open Road's Italy with Kids, $14.95
Open Road's Paris with Kids, $16.95
Open Road's Caribbean with Kids, $14.95
Open Road's London with Kids, $12.95
Open Road's Best National Parks With Kids, $12.95
Open Road's Washington, DC with Kids, $14.95

Order now at and get big savings at:
www.openroadguides.com